MISSION AND WITNESS

MISSION AND WITNESS

The Life of the Church

Selected and Edited with Commentary and Preface
by Patrick J. Burns, S.J.

THE NEWMAN PRESS
WESTMINSTER, MARYLAND
1966

6th Printing September 1966

Imprimi potest: JOHN M. DALEY, S.J.
February 1, 1963

Nihil obstat: JOSEPH ZALOTAY
Censor deputatus

Imprimatur: LAWRENCE J. SHEHAN
Archbishop of Baltimore

Date: October 24, 1963

Preface

THIS IS a book of readings on the theology of the Church. It is aimed at the intelligent Catholic seriously interested in deepening his knowledge of the nature and activities of the Church. While the selections usually require only a minimum technical background, nevertheless they represent an attempt to summarize within the limits of a single volume a solid introduction to the latest and best thought on the Church. They demand close reading, analysis, reflection, and discussion. They will undoubtedly challenge some of the reader's previous impressions of the Church.

These writings, then, are intended to raise more problems than they solve. They are offered as open-end approaches—of the contemporary Christian understanding—to the Church, a many-splendored reality viewed in the dynamic and sometimes dazzling light of Faith.

The chapters which comprise this book are fundamentally dogmatic studies, not essays in apologetics. Their authors attempt to understand the realities of the Church as grasped by the light of Faith and authenticated in official Catholic doctrine. These writings presuppose Faith in the reader; they do not attempt to render the Faith credible, to indicate evidence which can ground a prudent assent of Faith, or to dispose the reader to accept such evidence. They aim at understanding *what is already accepted in Faith,* not at Faith itself. Yet because they are written by thinkers who work hard to communicate with their fellow men, these selections are automatically relevant to the contemporary mind, even without the light of Faith. To any man brave enough to encounter God wherever He chooses to reveal Himself, they will present a challenge.

An attempt has been made to give this book what may be termed an *ecumenical awareness*. The Church in general, and the Church's authority and apostolic succession in particular, are neuralgic points in current ecumenical discussion. Though none of the following studies deals explicitly with the ecumenical mission of the Church, all treat of ecumenical problems at least in passing. It is hoped that all observe proper ecumenical etiquette and avoid needless offense to anyone. This is no accident. The drive for Christian unity and an acute consciousness that the present state of separation is intolerable are part and parcel of contemporary Catholic thought.

Then too, Catholic thought on the Church is moving away from the post-Tridentine emphasis, born of controversy and bitter necessity, on the hierarchical, juridical, and a-historical elements in the Church. Without denying the importance of these elements, this new emphasis seeks a more balanced presentation of the reality of the Church by stressing that the Church is the community of *all* the faithful, whose juridical organization is a necessary but partial manifestation of those internal dynamisms through which the Church fulfills her mission to the world at the present stage of salvation history.

The chapters which follow reflect this stress, and strive for balance by scrupulously respecting all the biblical and patristic data on the Church. They strive for essentials by investigating what is of common concern to all members of the Christian community rather than merely to some class within that community. Finally, they strive for vitality and significance by investigating the Church not as some eternal essence but as the *continuation of Christ* working out our salvation in human history, dependent upon our witness and our dedication, so that He may accomplish the world's salvation in us and through us.

The structure of the book is five-fold. *Part 1* presents the biblical roots of the Church: the preparatory work of the Old Dispensation, the awareness on the part of the primitive Christian community of what Christ intended His Church to be, and the grand unifying insights of Paul's vision of the Church. *Part 2* investigates the nature of the Church in general terms, and from several angles: the Church as the continuation of Christ, the Church as a Eucharistic communion of the faithful, the Church as the fundamental sign of the presence and activity of the Trinity in the world. *Part 3* studies the role of authority in the Church as a meaningful reality for all her members: the nature of the Church's authority, the relationship between the authority of the bishops and the authority of the Pope, the problems which the Church's authority creates for contemporary Catholics. *Part 4* looks at the role of Christian understanding in the Church: the authentic presentation of Christ's Truth by the officials of the Church, the twin channels of that Truth in the Bible and the Church's twenty centuries of experience in living the biblical realities, and the phenomenon of growth in the Church's dogmatic presentation of Christ's Truth. *Part 5* investigates in detail various aspects of the Church's mission to the world: the role of the Holy Spirit in that mission, the place of the lay Christian in that mission, the special mission of religious within the Church, the role of the liturgy in fulfilling the Church's mission, and finally St. John's concept of the *era of the Church* as the last age of salvation history.

Seventeen articles in all, by different and differing authors, each with his own personal interests and emphases, in an organic and harmonious presentation of the Church as she is seen by contemporary Catholic thinkers.

Finally, I must take this opportunity to express sincere

gratitude to all who helped in the production of this book: to Avery Dulles, S.J., for his direction and support; to the numerous theologians who were so generous with their advice and suggestions, both pedagogical and theological; and to all those friends who made the book possible through their labors as translators, proofreaders, and consultants. Further acknowledgments to publishers and individual authors are made in connection with each selection. Except for slight omissions and abbreviated footnotes, the chapters appear as they did in the source indicated in the introduction to each article.

PATRICK J. BURNS, S.J.

Woodstock, Maryland
May 1, 1964

Contents

Contents

[xi]

PART V

The Mission of the Church

Contents

PART 1 *The Church in the History of Salvation*

CHAPTER 1 *From Synagogue to Early Christian Assembly**

by JACQUES GUILLET, S.J.

AUTHOR: Jacques Guillet is dean of the Jesuit theologate in Lyons, France, and an acknowledged leader in the extremely vital French biblical movement. He has published extensively on various biblical themes in *Christus,* the Paris journal of spirituality.

ARTICLE: The early Church did not suddenly spring out of nowhere. Christ intended the Church as a symbol of the fulfillment which his new dispensation of Charity brought to the old dispensation of the Law, which was itself institutionalized in the Jewish synagogue. Guillet traces the development of the synagogue in the course of Jewish sacred history and shows how the early Christian community utilized and gradually transformed this institution into a new reality which we know today as the Church. Building on this providentially prepared symbol of the Chosen People's unity and destiny, the Apostles created a new symbol of Christian unity and universality. The primitive Church incorporated the Scriptural liturgy characteristic of the worship of the synagogue into the paschal celebration of the Eucharist in which the Scriptures find their fulfillment. Here, then—in the Jewish synagogue— is the taproot of the Christian Church in sacred history.

READINGS: For the reader who wants to fill in any deficiencies in a gentleman's knowledge of the Old Testament and its

* "From Synagogue to Early Christian Assembly" originally appeared in *Life of the Spirit* 12 (1957-58), pp. 22-29 and pp. 64-72. It is reprinted here with permission.

connection with the New Testament, three sparkling books are now available: *The Two-Edged Sword* (Bruce, 1956), by John L. McKenzie, S.J., presents the world of the Old Testament and the role of that world in sacred history. *Themes of the Bible* (Fides, 1960), by Jacques Guillet, S.J., traces the central themes of the Old Testament to their fulfillment in Christ in the New Testament. *God's Living Word* (Sheed & Ward, 1961), by Alexander Jones, investigates various aspects of the Bible in a series of lively and fascinating essays.

O UR PURPOSE [1] will be to show how the Synagogue as an institution, as it was organized by the Jews on their return from the Exile in Babylon, not only provided the early Christian Church with a whole set of services, customs and ritual laws, but also supplied a certain kind of atmosphere which played an important part in the development of early Christianity.

Our Lord and the Apostles Preached First in the Synagogue

This appears at the very beginning, when we find our Lord Jesus Christ himself using the institution and attending the Synagogue. It was in the Synagogue at Nazareth that Jesus first proclaimed himself the Messias, when he read from "the book of Isaias the prophet: The Spirit of the Lord is upon me . . ." and added, "This day is fulfilled this Scripture in your ears." [2] Again on one of the first days—and a decisive one—in his public life (described by St. Mark [3]), after he had chosen his first apostles, Peter, Andrew, James and John, he went to Capharnaum and it seems that his first move, when he arrived there, was to enter the Synagogue and address the congregation.

Later in his public life, after the miracle of the loaves and fishes, and the subsequent outburst of enthusiasm, the important thing was that the crowd should go beyond the fact of the miracle itself and grasp what was the real Food which our Lord had brought them. This was one of the decisive moments in our Lord's life, for now the people would have to make their decision—and it was in the Synagogue that he asked them to do so, delivering the speech on the Bread of Life [4] which was to lead most of them in fact to break with him. It was also in the Synagogue that he strengthened the faith of the Twelve and there too Peter pronounced the words which marked such a decisive step for all of them: "Lord, to whom shall we go? Thou hast the words of eternal life." [5]

What our Lord did, his apostles did after him. They too went straight to the Synagogue, to announce the good tidings of Christianity. When we read the Acts of the Apostles, we find much the same thing as we find in the Gospels: in Antioch in Pisidia, as well as in Iconia, Lystra, Thessalonica and Philippi, St. Paul went to the Synagogue, and there, usually, came the division between those who were prepared to receive the message and those who rejected it. The author of the Acts does not attempt to conceal the fact that the majority of the hearers refused or rejected the Gospel tidings—broadly speaking, at least. It was there, nevertheless, that St. Paul made his first converts.

Thus it may be stated as a matter of sober fact, that Christianity was born of Judaism, not only because it was born in Palestine and born from Jesus, a Jew, but because wherever the apostles preached, they did so first in the Synagogues. No doubt in all these places it was the Jewish nucleus, however small, which formed the starting-point and center of the first Christian communities. We may regard this as a series of providential dispositions which provided the apostles with their first opportunities, but it was also quite natural for them to go to the Synagogues first. They gave them both the place and the opportunity: general meeting-places where they were sure to find an audience among their own countrymen, who were already well-acquainted with the Scriptures; and opportunity, since according to custom every Jew was welcome to address the congregation. As everyone knows, the ordinary meeting in the Synagogue consisted fundamentally in a reading from the Scriptures, followed, if need be, by a translation and commentary.

The Church has kept this pattern in her own liturgy. We still have the Epistle, which is normally a text from the Old Testament, the Gospel, which gives so to speak the tidings that the times are accomplished and the prophecies of the Epistle fulfilled, and finally a sermon (or better, homily), the expounding of the Scriptures.

The Life of the Synagogue and the Mystery of Israel

These facts show the undeniable mark of divine providence. Let us not, however, stop at these preliminary points. The Synagogue did much more than provide the suitable place and opportunity for the preaching of the Gospel. It reflected the very structure of Israel, her whole being and future destiny—what is sometimes called her *mystery*. This means not only that Israel was a people, and as such had her own assemblies, but also that she was a people specially created by God himself. In those of her institutions where God's influence exerted itself most vividly and deeply, such as the meetings in the Synagogue, let us now try to discover the supernatural being of Israel and her supernatural destiny.

Her supernatural character appears clearly when we compare the Synagogue with similar contemporary religions, likewise spread over the Greek and Roman world. Unlike ancient Judaism, the nation after the Exile no longer had its center in one place, Jerusalem. Its worship was no longer confined to the Temple but was scattered over cities and villages, and in each locality it had small groups of worshipers who gathered at definite meeting places. At about this time, a number of cults or self-styled religions likewise hailing from the East—such as the Egyptian cult of Isis, or more frequently, that of Mithra from Asia Minor—were gradually invading the Roman world. They took the place of the old Roman religion, which seems to have been a cold, utilitarian affair, consisting chiefly of a number of external rites. These new Eastern religions brought with them an element of passion and physical devotion, a kind of communion with a god or with divinity in general. This type of devotion or communion was fostered in small gatherings, in close circles whose members tried to kindle among themselves that religious fervor and spiritual enthusiasm which they missed in the religion of Ancient Rome. Such religious movements, incidentally, may have favored the expansion of Christianity in so far as they exalted the value of religious feeling and aroused dissatisfaction and a craving for true religion.

Yet although they had some features in common with the Synagogue, these religions were basically different from it. The devout souls who attended the pagan meetings and sought initiation into their mysteries were in search of a personal experience that would bring them into contact with such and such a divinity or such and such a place, but this never led them beyond the level of personal experience. Even when this experience was shared with others, there was no question of its being the religious experience of a whole *people,* as in the case of Israel. Furthermore, it was an experience lived in a state of exaltation, not, as with Israel, an experience lived in history.

The Jews, again, based their assemblies upon the Scriptures. It seems quite safe to say that the whole history of

Israel throughout the ages from the moment she was chosen by God and God wrought his work in her, and all the devotion of her saints from Abraham and the Patriarchs to the Judges, Kings and Sages, came to life again in the Synagogue. And there too we find all her institutions. There all her genuine religious life and religious experience, with God himself as its source, and without any trace of the illusions and perils inherent in all pagan experiences, were transmitted to those who attended the meetings. Here we are faced with supernatural facts, and the Apostles and early Christian missionaries who made use of them used something given them by God.

Let us now see what the Church inherited from this institution. There are two main points to investigate: first, how the Synagogue, in so far as it embodied the unity and universality of Judaism, enabled the Church to affirm her own unity and catholicity; secondly, how it gave the Church the Scriptures.

The Synagogue Embodied the Unity and Universality of Judaism

The Synagogue expressed both the unity and the universality of Judaism. Its origins are obscure. We do not know how far back it dates—perhaps to before the Exile. However that may be, it seems that the Synagogue developed with the Exile and with the first dispersion of the Jewish people into Babylon. Thence it spread throughout the world.

It is quite true to say that there was never a Jewish community anywhere without its Synagogue. Only ten Jews were needed to establish one and to organize the cult. It was therefore quite easy to start such an assembly as soon as there was a community, however small. The humblest township could have one. Even the Temple of Jerusalem seems to have had a Synagogue within its precincts (that is, definite places where the faithful could gather to read the Scriptures and meditate on them, independently of the public worship and liturgy).

There were hundreds and hundreds of them all over the Jewish world. According to the Acts there seem to have been a great number in Jerusalem itself; other sources say hundreds, but this is probably an exaggeration. It is certain at least, according to the Acts, that as soon as there was any community of Jews outside Israel, not necessarily with its own language but with local roots, the people concerned would gather together on their visits to Jerusalem and form a Synagogue. We can trace a number of different meetingplaces of this type from which a certain number of early Christians found their way to the Church. Something of the same kind exists in Rome today, for there each Christian nation has its own church and parish.

Before the Exile

Now it must be remembered that this institution of the Synagogue, spreading its network across the whole world, was quite a recent feature in the religious history of Israel. In a way, it was an intermediary stage between Judaism and Christianity. For the religious tradition of Israel, as we know it from most of the important passages in the Old Testament and as it was ordered by God himself, was one of great assemblies of the whole People—the great gatherings at the foot of Sinai, the march through the desert, the compact life under the Kings. When the people did happen to be divided, as at the time of the Judges, this was quite obviously not a normal state of affairs. The function of the Judges and the Kings was precisely to bring all the people together again. Then came the Exile, of course. But immediately after they returned, there were again great assemblies at Jerusalem under

Esdras and Nehemias, who endeavored to gather the People together in one great unity.

After the Exile

Running parallel with this aspect, which appears clearly in the Bible, is another feature of Israel's religious life: its existence in the shape of small communities, in which certain peculiarities of language, and even of race—the result of the dispersion—were stressed. Nevertheless, dispersed and separated though the people seemed to be, the Jewish Synagogue was an *instrument of unity*. All the Jews met there around something that linked them together. There was constant contact between the Synagogues throughout the Jewish world. There was much going to and fro. People knew one another, and when strangers came along, it was precisely one of the functions of the Synagogue to welcome them. It seems from the texts that in some cases even foreigners could be received and fed on the premises.

From Synagogue to Early Church

Similar customs prevailed in the early Church. The close and constant relationship between the Christian churches was certainly inspired by the example of the Synagogues, where news circulated and visits were exchanged. Possibly the Christian term "apostle" is simply a transcription of the Jewish word for these "envoys," delegated by the authorities in Jerusalem to visit the Synagogues and insure unity of relationship, doctrine and feeling between the various local communities and the People of Israel as a whole. And this seems to show that materially speaking, as seen from the outside, the existence and life of the Synagogue were very similar to those of the early Church, which was likewise dispersed throughout the world and yet maintained its own identity and unity. The Church of Philippi and the Church of Corinth were not two separate churches. Each was a separate community, but together they formed the same one Church of Jesus Christ. Just as the Synagogue expressed both the power of expansion of the People of Israel (world-wide, yet at home everywhere) and its belonging together, so with the Church: she adopted the same kind of *framework,* which expressed and effected, as it were, both her unity and her universality.

We must, however, go one step further and see how Christianity and the Church, while borrowing many points from the Synagogue, added a new element of its own. The Synagogue seems to have been a consequence of the Jewish community. Where this community existed, there the Synagogue appeared. The Synagogue followed the Jewish people: wherever there was a number of Jews, they met and formed assemblies. Not so with the Christian Church. The Church herself existed first: the various Churches appeared as a consequence of her existence. This has always been so. For instance, in missionary countries an apostle or a missionary has only to appear on the scene and the Church at once exists there. Wherever a baptized person lives his faith, Christianity is there and around this Christian living in the spirit of Christ a new "center" is formed—the Church. In this appears the proper character, the true creative power, of Christianity. Wherever a missionary arrives, he brings with him the Spirit and the living Church.

Choice and Mission

If we call the Synagogue the expression of a people elected by God, the Church may be described as the expression of a mission. The economy of Israel is characterized by the word *choice:* God "chose" a people. The econ-

omy of the Church is characterized by the word *mission:*
God "sends," Jesus Christ "sends," and because of this
sending there is his Church. The missionary character of
the Church resides in the fact that the Christian is conscious of the Spirit living within him and enabling him
to raise a Church wherever he goes. The Synagogue
needed a community of flesh and blood, this community
of the People of Israel; but the Church was from the beginning a spiritual institution.

She was born of the Spirit and in full consciousness of
her power and unity in the Spirit, took from the Synagogue those institutions of control and supervision which
were used by the apostles in the service of the Spirit.
St. John supervised the Churches in Asia Minor, St. Paul
the Churches he founded in Corinth and Philippi. Both
knew that they carried the word of the Spirit. It was their
function to tell their communities what things the Spirit
wished and what things the Spirit operated. Conversely, it
was the duty of the communities to follow the Spirit which
came to them through their ministers. Spontaneously, as
new Churches were founded, a deep understanding developed among them and they reacted in a similar way
both to the authority of the apostles and to the Spirit.
This was very characteristic of the Church. There were no
traditions whatsoever, to begin with, in the Churches that
sprang up in the steps of St. Paul; they did not even have
their own Scriptures, for the books of the New Testament
had not yet been written. Nevertheless the Church had a
unity, both through the visits and supervision of those in
authority and through their spiritual influence. It seems
to me that this profound spiritual unity of the Church
has been preserved throughout the centuries, down to our
own day. The Spirit of Christ expressed itself in the first
martyrs, and does so today in the Christians suffering persecution in Christ. There is a spiritual kinship which is
the mark of the Holy Spirit.

The Scriptures in the Life of the Synagogue

The primary object of the meetings in the Synagogue was the reading of the Scriptures, yet this was quite a recent innovation, seemingly introduced along with the new institution. In order to realize this better, we must go back to the time of the Temple.

In the old days, when Israel had been gathered together in her own land, leading a national life centered around the Temple in Jerusalem and the big annual festivals held there, the whole People used to go up to the Temple to offer sacrifice. The indissoluble bond between the Temple and the sacrifices made there was indeed one of the basic requirements of the Old Testament religion.

The Scriptures had a large place in this liturgy both before the Exile and after it, when the Temple was restored and the sacrifices and ceremonies were revived. A number of the books—Leviticus, for example—consist of codes of law, and particularly rituals, intended to fix the liturgy to be used in the Temple. The Psalms were largely a collection of hymns to be sung on liturgical occasions, especially as an accompaniment to festivals and sacrifices. Some of the historical books originated in these festivals and gatherings of the whole People: it is quite likely, though not certain, that the first fifteen chapters of Exodus, from the hardening of Pharaoh's heart to the Israelites' departure from Egypt and the Canticle of Moses, center around stories evolved and developed in connection with the Paschal festival. These stories were told at the Jewish Pasch (they may have been acted), and they concluded with the Canticle of Moses. It is also very likely that chapters 19 to 24 of Exodus, containing the great scenes on Sinai, were said on certain festival occasions whose object was the renewal of the Covenant. After the Exile, for instance, Esdras read the Law to the People assembled in Jerusalem on a holy day.

[13]

The preaching of the prophets too had the Temple as its principal setting. Amos was an exception: he did not preach in the Temple, but at the schismatic procession in Bethel, which he seems to have followed to remind the people of the demands made by the God of Israel. But Isaias and Jeremias certainly lived in the Temple and Jeremias preached there—which means that the People must have been gathered within the holy precincts.

All this goes to show how the Jewish Scriptures took shape around the liturgy that accompanied the festivals and sacrifices, and how they were intended to give inner significance to functions that might otherwise have been no more than external actions. Any liturgy or external worship runs the risks of degenerating into rites which are empty of meaning.

Yet so long as Israel was gathered together in one body, leading its national life without any hitch and remaining faithful to its traditions and customs, it does not seem to have been necessary to write down any of the things that were recited and sung. For the fundamental element in this liturgy was the sacrifice. This is a mysterious, universal and very profound feature of most religions: the object of worship, the encounter with God, is brought about by sacrifice. In the act of sacrifice, man consecrates all he is and all the results of his activity and culture to his Creator. The sacrifice consecrates his offering and assures his communion with God.

The Liturgy of the Book

But in post-Exilic Judaism, Israel could no longer offer up sacrifices, for they were possible only in Jerusalem. The novelty—and extraordinary novelty it was—was that a worship was in fact still being celebrated, and with rites whose object was not a sacrifice but the reading of the Word of God. For the Liturgy of the Synagogue now became entirely centered on the Scriptures. In point of fact the Word of God had always been regarded as something divine: the prophets had been convinced of that. Now, dispersed throughout the world, the Israelites had to live their own traditions and affirm their belonging together and their unity. They found themselves compelled to write their Scriptures down.

I will not say that this had not begun before the destruction of the Temple, but it does seem that it was the dispersion, and the founding of the Synagogue, that made it necessary to fix Israel's traditions in writing—the psalms as well as the laws—and thus create the Canon.

The Jews were convinced that the Scriptures were something God had given them, and so it was possible to use them as a proper form of worship. From now on worship in the Synagogue had a rite and liturgy of its own: the liturgy of the Covenant.

The Covenant Continues

All Israel's liturgies were, of course, liturgies of the Covenant, since the Covenant was the basis of Israel's religion. It was not only a bilateral contract of "give and take," God granting his blessing to the people if they remained faithful to the Law. The Covenant meant more than that: it meant a joint life lived together by God and his People. Previously such a Covenant had only been able to be lived in the Land of God, where the Lord received his People, for this land had been given to them so that God's People could live there as a holy People.

When the worship of the Synagogue took the place of the Temple, this alliance, this Covenant, which had formerly been sealed by sacrifices, was now sealed by the Worship itself. The People of Israel still received the Word of God, the pledge of God and the Law of God, but in return they now gave their faith. Their worship be-

[15]

came more inward and to a certain extent more spiritual. Israel gradually came to realize that animal victims could be of no avail without an interior offering and a real consecration of human life.

The Part Played by the Scribes

Thus the Synagogue was in fact the origin of the written Bible, which became the Sacred Book of the liturgy. From this point dates the great tradition of the copyists and scribes of Israel, a tradition so perfect that the Hebrew Bible has in fact been handed down to us much more faithfully than were the Books of the New Testament—a fact proved recently by the discoveries made in the Qumran caves. The Scriptures were regarded as things absolutely sacred. From this time dates the movement which tended to turn the religion of Israel into a religion of THE BOOK (a tendency which became a real aberration in the Islamic religion, where the Book itself became a divine object). Hence the importance of learning, which has been so great in all subsequent Judaism. The Synagogue was not only a place of worship, but also a school-house and a place of study. Here lay the source of Jewish culture and education throughout the centuries; and it explains why the Jews were able to keep their unity and their Scriptures. "Israel will have nothing to fear from her enemies," one Rabbi said, " as long as children's voices can be heard repeating the words of the Law in the Synagogues."

He Who Fulfilled the Scriptures

The fact that the Synagogue gave Israel the Scriptures may have been providential for Christianity. For Jesus certainly presented himself as the One who came to fulfill the Scriptures. And this did not simply mean that he was able to give the answer to enigmas or riddles posed by

Holy Writ, or to fulfill such and such a mysterious prophecy whose sense till then had been obscure. There is of course this element in the fulfillment of the Scriptures. But there is also something much greater and more wonderful; for what was meant was that Jesus manifested—in his own Person, in his movements, his words, his life and death—everything towards which the People of Israel had till then been tending. It meant that he was to show why God had chosen Israel, why he had given her the Law and inspired her with a certain expectation. The fulfillment of the Scriptures meant first of all, literally, that Jesus was the One who observed the Scriptures and kept the Law to perfection. It meant that it was Jesus whom the prophets had called for, when they had preached righteousness, for he alone achieved the righteousness they required. He alone was faithful to their teaching. He realized what no other Israelite had been able to realize: an utter faithfulness to the Scriptures and the perfect fulfillment of them.

It seems to me providential that Jesus should have revealed the meaning of the Scriptures at a time when they were taking the shape of a Book and forming a Canon. In a sense it may be said that the portrait of Jesus was taking shape and being traced in the Holy Book just when its original was being revealed in the living face of our Lord. Thus Israel was able to do all that God required of her in the Scriptures and at the same time to discover in Jesus Christ One who gave God his full due. It seems therefore quite natural that Jesus should have appeared in the Synagogue—where the Scriptures were read and re-read—as the One who came to fulfill them.

The Septuagint

There are a few minor points contained within this great providential fact which are worth emphasizing. The Synagogue for instance was responsible for the Greek text of the Hebrew Bible, the Septuagint, so called because it was done by seventy translators locked up in separate rooms and who, tradition says, were found in the end to have produced exactly the same text. This is certainly a legend, but it has an underlying truth behind it: the fact that the translation bears the mark of the hand of God. Whether it was inspired or not is a disputed question. Some excellent theologians and a number of Church Fathers have asserted that after all the translation of the Septuagint may have been just as inspired as the Hebrew original was. However that may be, the translation itself was made necessary by the existence of the Synagogue which had to provide an intelligible text for communities scattered in countries where Hebrew was not understood. And, important for us, it supplied the first missionaries with a vocabulary which enabled them to address the pagan world directly, and thus win it to Christ.

It is difficult for us to gauge the importance of a translation in the matter of evangelizing pagans. A missionary can understand the seriousness of the problem. When he lands in a new world he wonders what words he is going to use to convey the fundamental realities he has brought with him, how he is going to translate into the pagan language certain words which have no equivalent outside the Christian world, words like "God," "Sacrifice," "Penance," "the Spirit." This is a very difficult task and it means that the missionary has to be fully acquainted with the civilization he is entering.

There is an example of these risks and dangers in the life of St. Francis Xavier. When he first began to preach, Francis was given a word for "God" by a Japanese. He used it, only to discover later that it signified a dreadful and terrifying divinity, more demon than god, and that he had in fact been teaching his hearers to worship the devil.

Not all the early Christian missionaries were so well up in Greek civilization that they could speak to the people they approached in an intelligible religious language, and the Greek version of the Old Testament was therefore a first-rate instrument for establishing and spreading Christianity. And this was due to the deep and thoughtful work done two centuries earlier by the translators in Alexandria, who knew very well what they were about.

There is one very striking example of this. In translating the first commandment, "Thou shalt love the Lord thy God," a less thoughtful translator would naturally have rendered "love" by the usual word *eran*. If this had been done, the Greek world would never have grasped what it really meant to "love God." Fortunately the Jewish translators in Alexandria deliberately chose the verb *agapan*, a word less frequently used but one which enabled the Greeks to understand what the love of God and man really meant in Revelation and in the Bible.

The establishment of the Scriptures and the Greek translation for use in the Synagogues seems to have been providential. Pagan converts to Christianity were brought into contact with both the Jewish scriptural tradition of the true God and him who had come to fulfill the Scriptures. The importance of this double discovery becomes plain when we find St. Luke, a writer from the pagan world, faithfully adopting the Jewish Scriptures along with the Christian faith: the stories of our Lord's childhood, especially in the first two chapters of his Gospel, are closely interwoven with passages from the Old Testament. This is not surprising in the case of St. Matthew who was a Jew, but St. Luke had been a pagan and it shows that when he became converted to Christ he knew that he had to become converted to Israel too, and to the Bible which Israel gave him.

More Sacred than the Scriptures

In the first part of this discussion we remarked upon the essential difference between the unity of the Church and the unity of the Synagogue. Here is another remark-able difference. Although the Church accepted the Word of God in the Scriptures as something sacred, she had something more sacred than a written Book and that was the Eucharist. The Scriptures are made perpetual and eternally living in the Eucharistic Presence, and this fact appeared historically from the very first day. The Jewish Christians continued to attend the meetings in the Syna-gogue along with the other Jews, and for a long time they found no difficulty in this. However, they realized that they had something else besides the Scriptures, and they began to meet in their own homes to celebrate the Eucha-rist. Today these two meetings, the one in the Synagogue and the Eucharistic meeting, which used to be separate, are joined together: first we celebrate the reading service inherited from the Synagogue, then the Eucharistic service which forms the Mass proper. We saw earlier that the de-struction of the Temple deprived Israel of the encounter with God that took place in the Sacrifice. This the Chris-tian Church rediscovered, and with the Eucharist she re-introduced the Sacrifice of Christ into the religion of the Book. The Synagogue had sprung from the destruction of the Temple, as a providential but imperfect alternative to it, but it could not claim to take the place of the Temple; whereas the sacrifice of Christ contains and sums up the whole of the Temple liturgy.

Memorial and Expectation

Worship in the Synagogue, however, centered entirely around a tradition—the past surviving in the holy Book, and an expectation. The Eucharist has both these features: it is a memorial of the past but a memorial which really becomes present on the altar; it has a past history yet is perpetually present; and it is also an expectation, but what we, Christians, look forward to is ours already. This is possible because the Word became Flesh and the Word brings the Spirit. The Word of God is not fossilized in a book. It goes deeper than the written words: in the Sacrament it is a Life, the Life of Jesus, the Word of the Father. And in fact it is more than that, for in Jesus all was Life— his actions, his movements, even his times of silence. There are certain things that the Scriptures are unable to tell us; indeed, the Person of Jesus is absolutely necessary to convey the Mystery of God to us and to give us access to what God is: Father, Son, and Holy Spirit. This Person is given to us in the Scriptures, but he is given to us in a better way in the Eucharist. Thus the Sacrament, the Food of Christians, deeply modified the Synagogue as an institution.

The Christian Tradition

The Synagogue was based on a Book and a verbal tradition in which one man said something to another, and he in his turn said it to a third. The Christian tradition is not a verbal tradition. It still has the Scriptures as its nucleus and center and it never gets estranged from them, but it overlaps and completes them. Being broader and more extensive, it is bound to be more faithful to Jesus Christ as a living Person. This fidelity to the Spirit of the Christian tradition finds tangible proof in a fact to which I referred above when speaking of the Jewish copyists and scribes: the New Testament writings were not transcribed as carefully and faithfully as the Jewish Scriptures which had been copied in the Synagogues. This is not difficult to understand.

In the Jewish world, the Bible, precisely because it was a holy thing, was never taken out of the Synagogue, so that the number of copies remained comparatively small. The Christians, on the other hand, who were on the whole less well educated than the Jews, all wanted to have the

Scriptures at home. There was a great demand for copies of the Gospels and St. Paul's epistles. As these had to be produced for a wide public and as the Christians had no specialized copyists, the work was not done as carefully and faithfully as in the Synagogue. The Christian copyists sometimes took liberties with the text. While reading or copying one Gospel they would suddenly remember another, and they had no scruples whatsoever about changing a word here and there and substituting another which they thought better.

Technically this is a serious loss, yet nothing was lost to the faith. The miracle—if one may so call it—was that in spite of these occasional liberties the Gospel remained entirely unaffected; the worst Christian manuscripts— and some are very bad indeed—do not contain a single error. The Christian tradition was not affected because it had a living tradition to support it.

"What hast thou that thou hast not received?"

In conclusion let us remember one last thing we owe to the institution of the Synagogue: it forces us to be continually remembering our origins.

One of the great temptations for the members of any chosen group is to believe that they have deserved their election. Both Christians and Jews are prone to imagine that their privileges—Baptism in one case, Choice in the other—have been granted them because of their exceptional merits. It was Israel's temptation to believe that she had deserved her election, and it is a temptation facing the Christian today to believe that he has deserved his vocation.

The Bible reminds the People of God unceasingly that left to themselves they are nothing, that the Lord has made them what they are. They would have been reduced to nothing in Egypt had not God taken them out of that land of paganism and oppression. When the author of Deuteronomy describes the ideal life for Israel, he insists on the helplessness of the people and the free gifts they have received from God in "a land flowing with milk and honey." [6] The Jews were a peasant people and like all peasants attached to their own soil; yet the Holy Book did its best to root them even more firmly, reminding them that they had not been born in the land but brought there, finding "great and goodly cities which they had not built for themselves, houses full of riches which they had not set up for themselves . . . vineyards and oliveyards which they had not planted themselves," [7] a land where everything came from God and whose fertility was a result of the rain that fell from heaven, which man himself could not provide. And in this land of God they had to "do all his precepts before the Lord," so that they might enjoy the gifts of God.

The Prophets insist on this teaching too. We, Christians, should apply it to ourselves. As a help in this, the Church always finds herself facing a religion and a People which compel her to remember her origins. Everywhere she finds the Jewish People on the same path as herself, scattered as they are, competing with Christians and partly at least possessing the same riches as she herself does. This is a constant reminder that she does not hold these riches from herself but from the divine mercy.

Thus the Christian is continually being encouraged not only to be modest, which is only human, but to be humble: to acknowledge that he owes everything to God . . . and through the ministry and instrumentality of other men. The Church has received her inheritance from a People who suffered to preserve it and hand it on. This seems to me to be one of the chief services the Synagogue still renders the Church to this day. We Christians should never stop thanking God for it.

[23]

Notes

1 This is a translation of a talk given at Notre Dame de Sion, Paris, in July, 1955.
2 Lk 4:17-21.
3 Mk 1:14-29.
4 Jo 6.
5 Jo 6:69.
6 Dt 6:3.
7 Dt 6:10-11.

CHAPTER 2 *Kingdom to Church**

by DAVID M. STANLEY, S.J.

AUTHOR: David M. Stanley is professor of New Testament studies at the Jesuit theologate in Willowdale, Ontario, Canada. He has published numerous studies of Pauline theology, as well as a brilliant doctoral dissertation, *Christ's Resurrection in Pauline Soteriology*.

ARTICLE: "Kingdom to Church" investigates the structural development of apostolic Christianity by studying the New Testament accounts of this development. Employing all the subtle techniques of contemporary biblical criticism, Father Stanley traces the growing consciousness in the primitive Christian community of what Christ's Church was supposed to be and how it was to be structured to best fulfill its salvific mission in the world. Luke's account of the early Church in the first chapters of Acts is analyzed first; then Matthew's presentation of the life and mission of Christ in the light of the experiences of the apostolic Church is examined. The article is difficult, but well worth the effort needed to keep up with a master literary analyst unfolding one of the most important organizational developments of all human history.

READINGS: Besides re-reading Acts and St. Matthew's Gospel, the reader may like to look at another of Father Stanley's articles, "The Gospels as Salvation History," which appears in a volume similar to this book, *Faith, Reason, and the Gospels* (edited by John J. Heaney, S.J.; Newman, 1961), pp. 253-275.

* "Kingdom to Church" originally appeared in *Theological Studies* 16 (1955), pp. 1-29. It is reprinted here with permission.

The other articles in the final section of *Faith, Reason, and the Gospels* would also be pertinent.

———————————————

DURING HIS EARTHLY career Jesus Christ proclaimed the coming of the kingdom of God. In the years immediately following his departure from this world the Christian Church made her appearance in history. What relation does the Church bear to the kingdom preached by Christ?

The question poses a problem which has been of paramount interest to the Christian theologian and the New Testament critic alike.[1] Our study attempts to redefine the continuity between Christ's preaching of the kingdom and the founding of the Church by tracing the lines along which, on the evidence of the New Testament, the Christianity of the Apostolic Age evolved, and by formulating the term of that evolution as perceived by the faith of the primitive Church.

The principal sources for such an investigation are the Acts of the Apostles and the Greek Gospel of St. Matthew. Acts recounts the series of events through which the primitive community was gradually liberated from the influence of Judaism and became increasingly conscious of its missionary vocation towards pagan peoples. This experience led it to perceive that by this divinely guided growth it was realizing the notion of the kingdom announced by Christ. Moreover, it was the utilization of this experience of the Christian community in the first decade after Christ's death which had enabled Greek Matthew to express in his Gospel his very profound intuition of the kingdom's actualization in the Church.

Loisy once remarked with characteristic acerbity that the only "miracle" of Pentecost was the origin of the myth of the Church; the answer to the disciples' vain expectations of a parousiac coming of Christ in his heavenly kingdom was the disillusioning arrival of the Spirit with plans for the erection of a Church upon earth.[2] Apart from its evident cynicism this statement has the merit of picking out one of the essential elements in the problem before us. Loisy was at least right in perceiving that the relation of kingdom to Church involved a psychological question: how did the apostolic community become aware that the kingdom of God manifested its coming through the organization of the Church?

Another important aspect of the question is the phenomenological one: by what stages did the Church finally emerge as an entity distinct from the Judaism in which she was born, and what bearing had this emergence upon the growing consciousness of the early Church that in her life the kingdom had come upon earth?

Such elements which pertain to the existential order do not readily admit of definition. But they must not, for that reason, be neglected. It is only by a study of the coming-to-be of the Church, a development of its very nature extended over a period of time, that the coming of the kingdom in the Church can be properly perceived.[3] For the coming of the kingdom, like the founding of the Church, is an existential process, not a static thing, and their relation to one another can be grasped only through an insight into experience. To recapture the salient features of that experience in the first age of Christianity is the purpose of the following pages.

The Apostolic Community in Jerusalem

The present editorial arrangement of the New Testament, by which Luke's Gospel is separated from Acts, tends to obscure the fact that they constitute a two-volume work on Christian origins. By using the closing scene of

the one to form the prologue of the other Luke under-
scores the unity of conception which governs the whole
history. This repetition of the narrative of the ascension
extends to several of the circumstances attending it: the
mention of Christ's prophecy concerning the future universal character of the apostles' mission (Lk 24:47; Acts
1:8), the nature of that mission as a witnessing to the resurrection (Lk 24:48; Acts 1:8), the promise of the Spirit
(Lk 24:49; Acts 1:4, 5, 8), and the injunction to "remain
in the city" until the reception of the Father's promise.
By employing such a carefully constructed transitional
link Luke clearly indicates that he desires the reader to
appreciate not only the continuity existing between the
two great sections of his study but also the parallelism he
has seen between the movement of the one and the other
book.

The first contains the story of Christ's work for the
salvation of humanity. By laying its opening and closing
scenes in the Temple, as Dr. A. M. Ramsey has remarked,[4]
Luke points out the complete transformation in the conception of divine cult and of religion itself which has occurred in the course of the events he has related.

I suggest that the second volume has been constructed
according to a similar plan. In the opening scenes of Acts
the risen Christ instructs his apostles about the nature of
the kingdom of God (Acts 1:3), while its closing lines describe Paul in Rome "heralding the kingdom of God"
(Acts 28:31). Consequently it is not unreasonable to suppose that Luke, with whom it is common practice to present similar sequences as a kind of diptych,[5] proposes to
trace the evolution which occurred in the notion of the
kingdom during the first generation of the Church's life.
From the beginning of Acts he clearly enunciates this
theme: the propagation of the kingdom through the apostolic testimony under the direction of the Holy Spirit.[6]

What promise for the future does Luke find in the

little group which returned to Jerusalem to await "the promise of the Father"? Following an ancient source at his disposal, he points out that they numbered one hundred and twenty, sufficient in Jewish law to form a distinct community with its own sanhedrin. This sanhedrin is indicated by a repetition of the list of the apostles with Peter at their head. They are conscious of their office, which is to witness to Christ's resurrection before the Jews and within the community.[7] With this in mind, Peter declares that a twelfth must be elected to replace the unfortunate Judas (Acts 1:21-22). The stringent conditions laid down for eligibility prove the importance of this function; and, in fact, only two of the disciples appear to qualify as candidates.

Yet the limitations of the apostles' awareness of what lies before them is only too evident in Luke's account. Their question put to the ascending Christ, "Lord, is it at this time that you will restore the kingdom to Israel?" (Acts 1:6), betrays a crassly material view of the kingdom of God, a view which may well have been operative in their election of Matthias. Why was it so necessary to have twelve witnesses rather than eleven? When, some twelve years later, James is executed, there is no move to replace him. The reason may have been that James had faithfully executed, as Judas had not, his function as witness. It is possible, however, that prior to Pentecost the apostles were concerned with filling those twelve thrones to be occupied by them in the great eschatological judgment of Israel.[8]

Another point, to which we shall return later, deserves mention here: Peter's insistence that the candidate for apostleship should have received the baptism of John (Acts 1:22). Several of the original Twelve had been disciples of the Baptist (Jo 1:44 ff.), and Peter's remark implies that the others had also received the same type of baptism. This will prove an important factor in the constitution of Christian baptism.

[29]

Luke depicts the little community as "at one in perse-vering in prayer" (Acts 1:14); but it does not appear that they celebrated the "breaking of the bread," or that they attempted to win any new adherents to their way of life. They were full of expectancy, as they awaited the mysteri-ous baptism in the Holy Spirit and the return of the Master, predicted by the angels (Acts 1:11). Their con-sciousness that in electing Matthias they were accomplish-ing what had been foretold by the prophets (Acts 1:20) proves that they somehow knew that they were assisting at the consummation of Israel's sacred history. Beyond that, they had no inkling of what was shortly to happen to them.

The Jewish feast of Pentecost brought a transforma-tion of the community into something very different from what it had anticipated. It is likely that the disciples had conjectured that the baptism of the Spirit was to usher in the parousia of the Lord, come back to restore the sover-eignty to Israel. Luke has taken pains to disclose the revo-lutionary character of the descent of the Holy Spirit. Tongues of fire appeared, accompanied by a great noise as of wind: "dividing," they sat upon each of the disciples, with the result that all present fell into ecstasy and began to pray aloud in praise of God and of the wonder he had wrought (Acts 2:4).[9]

Two facts emerge clearly from the account: the com-munity was caught up in ecstasy, and they were endowed with the gift of prophecy. Recent exegesis of the passage has shown conclusively that the gift of "tongues" had no relation to preaching but was "the voice" which attracted the attention of the crowds assembled in Jerusalem for the feast of Pentecost. It was the prophetic charism,[9a] as Luke indicates, which was later exercised by Peter in his address to the multitude: "Peter then advanced with the Eleven. He raised his voice and began to prophesy to them" (Acts 2:14).[10]

The greatest change perceptible in the attitude of the disciples is their realization that the messianic times have thus been inaugurated by the descent of the Spirit and not by the Lord's second coming. It was of this hour that Joel had spoken when he declared that Yahweh's Spirit would be poured forth, prophecy would again return to Israel, and salvation would come to all men through the Name of the Lord already identified as the risen Christ (Acts 2:16 ff.). The prophet had moreover foretold the creation of this group of God's servants, filled with the Spirit, who were the "little remnant of Israel," the messianic community. Dr. Joseph Schmitt has rightly seen how this realization dominates the first five chapters of Acts and has insisted upon its importance as the first link between the preaching of Christ and the ecclesiology of Paul.[11] It remains to point out the limitations of this Pentecostal revelation to the apostles.

The new Israel has been born in the fire of the Spirit, and Peter and the Eleven are prophets of the new Israel. But they are prophets "to the house of Israel" (Acts 2:36), to whom the messianic promise primarily belongs (Acts 2:39); and if Peter refers at all to the call of the Gentiles "in as large a number as the Lord our God will call them" (Acts 2:39), the reference is certainly obscure.

While Luke does his best to stress the universality of this first proclamation of salvation to "men of every nation under heaven" (Acts 2:5), it must be remembered that those who heard Peter on this occasion, during one of the great national pilgrimages to Jerusalem, were all Jews of the Dispersion. Isaias had made the Temple the focal point of reunion during the messianic age (Is 2:2 ff.), and the Jerusalem Christians can hardly have failed to be deeply impressed by the verification of this prophecy. The holy city must have seemed destined to be the center of the new religion on the day of Pentecost, and their experience in gaining converts during the period which followed served to heighten the impression that the expansion of Christianity was to result from a centripetal movement towards Jerusalem.[12]

Thus what is emphasized in the Lucan account of Pentecost is the function of the Jerusalem community in the formation of the church until the Council mentioned in chapter 15: her role as symbol of unity in early Christianity. This is clear also from an allusion in Luke's account to the tower of Babel, mentioned in the Canticle of Moses (Dt 32:8).[13] The miracle of "tongues" is presented as a supernatural reversal of Babel's baleful influence upon the nations of the earth. In Genesis the story was made the vehicle for a religious explanation of the diversity of language upon earth with its resultant hostility between peoples. In Acts the tongues which became "divided" cause the disciples to speak one miraculous language of ecstatic prayer, which summons the men of various nations to receive, in the charismatic gift of interpretation, a share in the outpouring of the Spirit.

Finally, Luke's narrative suggests that the coming of the Spirit was the promulgation of the Christian law: the references to fire and to the sound which marshals the crowd are reminiscent of the giving of the Mosaic Law upon Sinai.[14] In his Gospel Luke refrained from giving to his "sermon on the plain" the interpretation which Matthew plainly put upon the "sermon on the mount," that of a proclamation by the new Moses of the new law. In the chapters of Acts which follow the Pentecost narrative the evidence which has been collected from earlier sources points to the disciples' preoccupation with their status as the new assembly of Israel (cf. esp. Acts 2:47), an attitude which is one of the results of Pentecost.[15] It can only be explained on the supposition that they looked on the descent of the Spirit as the imparting of the messianic law.

The first five chapters of Acts, which describe the

fruits of the Pentecostal experience during the first years of Jerusalem Christianity, depict an ideal, even idealized, state of affairs. There is a continued and quite remarkable increase in the number of the disciples, who enjoy popularity with their Jewish neighbors, and who practice under apostolic direction herioc charity towards one another. Persecution, when it comes, is welcomed as a further proof that they constitute the messianic community of the "last days" (Acts 4:24-31), and the wonders of Pentecost recur, endowing them with new courage and patience. A brief reference to what is almost certainly a personal reminiscence of one of the apostolic group reveals the attitude of this heroic age as one of joyfulness, "for having been judged worthy to suffer outrages for the Name" (Acts 5:41).

Three relatively long summaries with which the author punctuates his narrative serve to mark the passage of time and also to draw attention to the marvelous advance of Christianity (Acts 2:42-47; 4:32-35; 5:12-15). As has been pointed out,[16] some earlier document is the source of these résumés, but in each case their scope has been enlarged by the interpolation of an additional theme. To discover the reason for these insertions is to gain an insight into the spirit of primitive Christianity.

The first summary (Acts 2:42-47) follows the narrative of Pentecost and shows its effect upon the social-liturgical life of the disciples. It depicts them as following a course of instruction which is called "the teaching of the apostles," a presentation of the truths of the faith in the light of the exaltation of Christ and the descent of the Spirit.[17] The author of the summary insinuates that this teaching was ordinarily connected with the celebration of the Eucharist. While the Temple remained the center of public worship for these Jewish Christians, the "breaking of the bread" was the heart of their more properly Christian life. Carried out in the privacy of their homes during the course of a meal, it was characterized by joy. The disciples retained the vivid memory of how the risen Christ had come to them habitually in the course of a repast, and this sacramental coming of the Lord would remind them for a long time, as Paul testifies (I Cor 11:26), of the much-desired second advent of the Master.[18]

The community's keen sense of the social aspects of the Eucharist is also apparent in the practice of what Luke calls the *koinonia,* a word which may be translated by "common life" in the sense in which it is used in religious orders. A description of it has been interjected into this first summary (Acts 2:44-45): "the faithful shared everything in common; they sold their properties and their goods, and divided the proceeds amongst the community, according to the need of each one." By this interpolation its author wishes to correlate the teaching of the apostles and the Eucharist with this "communism" of the primitive Christians. Stanislas Lyonnet in a recent article has further specified this relation of the *koinonia* to the Eucharist: the "common life" was a necessary prerequisite for participation in the "breaking of the bread." [19] The fellowship with Christ in the Eucharist demanded that disposition by which each of the first disciples refused "to call his own what appertained to him" and regarded "everything as held in common."

The second summary (Acts 4:32-35), originally devoted entirely to the social features of the community's life (Acts 4:32-35), has been enlarged by an intercalated reference (v. 33) to the dynamic nature of the apostolic teaching. It is linked to the "little Pentecost" (Acts 4:31) and is thus presented as one of the tangible results of the presence of the Spirit in the community. By this procedure the author stresses the fact that the "common life" is one of the fruits of early Christian theological thought, which in its turn stems from the Holy Spirit. This testimony given by the apostles "with great display of power" was accompanied not only by the miracles performed upon the sick but also by those less tangible, spiritual wonders, like the *koinonia*,[19] which this teaching evoked in the hearts of the disciples.

The third résumé (Acts 5:12-15), which sketches the thaumaturgical work of the apostles, is significant because of its remarkable reference to the privileged position Peter held in the esteem even of outsiders. They realize somehow that he has taken Jesus' place amongst the disciples, and they bring to him their sick and possessed as formerly they had to Christ (Acts 5:15-16).

The fact that each of these summaries insists on the great favor which the community enjoyed with "the people" enables us to form some estimate of the relationship between the Jews and the Jerusalem Christians. To their fellow-countrymen the little group was simply a more fervent "sect" of Judaism, as Paul will later term them, like the Essenes or the Pharisees (cf. Acts 24:14; 28:22; 26:5). It may also be that the Jews tended to confuse them with the movement headed by John the Baptist. The fact that the Christian community was known in Palestine as "the Way," a title probably deriving, as we shall see, from the Baptist's preaching, seems to indicate this.

What may be gathered from Luke's narrative about the Jerusalem community's conception of itself? As we have observed, the Pentecostal experience revealed to the apostles the inauguration of the messianic age and the community's identity with the new Israel. The apprehension of this truth drastically altered their entire historical perspective: the Lord, they perceived, had begun his work as Messias and Redeemer, not by a personal reappearance in the world, but by the mission of the Spirit.[20] The old Jewish scheme of history they had already recognized as obsolete on ascension day; instead of one, there were to be two comings of the Christ. But now the commencement of the messianic times without this second coming made it clear that the "last age" comprised two moments.[20a]

There was a time of preparation, during which the invisible Lord by the Spirit worked through the community for the building up of a spiritual kingdom. Consequently, their role in this period was to assist in aggregating Israel-as-a-whole to the new faith. The second period was to be marked by Christ's second coming, when he would "bring the times of refreshment" and "the restoration of all things" (Acts 3:20-21). While the disciples did not know the date of this parousia, they were certain of one thing: the Lord's coming was contingent upon the conversion of Israel (Acts 3:19).

In the first flush of their enthusiasm and by the phenomenal success which attended their early efforts to convert Israel, they naturally considered that the period of preparation for the Lord's advent would be a matter of comparatively little time. For as yet they were unaware of the place to be occupied by the pagan nations in the divine plan of salvation. It was to be Stephen's privilege to begin the community's education on this important point.

For the moment, they regarded themselves as the "little remnant" whose duty it was to rescue as many as possible of the "wicked and perverse generation." They called themselves "the Way." This title, I believe, they took from II Isaias, whose prophecy was a favorite commonplace in their preaching: "Prepare the way of the Lord . . ." (Is 40:3 ff.).[21] Since John the Baptist had been the first to use the passage in his call to penance (Mt 3:3), the designation of Jerusalem Christianity as "the Way" may be an indication of the close connection between it and the Baptist movement in the eyes of contemporary Judaism.

The community life of the disciples was, as we have noted, a paradisiac existence such as the prophets had foretold (Is 11:6 ff.). Full of joy, living in closest union with one another, having banished want by the sharing of their material goods, strengthened in time of persecution by the presence of the Divine Spirit, they seemed to enjoy the fullness of that messianic peace which was to mark the restoration of Israel. It is true that these Jerusalem Christians possessed a religion and a form of divine worship surpassing that of Israel; their evident belief in the divinity of Christ, their awareness of the personality of the Holy Spirit, and the "breaking of the bread" are evidence of that. Still it was the continuity between Christianity and the ancient religion which remained uppermost in their minds. The idea of receiving pagans, who had not first been converted to Judaism, was still inconceivable. The foundations of the kingdom had been laid, but the nature of the superstructure which the Lord intended to erect upon it was hidden in the future.

The Hellenistic Element in the Jerusalem Community

The picture present in the opening chapters of Acts is an idyll. Such a state of things was not to last. Indeed it could not last, if the primitive community was to discover its full destiny and to develop that independence of Judaism which the complete universal coming of the kingdom of God demanded. It was the vocation of a group of Greek-speaking Jews amongst the Jerusalem disciples, whom we may call the Hellenistic element, to dispel the idyllic atmosphere of the first years, which, however beautiful, tended to confine the new religion within the ambit of Judaism. These men, who were to commit Christianity to a course of action which would ultimately result in the admission of Gentiles within her ranks, make their appearance in Luke's story, characteristically enough, with the first signs of real dissension within the Jerusalem community (Acts 6:1).

However, the impact of this group of Hellenist Christians has already been felt in Acts' earlier chapters. The
so-called Hellenistic character of some of the most ancient
sources used by Luke has long been a puzzle to the critics.
It is now explained by the presence of these men in the
Jerusalem community from its inception. Among their
more important contributions to early Christian theological thought were the elaboration of a rudimentary apologetic, based on the Greek Bible, the working-out of the
theology of the name "Lord," *Kyrios,* one of the clearest
proofs of the primitive faith in Christ's divinity, and the
speculation upon the servant-role of the suffering and
glorified Christ.[22] It may also be that the presence of anti-
Jewish feeling in the examples of the Jerusalem kerygma
found in Acts should be credited to them. At any rate, by
their creation of a series of scriptural arguments for the
truth of Christianity, which were intended for use
amongst Greek-speaking peoples, and their reflections
upon Christology, the Hellenists were already forging
weapons that could be used in the great missionary enter-
prises of the future Church.

The greatest figure in the group was undoubtedly that
of Stephen, a man "full of grace and of power," endowed
with many of the charismatic gifts displayed by the apostolic college (Acts 6:8) and possessing the clairvoyance
and fearlessness of the ancient prophets. A Jew, he was
versed in the Scriptures; a Hellenist, he was without any
of the narrow chauvinism which tended to cramp the
Christian spirit of many of the "Hebrews." If the long
discourse attributed to him in Acts be characteristic of his
doctrine, Stephen liked to dwell upon the infallible triumph of the divine plan over every obstacle that human
malice could devise to thwart its execution. At the heart
of such a conception of sacred history lies a profound intuition of the central truth of the apostolic preaching:
Christ's death at the hands of the Jews and his resurrec-

tion by the power of God the Father. This insight resulted in the first Christian interpretation of the Old Testament; and the histories of Abraham, Joseph, Moses, and the prophets revealed to Stephen the relative, ephemeral nature of Judaism, as well as the basic incompatibility between the practice of Christianity and Judaism. In the context of Acts Stephen's defense is addressed to his Jewish judges, and as such it insists upon Israel's characteristic sin, the clinging to what is of passing value in code and cult as if it were definitive. Actually, however, the martyr's interpretation of Old Testament history contained a warning to his fellow-Christians, pointing out the anomaly of their position vis-à-vis Mosaic customs and the danger attendant upon the clinging to such practices.

But it was through his death that Stephen was destined to fix this lesson firmly in the mind of the primitive Church. Luke's account of the first martyrdom, drawn from an earlier source, proves that the disciples had been impressed by its close resemblance to the Master's passion. By dying on the charge of teaching that "Jesus will destroy this Place and change the traditions which Moses bequeathed to us" (Acts 6:14), Stephen reminds his brethren that Jesus had been condemned by official Judaism for declaring himself "greater than the Temple" (Mt 12:6; 26:59) and setting himself above the Law of Moses (Jo 19:7).[23]

If the community of Jerusalem was slow to realize the inexorable logic of Stephen's teaching, the leaders of the Jews were not; and the persecution which broke out as a result of Stephen's death put an end forever to the ideal conditions in which hitherto the Christians had lived. Except for the absence of their exalted Lord, they had seemed almost to dwell in heaven, possessing the best of the two worlds of Israel and Christianity. Stephen's message brought the community down to earth, reminding them that it was in this world that they must struggle, even to death, to establish the kingdom, before they might hope to enjoy its glories in another world. In the divine call of Abraham, of Joseph, of Moses, with its peremptory demand to sever all attachment to people or country, Stephen had perceived types of the Christian vocation. But before this little seed which he implanted in the minds of the Jerusalem community could germinate into the missionary spirit of Antioch, a further divine intervention was required.

The Community's Gentile Mission Revealed to Peter

Pentecost had revealed to the apostolic community the spiritual nature of the kingdom. Stephen had hinted at a further stage of development in suggesting a broader and more universalist outlook. It was Peter's experiences at Joppa and Caesarea which were destined to add a new dimension to the plan of Christian expansion.

The episode connected with the baptism of Cornelius the pagan is clearly of great importance in Luke's eyes. Like the conversion of Paul, it is recounted three times, and with each retelling fresh light is thrown upon its meaning. Logically, if not chronologically,[24] it takes precedence over a similar phenomenon at Antioch. The initiative in admitting pagans directly into the Christian communion belongs, as of right, to the head of the Jerusalem community. Luke is at pains to point out that this unprecedented event is clearly willed by God. Before answering the call of Cornelius, Peter is supernaturally informed that a creative act of God himself has abolished the impurity formerly attaching to non-Jews: "What God has purified, call not impure" (Acts 10:15). And this principle is seen to operate effectually in Peter's subsequent attitude towards social intercourse with the Gentiles (Acts 10:28; 11:3, 9, 18; 15:9).

In obedience to the vision, Peter accepts the hospitality of Cornelius, preaches the Gospel to his household; and, when the Spirit descends upon the group as upon the first Pentecost, he orders that they be baptized.

This admission of Gentiles who had not come to the Christian faith by way of Judaism was a remarkable step towards the realization of the universal character of the Kingdom. The disciples who had followed Jesus in Galilee were aware that somehow the Gentiles were to be called to a share in the messianic blessings as the prophets had foretold. Still it seems, from the explanations Peter is forced to give upon his return to Jerusalem, that they had not conceived it possible that pagans should be admitted *ex aequo* with the chosen people. Despite Luke's characteristic remark that the community "glorified God" (Acts 11:18), it appears, from the difficulties that arise at Antioch, that for some time they regarded Cornelius' conversion as an exception to the general rule. What is significant, however, is that the issue, in Peter's mind, is settled once for all; when he appears at the assembly in Jerusalem some years later, he will merely reassert the principle revealed to him that day by the sea in Joppa.

A curious remark of Peter's in his account of the Cornelius episode to the brethren of Jerusalem deserves to be noted for the light it sheds upon the process by which the apostles had come to recognize the institution of the sacrament of baptism. ". . . The Holy Spirit descended upon them, just as upon us at the beginning. And I recalled the Lord's remark: 'John,' he said, 'baptized with water, but you will be baptized in the Holy Spirit'" (Acts 11:15 ff.). His recollection of this saying of the Lord is given by Peter as his reason for allowing Cornelius and his famliy to be baptized.

What led Peter to such a conclusion? Why not consider these pagans who had received the Spirit, just as the apostles themselves had, members of the Church? It would seem that those who received the Holy Spirit on Pentecost were considered to constitute the messianic community without any reception of baptism. Moreover, in the very words of Christ which Peter recalls, the Johannine baptism with water is opposed to the baptism with the Spirit. Yet Peter had said at Caesarea: "Can we refuse the water of baptism to those who have received the Holy Spirit even as we did?" (Acts 10:47).

What led the apostles to practice a sacrament, defined in the fourth Gospel as a rebirth of "water and the Spirit" (Jn 3:5)? As we have already remarked, the reception of John's baptism had been a condition for candidature to the apostleship. Peter, Andrew, John, Philip, and Nathanael seem to have been disciples of the Baptist; and since the disciples of Christ had also practiced this rite (Jn 4:2), the rest of the Twelve as well as the other disciples gathered in the upper room had also received it. With the reception of the baptism in the Spirit, the apostles were given a more profound insight into the antithesis: John with water, Christ with the Spirit. They had received the waters of Johannine baptism, and now Christ had baptized them in the Spirit. It was a "validation," a "sacramentalization" of the Johannine baptism. Water and the Spirit were henceforth to form a new reality, the Christian sacrament of baptism.[25]

The "New Creation" of Antioch

With the sure instinct of the true historian, Luke connects the foundation of Antiochian Christianity with the death of Stephen (Acts 8:4; 11:19). Stephen's influence is felt not only in the fact that the founders of Antioch were Hellenists, but also in their departure from the ordinary rule of preaching only to the Jews (Acts 11:20). Their evangelization of the pagans met with unprecedented success, and the result was a community predominantly pagan in origin. Furthermore, three factors in the formation of the Antiochian church resulted in a strikingly new formula of Christianity.

Joseph Barnabas, a Levite of Cypriot origin (Acts 4:36), who enjoyed the confidence of the heads of the Jerusalem community, was sent to supervise the new foundation at Antioch. As leader of the new church, he displays the qualities which had earned him the sobriquet "Barnabas," [26] by encouraging the novel experiment at Antioch whereby Jewish and Gentile Christians lived in Christian fellowship, and by promoting a marked growth in the congregation. Barnabas possessed, moreover, a rare gift for judging men; and the man he picked as his lieutenant was Saul of Tarsus, whom he had already sponsored in Jerusalem when Saul had been an object of fear and suspicion to the other Christians. Barnabas knew that Saul had retired to his own city of Tarsus because of his failure at evangelization in Jerusalem. There he sought him out and succeeded in getting Saul's cooperation. Barnabas' realization that Saul's talents could best be used in a mixed community like that of Antioch was a stroke of genius, from which both Saul and the Antiochian Christians were to profit.

Saul had returned to Tarsus with only the memory of a vision in which Christ had informed him that his vocation was to preach the Gospel to the pagan world (Acts 22:17-21). Perhaps also he still remembered Stephen's conception of a Christianity conscious of its freedom from the Mosaic Law and the Temple cult. In any case, it was at Antioch that Stephen's principle was being put into practice for the first time; and the year Saul spent there under Barnabas' direction prepared him for his future mission to the pagans. The example given him in the art of governing a congregation composed of some Jewish and many pagan Christians would serve him later in founding churches like Philippi, Thessalonica, and Corinth. The development of a completely Christian liturgy, centered in the Eucharist, would provide Saul with a form of cult that could be easily transplanted to new foundations. His period of training came to an end the day the Holy Spirit manifested his will regarding himself and Barnabas. The great missionary era of the Church had begun.

Luke points out that the completely distinctive character of Christianity was realized for the first time not at Jerusalem but at Antioch (Acts 11:26). There the group of disciples appeared as a "new creation" by contrast with both paganism and Judaism. This was due to the absence of the Temple's influence in their Christian life, together with the fact that the majority of the disciples were converts from paganism. The Jerusalem community had been, in fact, no less Christian, but it remained to some extent under the shadow of the Temple. At Antioch it was easier to forget the ancient discrimination between Jew and Gentile, where there was no "wall of separation" to divide Jewish Christians from the rest, as when the Jerusalem community assisted at the public liturgy of Israel. Until certain Christian pharisees invaded Antioch (Acts 15:11), there were no such distinctions.

The most important feature of the new spirit manifested by Christian Antioch was her answer to the divine call to the missions amongst the Gentiles. In Jerusalem the community tended to await the coming of the pagans to the center of the new religion, the Temple. It is Antioch which first obeys the command of Christ to carry his Gospel "to the end of the earth." Her Hellenist founders had not forgotten Stephen's teaching that the Almighty had been a wanderer himself during the greatest period of Israel's religious life, the march through the desert, that he "does not dwell in structures built by human hands" (Acts 7:48). They were aware that the Eucharistic liturgy, which was the center of their Christian life, could be carried out wherever the preachers of the Gospel were to be found. It was scarcely an accident that the Spirit should summon the first missionaries of Antioch while they were engaged in the Eucharistic cult.

This divine revelation of the fully universal nature of the kingdom of God was to be brought home to the apostolic Church through the missionary experiences of Paul. His travels throughout Asia Minor and Europe illustrate, in Luke's story, the witnessing "to the end of the earth" which the risen Christ had mysteriously pointed out as an element in the coming of the kingdom. Moreover, as events were to prove, Paul was destined to enlarge considerably the early Christian view of the history of salvation.

The Jerusalem community had held firmly to two principles which she knew to be divinely revealed: the Gospel must first be preached to Israel (Acts 2:39; 3:26; 5:31), and the parousia of the Lord was delayed only until Israel as a collectivity had accepted Christianity (Acts 3:19-20). Paul made the first of these his guide in preaching the Gospel; wherever he went, he first announced the kingdom to the Jews of the Dispersion. Yet everywhere, as Luke testifies, he met their almost unanimous opposition to Christianity. In many places the only obstacle to their killing him out of hatred for his message was the power of imperial Rome (Acts 17:5 ff.; 18:12 ff.; 21:31 ff.; 23:12 ff.; 25:2 ff.).[27]

By contrast Paul was very successful in his attempts to convert the pagans. According to Acts, Paul's most sustained effort to convince the Jews of the truth of Christianity was at Ephesus, where he devoted three months to the task (Acts 19:8); it seems that he did not succeed in making a single convert amongst his own race. Now it is interesting to note that it was around this point in his career, in the opinion of many commentators,[28] that Paul seems to have undergone a change of opinion with regard to the proximity of the parousia. At any rate, by the time he wrote to the Roman Church from Corinth, about the year 56, he had clearly formulated a theology of history according to which, by her rejection of the Gospel, Israel had yielded her place in the kingdom to the pagan nations and would only accept Jesus as the Christ "when the full number of the Gentiles has come in" (Rom 11:25-26).

Whether Paul had been granted a special revelation on this point, we do not know. It is, however, not improbable that this conclusion was simply the result of his missionary experiences during the height of his career as an apostle. Once he had arrived at this conclusion, he must have seen the conversion of Israel as a hope indefinitely deferred, and with it the second coming of the Lord. For the earlier belief, stated by Peter, was not found to be incorrect: the parousia was still contingent upon the collective entry of the Jews into the kingdom. Paul's discovery was that this conversion itself was, in its turn, contingent upon that of the Gentiles. In the early days of Palestinian Christianity Israel's acceptance of the faith would, it had seemed, be almost spontaneous, a matter of no time at all; and the Lord's coming had in consequence appeared at hand. It took the greater part of Paul's missionary activity to change that outlook. By the time Matthew's Gospel, as we possess it in Greek, came to be written, the divine plan for the propagation of the Gospel was known throughout the Christian Church. This realization of the delay in Christ's second coming was, I believe, an important factor in turning Paul's attention to the mysterious phenomenon of the Church herself and in promoting, perhaps chiefly through his instrumentality, the conviction in apostolic Christianity that the coming of the kingdom was to be identified with the organization of the Church.

The End of Jerusalem's Importance in Apostolic Christianity

In the early years Jerusalem had seemed destined, with the Temple, to be the center of Christianity. But Acts reveals a gradual movement away from the capital of Judaism. The Hellenistic element is driven out by persecution. Peter, more and more occupied with his pastoral visits to new foundations, finally goes off "to another place" (Acts 12:17). About the same time the apostles themselves appear to have sought new fields of evangelization; Paul, frustrated in his apostolate in Jerusalem, lives a year at Antioch and then begins a series of expeditions which lead him eventually to Rome.

Jerusalem had but one more function to perform in the history of the early Church: to promulgate the definitive character of Gentile liberties. This she did in the Council of Jerusalem, in the presence of Peter, Paul, and others, if not all, of the apostles. Luke makes it clear that this formal acknowledgment of the fully revealed divine plan for the coming of the kingdom emanates not from Peter but from the Jerusalem community, in the person of James, her bishop. Peter, for whom the question was settled long ago at Caesarea, is simply present as "the legate of Christ." [29] It was fitting that Jerusalem, the mother-church and primitive guardian of orthodoxy, should publicly accept the declared will of God before disappearing, as she would soon after, with the advance of Titus' armies, into history. Her chief glory was ever to have submitted to that divine will, no matter what it cost her. Her original conception of the kingdom of God had been very different from the reality as it evolved under the impact of events. Once the tide turned in the direction of the Gentiles, Jerusalem's task was ended, and the focal point of Christianity was henceforth to be located elsewhere.

In Acts Luke sketches the gradual revelation to the early Church of what Christ had meant in his post-resurrection discourses by "the kingdom of God." It is consonant with our author's purpose that, after its recurrence in this place (Acts 1:3), he makes no reference to the phrase during the part of his narrative which deals with the Jerusalem period, but only when he comes to Paul's missionary activity.

The phrase is first mentioned upon Paul's return to Lystra from Derbe; he and his companions "encouraged the spirits of the disciples, urging them to persevere in the faith, 'for,' they said, 'it is by many trials that we are to enter the kingdom of God'" (Acts 14:22). It is clear from the context that by perseverance in "the faith" Paul means continued loyalty to the Church which he has organized among the disciples (v. 23 speaks of his establishing a hierarchical body), the only means of entry into the kingdom. In Ephesus, as has been pointed out, Paul spent three months, as Luke remarks, "trying to persuade them [the Jews] about the kingdom of God. But . . . some hardened their hearts and refused to be convinced, vilifying the Way before the assembly . . ." (Acts 19:8). This passage shows that to reject the Way is to reject the kingdom of God. In his farewell discourse to the "seniors" of the Ephesian Church, Paul describes his part in organizing the Church amongst them as a "heralding of the kingdom" (Acts 20:25). The preaching of the kingdom, rejected by the Jews, has resulted at Ephesus in the founding of a Gentile Church.

These three passages depict in miniature the connection between the kingdom of God and the Church which Luke has revealed to his reader by recounting the missionary experiences of Paul. The Church is the Way to the kingdom; to reject the Church is to refuse God's kingdom; the coming of that kingdom upon earth was effected by the apostolic organization of the Church among the Gentiles. In Christ's earthly life, as Luke has shown in his first volume, the preaching of the kingdom was greeted with incredulity on the part of his fellow-countrymen. When it ripened into hatred for his message, this incredulity compassed his death. But it was by the death of Christ and his resurrection that the coming of the kingdom into this world was definitively inaugurated. In Paul's lifetime the preaching of the kingdom met with this same Jewish incredulity and hatred. Through this apostolic experience Paul came gradually to comprehend the successive stages in the divine plan for the establishment of the kingdom. From all eternity God had decreed that Israel's exclusion from the kingdom through lack of faith should lead to the call of the Gentiles, whose conversion in turn would provoke that of the Jews. Such a scheme of things was necessary in order that Christianity should be liberated from the thrall of Judaism, and by withdrawing herself from the shadow of the Temple should actualize the potentiality for true universalism which was an essential quality of the kingdom of God.

All of this Luke implies when at the very end of Acts he describes Paul's activity in Rome as a "heralding the kingdom of God" (Acts 28:31). A few days after his arrival in that city Paul had, in the Jewish assembly, "borne testimony to the kingdom of God" (Acts 28:23), by trying to persuade them by scriptural arguments about the messianic character of Christ. When he meets with this last refusal, he states that "God's salvation has been sent to the Gentiles" (Acts 28:28). Acts closes with the preaching of the kingdom to the Gentiles, thus reminding the reader that the divine revelation concerning the coming of the kingdom, with which the book began, has reached its term.

Kingdom and Church in the Gospel of Matthew

A brief review of the first Gospel will clarify the relation between the coming of the kingdom and the founding of the apostolic Church. It will also, in addition to providing a confirmatory argument for Luke's interpretation of the experience of the apostolic Church, throw considerable light upon the purpose of Matthew, who writes at the close of the developments we have been describing.

Like any other Gospel, that of Matthew narrates the story of Jesus' public life culminating in his passion, death, and resurrection. What is peculiar to Matthew's Gospel, however, is a very clearly marked progression in the dramatic movement centering in Jesus' preaching of the kingdom of heaven.

This proclamation of the kingdom arouses greater and greater opposition during the Galilean ministry, which reaches its peak in Jesus' refusal to give any sign "except the sign of the prophet Jonas" (Mt 12:38-42), and his terrible warning "to this wicked generation" that the state of having positively rejected the kingdom will be worse than their first state of ignorance regarding it (12:43-45). In the sequel Jesus devotes himself to the instruction of his faithful disciples; apart from certain controversial episodes, he leaves the Jews to themselves. Meantime the Jewish opposition turns to hatred, draws down upon itself the angry fulminations of the seven-fold woe in chapter 23, and achieves its purpose in the passion and death of Jesus.

During this latter part of his Gospel, Matthew dwells with increasing insistence upon another theme: to replace the Jews who have rejected the kingdom, the divine plan calls for the admission of the Gentiles. This motif appears in a series of parables, most of which are found only in this Gospel: the parable of the eleventh hour (20:1-16), of the two sons (21:28-32), of the vineyard (21:33-46),[30] of the wedding feast (22:1-14).[31]

Matthew had made use of another device to highlight this presentation of the drama of Jesus' preaching of the kingdom: five lengthy discourses, artificially constructed from the sayings of Christ scattered throughout the traditions of the public life, which form a kind of commentary on the narrative sections which precede and delineate various aspects of the kingdom of heaven.[32] The sermon on the mount (5:1 to 7:29) prepares for the coming of the kingdom and promulgates its new code. The missionary discourse (10:5-42) contains Jesus' plan for the promotion of the kingdom amongst the Jews of Palestine. The discourse in parables (13:3-52) portrays the mysterious nature of the kingdom and explains, in effect, why it is rejected by the Jews, and why during the rest of the story Jesus will content himself with instructing only his faithful followers. The fourth sermon (18:1-35) is an instruction to the disciples on the mutual duties of the members of the kingdom. The final discourse (24:3 to 25:46) contains Christ's prediction of the end of the world of Israel, the ruin of the Temple, which is present as the externalization of the coming of the kingdom in his death and resurrection.

A re-examination of these discourses in the light of form criticism reveals another source upon which Matthew had drawn: the experience of the apostolic Church. The recognition of this element in the Matthean picture of the kingdom of heaven gives a completely new insight into the purpose of the evangelist. By adding this new dimension to his picture of the kingdom as preached by Christ, Matthew has set in parallel the experience of the Apostolic Age and that of Jesus' earthly life. This experience of the primitive Church during the thirty years which followed the Master's death has verified what he stated about the coming of the kingdom. Thus within the description of the coming of the kingdom we are enabled to discern the figure of the nascent Church.

The sermon on the mount teaches the proper dispositions for the receiving of the kingdom when it comes, and presents what we might call the "pre-history" of the kingdom. The beatitudes which form its exordium recall the two great classes of Israel who were types of the subjects of the kingdom, "the poor" and the prophets.[33] Christ insists upon the exact observance of the Law of Moses, as he did throughout his earthly career (5:17-20). By this means alone the will of God will be perfectly accomplished, and this is the *conditio sine qua non* for the coming of the kingdom, as the "Our Father" (6:9-13) shows.

Yet the passage which immediately follows the exhortation to observe the old Law promulgates, by a series of six antitheses, the new Law of the kingdom. It is a code of perfection, but a code which concerns those who live in this world. It outlaws hatred, impurity of mind, divorce, perjury, vengeance; it insists on love of enemies (5:21-48). Like the command to leave to God all care of material needs (6:25), which Acts testifies was carried out in the apostolic *koinonia*, this new legislation is the charter of the primitive Church. Yet, in this first discourse, which occurs in Matthew's Gospel before the constitution of the apostolic college (10:1-5), the picture of the future Church is only discreetly hinted at. The disciples are to be the prophets of the kingdom (5:12), a theme which Matthew introduces immediately after the beatitudes; he will refer to it again in three subsequent discourses.[34] For the present, until "heaven and earth pass away" (5:18) as a result of Christ's death and resurrection,[35] the kingdom is still in the future.

With the missionary discourse there appears a curious blending of the experiences of the little band of apostles, sent to preach the coming of the kingdom, with that of the Apostolic Age. The instruction of the newly-chosen Twelve concerns at first only their immediate mission in Galilee (10:5-16). They are forbidden to evangelize pagans or even Samaritans; their message, like that of John the Baptist and Jesus himself, concerns something still in the future: "The kingdom of heaven is near at hand." Abruptly, without warning, the whole setting is shifted (17-42); the apostles are dragged before "governors and kings" to present the testimony (18) to Christ's resurrection described in Acts. Thus there is no longer any question of announcing the coming of the kingdom: it is now proclaimed as having come, through Jesus' death and exaltation. The "coming of the Son of Man," the divine visitation identified with the destruction of Jerusalem, will find the apostles still engaged in this missionary activity.[36]

This deliberate foreshortening of historical perspective reveals a deep insight on the part of the evangelist. He has perceived that the kerygma of the apostolic Church is a continuation of Jesus' preaching of the kingdom, although he is aware that the kerygma is centered upon the historical act of man's redemption by which the kingdom is come upon earth, and is aimed at attracting new members to the community. In short, Matthew has seen that the organization of the Church is an integral part of the coming of the kingdom.

By the time the instruction in parables is reached in the first Gospel, Jesus' preaching has been rejected by the majority of the Jews; in consequence, the rejection of Israel comes very much to the fore. Matthew cites Isaias 6:9-10 at greater length than Mark. He includes two parables, not found elsewhere, which bear upon Jewish incredulity—that of the hidden treasure and the pearl of rare value—which insist that entry to the kingdom entails the sacrifice of everything, even of the Law of Moses. Matthew still has Israel in mind when at the end of the sermon he recalls a personal experience of his own, the riches of the "scribe become a disciple of the kingdom," possessing the old as well as the new (52).

Two other properly Matthean parables describe the kingdom existing in this world as found in the apostolic Church at the date of writing. It contains the wicked as well as the good, "all sorts of things" (13:47), the just with the "promoters of scandals and iniquity" (41). Included in this sermon is the parable of the sower with the explanation of it that was current in the primitive Church. Here we find allusions to the presence within the kingdom-become-Church of the lukewarm who have been seduced by riches (22) and of the half-hearted who apostatize in time of persecution (21).

The point of departure for the fourth discourse is the disciples' question concerning "the greatest in the kingdom of heaven" (18:1 ff.). The narrative section preceding this exhortation on the mutual duties of members of the kingdom has recounted the promise of the primacy to Peter (16:18-19) and the incident of the Temple tax (17: 24-27), which proves Peter's privileged position among the Twelve. The lessons which Christ gives are for the community which Peter will shepherd: the dangers of scandal, solicitude for the "lost sheep" (Jesus has already described his own mission in these terms, 17:24-27), fraternal correction (here the word 'church,' mentioned in the promise of the primacy, again occurs), the spirit of forgiveness (illustrated by a Matthean parable, the two debtors, 18:23-35, which probably concerns relations between Gentile and Jewish Christians). There is an imperceptible transition in this sermon from the real child, present at the beginning, to the humble and simple members of the future Church.

The last discourse, which foretells the end of the world of the Old Testament, dramatically depicts the definitive coming of the Church in the divine visitation of the glorified Christ which terminates the existence of the Temple. Throughout the greater part of the Apostolic Age, the Christian community still clung to the traditions and cultic practices of Judaism. In this apocalyptic event Matthew sees the vindication of the universality of the new religion. The "Sign of the Son of Man" (24:30) displayed triumphantly above the devastation of Jerusalem is that Sign which Isaias foresaw raised up by the Lord for the Gentiles, and for those lost of Israel and the dispersed of Juda (Is 11:12): the kingdom come as the Church.

Three parables, which seem to reflect the organization of the Church at the time this Gospel was written, are inserted towards the end of the eschatological discourse. All three concern the eschatology of individuals, and thus provide a valuable insight into the Church's realization of the indefinite period of time during which she must exercise her mission before the parousia of her Lord. The parable of the steward (24:45-51) concerns the particular judgment of the apostles and the other administrators of the kingdom upon earth; that of the ten virgins, who appear as spouses of Christ (25:1-13), suggests that there are already groups of specially consecrated contemplatives, of whom Tabitha and the widows of Joppa may well be an earlier example (Acts 9:36 ff.); the parable of the talents (Mt 25:14-30) depicts the particular judgment of those who form the body of the faithful. By the time this Gospel was written, therefore, the death of individual Christians before the parousia was an accepted fact. The doctrine which we saw stated by Paul concerning the unlimited delay of the Lord's second coming is now common to the whole Church.

This eschatological discourse upon the ruin of the Temple performs a double function in the framework of the first Gospel. It serves to introduce the claims of the kerygma, the passion and resurrection narratives; as such, it explains the cosmic effects of the redemption depicted as a passing of the old heavens and the old earth in the creation of the new world. But it sets a term as well to the experience of the apostolic Church which Matthew has also depicted in these five sermons—the experience of the coming of the kingdom in the Church as a result of the preaching of the Gospel. Matthew composed his Gospel at a period when the whole evolution of primitive Christianity described by Luke in Acts has resulted in a Church, in which pagans have replaced the Jews who have rejected the good news of salvation. The center of religious interest has already shifted from Jerusalem to distant Rome, whither Peter and Paul have migrated. As a result the mystery of the establishment of the kingdom of heaven upon earth has been clarified for the apostolic Church; the entry of the pagans into the kingdom has taken precedence over that of Israel, and with it the unlimited duration of the life-span of the Church has been recognized.

The purpose of the twofold theme, or rather of a single theme developed on two different historical levels, now becomes clear to us.

Matthew has attempted in one volume what Luke has accomplished in two books: to show the coming of the kingdom of heaven as realized in the organization of the apostolic Church. He uses the literary scheme of presenting the preaching of Jesus in five great sermons primarily to expose the meaning of the passion and resurrection of Christ: Jesus' proclamation of the coming of the kingdom fulfills Old Testament prophecy in a way so unexpected by the Jews that they reject him, and so yield place to the Gentiles. A secondary purpose appears, however, in the references made in these same sermons to the apostolic preaching of the Gospel: the heralding of the kingdom of God, as come definitively upon earth through the principal act of Christ's redemptive work, is the principal means of organizing the Church. The apostolic community has perceived, Matthew tells us in effect, that the rebuff met by Jesus in his attempts to convince Israel of the truth of his message is paralleled by the failure of the nascent Church to win over the majority of the Jews to Christianity. In the case of Christ personally this attitude of Judaism led ultimately to his death; in the case of the apostolic community it led to the establishment of the Church as it existed when Matthew's Greek Gospel was written.

The date of the founding of the Church is a matter of much debate among theologians. Christ is considered by some to have founded it upon the cross; by others, when he rose as the glorified Head of the Mystical Body on the first Easter; by a third group, when he sent the Holy Spirit upon Pentecost. Luke's account of Christian origins in Acts indicates a solution to the problem along quite different lines: the coming of the kingdom which coincided with the founding of the Church was an evolutionary process extended over a period of time. Greek Matthew, who constructed his Gospel to underscore this same truth, has carefully marked the beginning and the end of the continuous movement which is the founding of the Church, by means of the first and the last of five great discourses:

The *terminus a quo* is the sermon on the mount by which Jesus inaugurates his preaching of the kingdom.

The *terminus ad quem* is the destruction of the Temple, the divine manifestation of the coming of the glorified Son of Man in his kingdom-become-Church.

Notes

1 One of the principal aims of the treatise *De Ecclesia* is to establish a relationship of identity between the kingdom and the Church. The bibliography given by W. G. Kümmel in a recent article shows present-day interest in the problem amongst non-Catholics; cf. "Jesus und die Anfänge der Kirche," *Studia Theologica* 7 (1953), pp. 1-27.

2 A. Loisy, *Les Evangiles synoptiques*, II (Ceffonds, 1908), p. 9; *Les Actes des apôtres* (Paris, 1920), p. 153.

3 For this reason the tendency of some treatises on the Church to express the relation of kingdom to Church in a neatly conceptualized equation based on a text like Mt 16:16-19 cannot be regarded with complete satisfaction. What must be demonstrated is that, on the view of the writers of the New Testament, the coming of the kingdom coincides with the developments which resulted, towards the latter part of the Apostolic Age, in the organization of the Church.

4 Arthur Michael Ramsey, *The Resurrection of Christ: An Essay in Biblical Theology* (2nd ed.; London, 1946), p. 80.

5 Cf. the remarks of Lucien Cerfaux in his *Introduction to Les Actes des Apôtres* (BJ; Paris, 1953), p. 11; also Stanislas Lyonnet, S.J., *Le récit de l'annonciation et la maternité divine de la Sainte Vierge* (Rome, 1954).

6 Pierre Benoit, O.P., "L'Ascension," *Revue Biblique* 56 (1949), p. 191.

[7] Lucien Cerfaux, *La communauté apostolique* (2nd ed.; Paris, 1953), p. 26 ff. I wish to acknowledge my indebtedness to this unpretentious but excellent little study of the Jerusalem community. Many of the ideas which I have developed in this essay are due to Msgr. Cerfaux's insights.

[8] Alfred Wikenhauser, *Die Apostelgeschichte* (2nd ed.: Regensburg, 1951), p. 30.

[9] The meaning of *kathos* in this verse is obscure. It may signify "just as": the disciples began to speak with other tongues *just as* the Holy Spirit was giving them to prophesy, i.e., two charismatic gifts were bestowed upon the group, ecstatic prayer and prophecy. It may mean: the disciples began to tell in other tongues *how* the Holy Spirit was giving them to prophesy (cf. Acts 15:14 for this use of *kathos*). The word *apophthengesthai* means to prophesy here and in v. 14, as it does in Acts 26:25.

[9a] Not the charism of "tongues," essentially an ecstatic prayer of divine praise, as the accounts of a repetition of the phenomenon at Caesarea in Acts 10:46, and at Ephesus, Acts 19:6. In composing his Pentecostal account, Luke has so closely interwoven the data of two sources (one describing the gift of tongues, another providing him with the substance of the Petrine discourse), as to give the (unwarranted) impression to not a few readers that when Peter preached he spoke "in tongues."

[10] The "speaking with tongues" is understood as ecstatic prayer by two prominent Catholic exegetes of the present day, Lyonnet and Wikenhauser; cf. Stanislas Lyonnet, "De glossolalia Pentecostes ejusque significatione," *Verbum Domini* 24 (1944), pp. 65-76; Alfred Wikenhauser, *op. cit.*, p. 34 ff., "Das Reden in Zungen ('Zungenreden')."

[11] J. Schmitt, "L'Eglise de Jérusalem ou la 'restauration' d'Israël," *Revue des Sciences Religieuses* 27 (1953), pp. 209-218.

[12] A. Causse, "Le pèlerinage à Jérusalem et la première Pentecôte," *Revue d'Histoire et de Philosophie Religieuses* 20 (1940), pp. 120-141.

[13] The word *diamerizomenai* (Acts 2:3) used to describe the tongues is borrowed by Luke from the LXX translation of Dt 32:8, where allusion is made to the tower of Babel.

[14] Cf. the account in Ex 20:18 ff. A patristic tradition, represented by Severus of Antioch (cf. Cremer, *Catena*, p. 17), points out this parallelism also. Pierre Benoit refuses to attribute this significance to Luke's account: cf. *art. cit.*, p. 193, n. 2.

[15] J. Schmitt, *art. cit.*, pp. 212-217, has reviewed this evidence provided by the first five chapters of Acts. The results of his investigation are most impressive.

[16] Pierre Benoit, O.P., "Remarques sur les 'sommaires' de Actes 2.42 à 5," *Aux sources de la tradition chrétienne*, pp. 1-10.

[17] This "teaching of the Apostles" is the fruit of the deeper understanding of the mysteries of Christ's earthly career promised in the discourse after the Last Supper (Jo 14:26; 16:25).

[18] The connection between the *fractio panis* and the post-resurrection repasts shared by the disciples with the risen Christ is suggested by Oscar

Cullmann, "La signification de la sainte cène dans le christianisme primitif," *Revue d'Histoire et de Philosophie Religieuses* 16 (1936), pp. 1-22. Cf. also Yves de Montcheuil, S.J., "Signification eschatologique du repas eucharistique," *Recherches de Science Religeuse* 33 (1936), pp. 10-43.

19 Stanislas Lyonnet, S.J., "La 'Koinonia' de l'Eglise primitive et la sainte Euchariste," *Actas del XXXV Congreso Eucaristico Internacional-Barcelona 1952, Sesiones de Estudio,* I, pp. 511-515.

20 Peter's speech on Pentecost shows that the disciples first perceived the redemptive character of Christ's passion, death, and resurrection as a consequence of the descent of the Holy Spirit. The coming of the Spirit, they realized, was due to Christ's exaltation to the Father's right hand (Acts 2:33). This proved his constitution as Lord and Messias (v. 36) and, moreover, his *new mission,* through the working of the Spirit, as *Savior* of Israel (Acts 3:26). As far as I can ascertain, the importance of this last cited text has not been noted hitherto. It sheds much light upon the psychological process by which the apostles arrived at their conception of Christ's death and resurrection as redemptive. They first recognized him as Redeemer through his sending of the Holy Spirit, i.e., in his exaltation at the right hand of the Father. Further reflexion revealed the salvific character of the two greatest acts of his life, his death and resurrection. But for a fully thought-out presentation of such a soteriology, we must await the writings of Paul.

20a J. Schmitt, "Les sources et les thèmes de la naissante foi apostolique au Christ Sauveur," *Lumière et Vie* 15 (1954), p. 39 f.

21 Wilfred L. Knox, *The Acts of the Apostles* (Cambridge, 1948), p. 72 ff.

22 E. G. Selwyn, *The First Epistle of St. Peter* (London, 1949), p. 93.

23 It is surely one of the conundrums of early Church history that, although the Jewish Christians knew that these charges had been expressly declared as cause of Christ's death by the Jews, still they were so slow in realizing that to follow Christ entailed the abandonment of Temple and Law.

24 It is impossible to decide the chronological order of the events subsequent upon the persecution of the Hellenist Christians in Jerusalem. However, Luke clearly indicates the literary (and hence, on his view, the logical) sequence by the use of the phrase *hoi men oun diasparentes* in Acts 8:4 and again in 11:19.

25 The apostles were aware that, upon emerging from the Jordan after his baptism by John, Christ had received the Holy Spirit, who descended upon him (Mt 3:13 ff.; Mk 1:9 ff.; Lk 3:21 f.). Moreover, in the Fourth Gospel, it is instructive to observe the marked connection between John's identification of Christ by the descending Spirit and the antithesis (John-water: Christ-Spirit) we have mentioned; cf. Jo 1:33. Thus the New Testament seems to indicate that the institution of the sacrament of baptism was begun in the Jordan but was only fully completed at Pentecost. The intuition of some of the Fathers of the Church (*Summa*

Theologica III 66, 3) that Christ somehow instituted baptism at the river Jordan is substantially correct.

26 The meaning of the name is explained in Acts 4:36 as "clever at encouragement" or "exhortation."

27 It may be that this experience of Rome's protective might is the origin of Paul's doctrine about the "obstacle" to the appearance of the "man of lawlessness" and the great apostasy (II Thess 2:6). At any rate, a most ancient Christian tradition has long identified this "obstacle" with the Roman Empire.

28 C. H. Dodd, "The Mind of Paul: A Psychological Approach," *Bulletin of the John Rylands Library, Manchester* 17 (1933), p. 104.

29 The phrase is that of Msgr. Cerfaux, *La communauté apostolique,* p. 96.

30 Although this parable is common to all the Synoptics, it has a special Matthean conclusion, v. 43: "Thus I declare to you: the Kingdom of God will be taken from you and given to a people who will produce its fruits."

31 This parable is found in Luke but without the special Matthean note (v. 7) about the slaying of the murderers by the king and the burning of their city, and without the strange addition (vv. 11-14), which would appear to be a warning to the Church's Gentile converts against presuming too much upon their vocation to the Kingdom.

32 Cf. the very illuminating discussion by Pierre Benoit, O.P., in his *Introduction* to *L'Evangile selon saint Matthieu* (BJ; Paris, 1950), pp. 7-11.

33 A. Lemonnyer, O.P., "Le Messianisme des 'béatitudes,'" *Revue des Sciences Philosophiques et Théologiques* 11 (1922), pp. 373-389.

34 The missionary discourse, Mt 10:41; that in parables, 13:17; that of the seven-fold woes, 23:34.

35 André Feuillet, P.S.S., "Le discours de Jésus sur le ruine du Temple," *Revue Biblique* 56 (1949), p. 85, n. 2.

36 André Feuillet, P.S.S., "Le triomphe eschatologique de Jésus d'après quelques textes isolés des Evangiles," *Nouvelle Revue Théologique* 71 (1949), pp. 704-707.

CHAPTER 3 *Paul's Vision of the Church in* Ephesians*

by CHRISTOPHER F. MOONEY, S.J.

AUTHOR: Christopher F. Mooney is currently completing advanced studies in dogmatic theology at the Institut Catholique de Paris. Prior to this he was an instructor in theology at Canisius College, Buffalo, and St. Peter's College, Jersey City.

ARTICLE: "Paul's Vision of the Church in *Ephesians*" locates and analyzes the three great Pauline symbols of the Church: the Church as the Body of Christ, the Church as Temple of God, and the Church as Bride of Christ. Father Mooney examines the place of *Ephesians* against the background of Paul's apostolic experiences on those three missionary journeys which contributed so much to the development of the early Church. He studies Paul's theological reflection on the Church and its role in salvation history and presents the Pauline symbol of the Church as Bride of Christ as the final unifying approach by Paul to the grand but mysterious reality which is the Church.

READINGS: A close reading of *Colossians* and *Ephesians* is required to provide even the minimum background for Father Mooney's study of the Church in Paul. The next book to look at would be Lucien Cerfaux's concise synthesis, *The Church in the Theology of St. Paul* (Herder & Herder, 1959). The best way for the busy reader to keep abreast of current biblical studies is to read *The Bible Today* (6 issues a year; $5.00

* "Paul's Vision of the Church in *Ephesians*" originally appeared in *Scripture* 15 (1963), pp. 33-43. It is reprinted here with permission.

for 12 issues; Collegeville, Minnesota), an excellent periodical with just the proper blend of scholarly competence and pastoral concern.

TODAY THE trend toward a strong realism in explaining Paul's theme of the Church as the Body of Christ seems to have gained a very wide acceptance among exegetes, Catholic and Protestant alike. Far from interpreting it as a mere metaphor signifying the collectivity of Christians as an organization, Pauline scholars explain it as a literal designation of the risen Christ in all his concrete reality. Msgr. Cerfaux affirms again and again that for Paul, Christians do not form a "moral body," a "mystical Christ," but rather belong to the real organism of his risen Person.[1] And Professor Robinson, in his fully rounded coverage of this theme, emphasizes that Paul's "underlying conception is not of a supra-personal collective, but of a specific personal organism." The Church for Paul "is in fact no other than the glorified body of the risen and ascended Christ." [2]

The position of the Dominican scholar, Pierre Benoit, is essentially that of Robinson and Cerfaux: the Body of Christ for Paul is not a supra-personal collectivity but the full organism of the real historic Body-Person who rose from the tomb and now reigns gloriously in heaven.[3] In fact, the only objection today to this realistic thesis seems to be from those who argue not from exegesis but from the apparent lack of harmony between such an understanding of Paul and the fuller theological development found in the Fathers and especially in the encyclical *Mystici Corporis*. These objections, however, seem to be merely an example of what has already occurred fre-

[62]

quently enough: a simple misunderstanding on the part of theologians of thought patterns discovered by the exegetes.[4]

The Place of Ephesians in Paul's Thought

Along with this wide agreement regarding the realism of Paul's theme of the Body of Christ, there is also general acceptance of the fact that the *Epistle to the Ephesians* represents the deepest and most profound development of Paul's thought on the Church. It is this development of Paul's thought and its implications in our own outlook which we wish to examine in this chapter.

At the end of the major epistles, says Cerfaux, the thought of Paul is that all Christians as a group, in so far as they are a spiritual organism, are mystically identified with the Body of Christ. It would be to go beyond the bounds of Paul's thought in these letters, he continues, either to identify this organism with the Person of Christ or to speak of a Mystical Body of Christ as a collective person which forms the Church.[5] This is also the conclusion of Benoit.[6] In the key texts of I Corinthians 12 and Romans 12, Paul concentrates on the fact that every Christian is united really and corporally to the risen Body of Christ. Within this limited thought pattern Paul can only say that all Christians together must be the Body of Christ. How this is possible is simply not his concern at this period. In the captivity epistles, however, there appears quite suddenly a totally new dimension. To appreciate fully what this new dimension is and its effects on Paul's conception of the Church, it would be well first to review the two sources of Paul's thinking on the Body of Christ, and secondly to indicate some of the events in Paul's own life which undoubtedly contributed to the development and precision of his thought.

Sources of Paul's Thought on the Body of Christ

With Professor Robinson and Father Benoit we can discern two ideas constantly governing Paul's treatment of the Body theme. First of all, because he is a Hebrew writing on religious themes, Paul uses the word "body" not as a neutral element in the body-soul composite of Greek anthropology, but rather as an animated and corporeal person, whose thoughts and desires are contained and revealed under the sensible aspect of bodily experience.[7] Or to look at it from another viewpoint, because Paul is a Hebrew "he cannot imagine a man without his body, and therefore associates the body with the whole work of man's ultimate salvation."[8] Using the word "body" in a religious context, the Hebrew mentality includes in that term the whole person, with emphasis on what is sensible and somatic.

The second concept influencing Paul's thought, one quite familiar to the Old Testament, is that of the corporate personality. According to this theory, the Semites conceived their nation or community, including its past, present, and future members, as a single individual, who could be represented in turn by any one member of the nation. As a result there was frequently a natural oscillation in speech between group and individual, as can be seen for example in the Servant Songs of Deutero-Isaias. Originating most probably from the role of the chief in Israel's tribal life, this concept is most important for understanding Paul's presentation of Christ as the new Adam who died and rose again with vicarious efficacy.[9]

These two concepts are quite sufficient for understanding Paul's teaching, nor is it necessary to think of the Body theme as ambiguous or, as some have done, to search for its source in the Persian myth of celestial man.[10] This is not to say that there was no influence on Paul's thought from the doctrine of the Eucharistic Body of

[64]

Christ. On the contrary, in I Corinthians 10:17 Paul himself directly grounds the unity of the Church in the Eucharist, "The one bread makes us one body, though we are many in number; the same bread is shared by all." Such an emphasis moreover highlights again the intense realism of Paul's concept of "Body of Christ." In so far as the Christian community feeds on the Body and Blood of Christ, it actually becomes the glorified Body of the risen and ascended Christ. But as Robinson points out, there is a jump here from "feeding on" to "becoming" which is taken by no other New Testament writer, all of whom must have been as familiar with the words of institution as Paul himself. The Eucharist, therefore, however significant it may have been for Paul's theology of the Body, is in no sense a full explanation of its development. Some prior experience is necessary to explain the jump in thought just indicated, and this experience Robinson places on the Damascus road. "The appearance on which Paul's whole faith and apostleship was founded was the revelation of the resurrected Body of Christ, not as an individual, but as the Christian community." [11]

The Influence of Paul's Apostolic Experience

With these two main sources of Paul's thought in mind, we may now look briefly at the experiences which Paul himself underwent between the time he wrote Romans, probably in the winter of 57-58, and his arrival in Rome in the spring of 61, where he was to write the captivity epistles. In the first place, during these years Paul must have been impressed with the phenomenon of the Church, successfully organized in many places under its own hierarchy, yet very consciously united with the Mother-Church in Jerusalem.[12] Moreover these years are years of suffering and danger and finally imprisonment for Paul. His life was threatened by the Jews at Corinth,

Jerusalem, and during his more than two years of captivity in Caesarea.[13] The long journey to Rome, lasting all winter, brought shipwreck off Malta and three months there in hardship and danger.[14] He finally sailed to Puteoli, where he was met and welcomed by the Roman Christians. Such experiences must have impressed on the apostle the solidarity of all "in Christ" as well as the universality of the Church.

Secondly, judging from Luke's account, Paul's mystical experiences must have increased considerably during the whole period which led up to the Roman captivity: he seems to live more continually under the guidance of the Holy Spirit. He goes to Jerusalem on the last trip from Greece "under compulsion by the Spirit" and "in every city the Holy Spirit assures me that imprisonment and persecution are awaiting me." [15] In Jerusalem even some of the scribes and Pharisees sense Paul's intense spiritual life, and in prison he is comforted by a vision of Christ.[16] Finally, on the journey to Rome, he prophesies, receives the vision of an angel, prophesies again.[17] All this seems to indicate how deep was Paul's spiritual growth during these years, a growth which, to judge by the captivity letters, had for its object the contemplation of Christ present in his Church.

Relation of Colossians to Ephesians

Paul's thought on the Church in Ephesians is best put in perspective with a word on Colossians, since the two letters are linked so closely. While Paul was captive in Rome, the Church at Colossae began to be threatened by dangerous speculations on the heavenly powers, basically Jewish in origin, but highly colored by Hellenistic philosophy. So much importance was being attributed to these "powers" in their control of the universe and the course of events, that the supremacy of Christ would seem to be compromised. The reaction of Paul was instantaneous, al-most belligerent. His letter to Colossae asserts with vigor the supremacy of Christ as *Kyrios,* Lord and Master, over the entire universe. From the very beginning, the primitive Church has applied to Christ this Greek translation of the name reserved in the Old Testament to Yahweh alone, and it has done so precisely to acknowledge the divinity of Christ and his equality with Yahweh in dignity and power. In I Corinthians 12:3 Paul himself points out that such an acknowledgment of Christ as *Kyrios* can only be made "through the Holy Spirit." What he wants to do now is to draw out the full cosmic significance of this name of Christ and to impress it upon the Colossian Christians. In the famous two-strophied hymn of Colossians 1:15-20, Paul went back to the pre-existence of Christ with the Father, in whose image he is the source as well as the instrument and final end of creation. The Incarnation, crowned by the triumph of the Resurrection, was seen as placing the human nature of Christ at the head not only of the whole human race, but also of the entire created universe, the latter indirectly concerned in the salvation of man as it had been in his fall.[18]

It will be noted that the movement of Paul's thought here was the result of a situation which was imposed upon him. He himself did not choose the heavenly spheres as a terrain on which to do battle. Yet in accepting the terms of the contest at Colossae he places himself on a psychological plane which was to have enormous consequences. For it was on this "celestial" level of thinking that he was soon to compose Ephesians, there to elaborate the full vision of the Church barely hinted at in Colossians.[19]

Doctrinal Advance of Ephesians

It is surprising that Msgr. Cerfaux sees nothing essentially new added to the idea of the Church in Ephesians.[20]

This is true only in the sense that the full flowering of the thought adds nothing essential to the seed of the idea. For throughout Colossians the perspective is clearly Christological. Paul's whole energy is brought to bear on the supremacy of Christ over the heavenly powers. The concept of the Church, on the other hand, is kept well in the background and indeed, in the key text of Colossians 1:18, seems to be added only as an afterthought, forced upon Paul by the very vastness of the canvas he was painting. The idea dominating Colossians therefore is one of subordination, with the idea of identification touched upon but left undeveloped. In Ephesians, however, it is precisely this latter notion of identification between Christ and his Church which is rethought under the full light of Paul's spiritual and intellectual maturity.[21] The perspective now becomes ecclesiological, and one senses immediately an atmosphere of serenity and calm reflection quite absent from the previous letter—as on the field of battle after victory has been won.

But what is of capital importance to recognize is that the ecclesiological perspective of Ephesians is itself situated within a new angle of vision, an angle defined by Benoit in Paul's own phrase: "in the spaces above the earth." [22] The errors at Colossae had forced Paul to turn his gaze toward the "powers" that ruled the heavens, and to affirm with full vigor that over them Christ was supreme. Forced by circumstances to think for the first time in these terms and sustained undoubtedly by his own growing mystical experience, Paul's attention focused more and more on heaven and away from earth. When his gaze had finally adjusted itself and he looked back again to the Church on earth from this new point of view, he found that he saw her under a completely new light. Her role in the plan of salvation had obviously not changed, but Paul's angle of vision had. Viewed from heaven, the drama being played out on the vast stage of the cosmos did not look the same as it did when viewed from earth. The scenery was indeed still the same; the lighting was quite different.

It is this change of lighting which must be taken into account. To read Ephesians from the perspective of the major epistles, without allowing for this new angle of vision, tends to produce the odd sensation that the book one is studying is slightly out of focus and that one is somehow seeing double. Initially this can be rather disconcerting and has itself been enough to make many serious exegetes doubt Paul's authorship, but this is another and more complex question. The point being made here is that when Paul looks back from heaven to earth on the members of the Church working out their salvation, he sees them now with a physiognomy quite different from that sketched in his earlier letters. They now appear more clearly distinct from Christ Himself and more strongly united among themselves. That which strikes Paul most is the Church's collective unity, and this he begins to vest more and more with the attributes of a living person. The Church is now seen in process of growing and building up *toward* Christ who watches and directs this growth from his triumphant seat "in the heavens." [23]

Does this mean that Paul now wishes to assert a *separation* between Christ and his Church? Quite the contrary. What he is trying to do in Ephesians is precisely to preserve that intimate and vital union between Christ and the individual Christian which so dominated his earlier thought, and at one and the same time to express what he now sees from the angle of vision forced upon him by the Colossian controversy. This is no easy task, and he accomplishes it by a skillful if sometimes laborious deployment of three images, the very ones he had earlier used to emphasize union: those of Body, Temple, and Bride. In Ephesians these images play a double role: they emphasize the collective unity of the Church, personified as it were and distinct from the Person of Christ, and they serve as well to recall and underline the Church's lack of autonomy, her intimate union with Christ and total dependence upon him for her very being and life.[24] Let us see how each of these images accomplishes this double purpose.

The Body-image

Paul first perfects the image of the Body until it is able to express the new physiognomy of the Church which he has discovered. To appreciate what he does, it is important to realize that until now the word "Church" had served almost always as a designation for local communities.[25] In the major epistles it had almost never appeared in the ecumenical meaning we take for granted today, that of universal Church, the entire assembly of Christians.[26] Originally linked in Paul's mind to the Old Testament concept of "God's people," the term "Church of God" had gradually been applied by him to the individual churches he had founded. Not until Colossians 1:18 did it suddenly take on a strong ecumenical sense, and it did so there as a result of a synthesis of the themes of Head and Body that seem hitherto to have undergone separate developments in Paul's mind.

The Head theme, for example, when it appeared in I Corinthians 11:2-4, was used to express not the union of Christians with or in Christ, but a certain hierarchy of subordination: "head" in the sense of "superior." Thus in I Corinthians 12:21, the "head" is simply a member of the body and is not identified with Christ at all. The Body theme, on the other hand, had always been used to express the idea of unity which was central to Paul's concept of salvation.[27] Through physical contact with the physical Body-Person of Christ through Baptism and the Eucharist, the Christian received as through a channel the life of the Spirit, and so in a very real sense became Christ, his members, his body. The linking of these two themes of Head and Body, therefore, was natural enough when it occurred for the first time in Colossians 1:18. Paul was emphasizing the superiority of Christ as Head of the heavenly powers, and there was an easy passage from the use of "head" in the sense of "superior" to its use in the physical sense as Christ himself, head of his Body the Church. The word "head," moreover, when applied to the body, already contained the idea of vital principle and source of nourishment.[28]

It is in the fourth chapter of Ephesians, however, that one finds the full implications of this linking of the three concepts of Head, Body, and Church. At the start of the chapter Paul affirms the collective unity of Christians along with their organic diversity (3-11), followed by an emphasis on the new idea that the Body of Christ grows and perfects itself. What enables Paul to assert this is precisely his identifying Christ not with the Body but with the Head. The Head does not grow, yet it is from the fullness of perfection already present in him that there comes the vital energy responsible for the Body's growth (12-16). This distinction between Christ as Head and his Church as Body had never before been made so strongly by Paul, and it illustrates in a most striking way the preoccupation of his thought in Ephesians.[29]

This is not to say that the intense realism of the Pauline conception of the Body of Christ is in any way lessened. He can still affirm without hesitation that the universal Church is identified with the physical Body of Christ in heaven.[30] This he can do because, as Cerfaux points out, the ontological distinction seen from his new angle of vision in no way excludes a "mystical" identification at one and the same time. The physical Body of Christ pours out its life on Christians and these become his Body in the sense that the mystically present cause is attributed to the effect.[31] The Church quite literally is Christ's Body because she is composed of all Christians who in their material personality are united to the risen Body-Person of Christ and receive through him the new life of the Spirit. It would be vain, says Benoit, even false, to force Paul's terminology here to mean exclusively either Christ's physical Body and Spirit, or his Body the Church, which is his Spirit communicated to men. In Ephesians Paul means both together, indissolubly united: the individual Body of Christ grown to include all Christians united to him in their own bodies through faith and Baptism, with the fullness of the Spirit flowing from the Head down through all the members.[32]

The Temple-image

What has just been said may be seen more clearly, perhaps, in the perfecting of the second of Paul's images of the Church, that of Temple of God. Never does Paul use this metaphor to describe the Christian's relationship to Christ, but always to God and to the Spirit, and in the earlier letters its chief function too was to bring home intimacy of union.[33] In Ephesians, however, it is rather distinction and growth which the image emphasizes, both key aspects of Paul's new angle of vision. In chapter 2, for example, Christ is already enthroned "above the heavens" and all Christians on earth are mounting up little by little toward Him, all the while receiving support from Christ's representatives on earth (vv. 6 and 19-22).

On the other hand in chapters 4:12 and 16, where, as we have seen, Paul develops anew the themes of Body and Head, Christ is seen as the key-stone of the Temple, toward which it is slowly rising. Head and key-stone are thus made to correspond in position as well as function, since both give strength and unity while yet remaining distinct from the whole.[34]

It is interesting to note how this second image of the Church is linked in chapter 2 with Paul's preoccupation with unity and his effort to underscore the collective aspect of salvation. His earlier synthesis, achieved with such anguish in Romans, is now rethought and fit into a larger horizon. The mental and visual adjustment necessary from the vantage point of Ephesians has enabled Paul to see Jew and Gentile united at last and integrated into the heavenly Temple mounting up toward Christ the keystone. The hateful division existing between them in the past has been blotted out by Christ's blood, which, by reconciling them to each other, has reconciled them to God (1-19). Salvation for both Jew and Gentile remains, as always for Paul, essentially human and moral, but now it becomes part of a much vaster setting. In Colossians Paul had insisted on a cosmic conception of Christ and the salvation he wrought, and this enables him now to see the Church too on a cosmic plane. Just as Christ is *Kyrios* over the whole universe, so the Church also comes to share in some mysterious manner this relationship of Christ to all creation. Always limited to a group of human beings, she appears nonetheless to guard within herself the destiny of the whole cosmos. It is in this way that the Church, as the risen Body of Christ, becomes extended, as it were, swelled in Paul's mind to the dimensions of the new universe, "the fullness of him who is filled all in all." [35]

But Paul has not yet said his last word on the Church. In chapter 5, through the moving image of the Bride, he brings to a focus all the disparate rays of his thought and presents us with a synthesis, a fusion of the themes of Head and Body and, implicitly, that of heavenly Temple. This remarkable text on marriage gives an extraordinary expression to the new angle of vision from which Paul views the Church in Ephesians. There is present, first of all, the fundamental idea of "Body of Christ" of which Christians are now "members," and which Christ has incorporated into himself by the purifying action of Baptism (26 and 50). But this baptismal action and salvation are presented in a collective fashion which gives to the group of Christians a personal quality: it is the "Body" which Christ has saved (23) and it is the "Church" which he has baptized (26).

And yet though so clearly attached to Christ as his Body, the Church is nevertheless distinguished from him as "Head." Subject to him always, she becomes the model of that obedience which every wife owes her husband (23-24). This image of "Head" as "superior," however, has a divisive connotation and Paul does not wish to insist upon it. For Christ is also the Savior, who "loved the Church and gave himself up for her," dying in the place of sinners so he could make them pure and holy by his sacrifices. At this point we should expect Paul to insist once more on the other meaning of "head" as vital principle. But no, he finds this too impersonal to express the closeness of the union, too weak to bear the weight of this gift of love. And so he employs a more striking image, one already found in the Old Testament, that of marriage, and we now see sketched in Paul's richest lines the theme of the Bride of Christ.[36]

This particular theme, so intimately bound up with that of the Body, had occurred explicitly only once before, though Paul had already twice used the metaphor of sexual union at least implicitly.[37] Moreover there is a chance, as Cerfaux says, that the virgin-Church of Ephesians is a personification of the heavenly Temple and the heavenly Jerusalem. Christ delivered himself up for the Church and purified and washed her, just as Yahweh purified Jerusalem and washed away its sins. He loved the Church as Yahweh loved his people in the Old Testament. He desires her to be glorious and holy and without flaw, just as Yahweh wished Jerusalem to be rescued and renewed.[38] This image of the Bride is thus far stronger than that of

Head-Body, since it contains, in addition to an intimate physical union, a union of hearts which can demand the total gift of oneself. The husband is not only the "head" whom the wife must obey, he is also and above all the intimate associate who loves his wife as his own flesh and sacrifices himself for her. This is what Christ has done for the Church which is his Bride (25-29). In this union, model of all human marriages, there is fully realized and definitively clarified the "mystery" seen by Paul to be present in the opening verses of Genesis (31-32).

Summary

In these final lines we may be allowed to see the ultimate flowering of Paul's thought on the Church as the Body of Christ. This thought, we have found, underwent a profound development between the period of the major epistles and the writing of Ephesians. One key to this development is very likely Paul's growing mystical experience. Yet this alone might never have sufficed were it not for the new angle of vision forced upon him by the Colossian controversy. It is this which enabled him to look down from "the spaces above the earth" and to see the Church at one and the same time identified with the risen Body of Christ yet clearly distinct from him. This new vision he communicates to his readers by a skillful transformation of three images in such a way that he preserves intact his prior vision of intimate union.

With Benoit we may summarize Paul's deployment of these images by picturing a diptych, the two panels of which are heaven and earth, the two personages, Christ and his Church.[39] On the one side is Christ, seated triumphantly in heaven as Head of the Church, communicating to his Body the life of the Spirit necessary for its growth. From here he constructs the heavenly Temple of God, of which he is the key-stone. More than that, he loves and cherishes the Church as a man does his wife, delivers himself up for *her* at the time of their marriage, and thus saves and purifies her and renders her immaculate.

On the other panel is the Church saved by his blood, a single Body with him, subject to him as a wife to her husband. Yet all the while the Church herself is in process of growth and development, as a body nourished by its head, as a spiritual edifice rising up toward heaven, to become at last "the fullness of him who is filled all in all."

It should be noted that each of these three images is linked in turn not only with the word "Church" used in an ecumenical sense, but also with the Person of Christ, thus showing the extent to which Paul's theology of the Church is simply an extension of his Christology. The images are likewise imposed one upon the other, a veil being lifted each time, as it were, revealing a new depth in the total mystery. And at every step too there are those expressions of wonder and love, so characteristic of mystical experience, which culminate at last in the image of the Bride, the ultimate development of Paul's thought on the relationship between Christ and his Church.

Notes

1 Lucien Cerfaux, *La Théologie de l'Église suivant Saint Paul* (2nd ed., Paris, 1948), pp. 206, 209, 210, 212, 254, 259; *The Church in the Theology of St. Paul* (New York, 1959). References are to French edition.

2 J. A. T. Robinson, *The Body* (London, 1952), p. 51.

3 Pierre Benoit, "Corps, Tête et Plérôme dans les Épîtres de la Captivité," *Revue Biblique* 63 (1956), pp. 7-12, 20-21.

4 For example, Th. Zapelena, "Vos Estis Corporis Christi," *Verbum Domini* 37 (1959), pp. 78-95, 162-170. A clear reply to Zapelena as well as an excellent statement of the relationship between Paul and *Mystici Corporis* has been given by J. Havet. "La Doctrine Paulinienne du 'Corps du Christ,' Essai de Mise au Point," *Littérature et Théologie Pauliniennes* (Louvain, 1960), pp. 186-216.

5 Cerfaux, p. 215. See also the excellent study of the major epistles by Barnabas Mary Ahern, "The Christian's Union with the Body of Christ in Cor., Gal., and Rom.," *Catholic Biblical Quarterly* 23 (1961), pp. 199-209.

6 Benoit, pp. 13-18.

7 J. A. T. Robinson, pp. 26-28; Ahern, p. 200.

8 Benoit, p. 18.

9 H. W. Robinson, "The Hebrew Concept of the Corporate Personality," *Werden und Wesen des Alten Testaments*, ed. by J. Hempel (Berlin, 1936), p. 58 ff. Also A. Feuillet, "Mort du Christ et mort du Chrétien d'après les épîtres pauliniennes," *Revue Biblique* 66 (1959), pp. 483-487.

10 Alfred Wikenhauser, *Die Kirche als der mystische Leib Christi nach dem Apostel Paulus* (Münster, 1940), pp. 232-240. Cf. Cerfaux, p. 281.

11 J. A. T. Robinson, p. 58. This is one of Robinson's most interesting hypotheses.

12 *Acts*, chapters 20-28, gives us a picture of well established communities in many places. In an unpublished text, David M. Stanley has developed at length the influence of these experiences on the captivity epistles.

13 Acts 20:3; 21:27 ff.; 23:12-21; 25:27.

14 Acts 28:11.

15 Acts 20:22-23.

16 Acts 23:9-11.

17 Acts 27:1-34.

18 Benoit, pp. 34 and 40. On Paul's use of *Kyrios,* cf. Cerfaux, pp. 350-359.

19 Pierre Benoit, "L'Horizon Paulinien de l'Épître aux Éphésiens," *Revue Biblique* 46 (1937), p. 508.

20 Cerfaux, pp. 221-222.

21 Benoit, "L'Horizon Paulinien . . . ," pp. 523-524.

22 *Ibid.*, pp. 511, 513; Ephesians 6:12. Also Ephesians 1:3; 1:20; 2:6; 3:10. These expressions do not appear in Colossians.

23 Paul had already hinted at this development in Colossians 1:18 and 24; 2:19; 3:1-4.

24 Benoit, "L'Horizon Paulinien . . . ," pp. 515-517.

25 Cerfaux, pp. 143-157, gives a full treatment of texts.

26 *Ibid.*, 241. Benoit, in "Corps, Tête . . . ," p. 22, finds the ecumenical meaning weakly asserted in three or four early texts, especially in I Corinthians 12:27 ff.

27 Confer I Corinthians 6:5; 10:17; 12:7-11; Romans 12:6-8.

28 Benoit, "Corps, Tête . . . ," pp. 23-29. For quite another interpretation see J. A. T. Robinson, pp. 65-67, and Benoit's answer in *Revue Biblique* 64 (1957), p. 585.

29 Again, there is a hint but no development of this idea in Colossians 2:19. Confer Benoit, "L'Horizon Paulinien . . . ," pp. 359-360.

30 Ephesians 1:22 is explicit, while Ephesians 5:23 is implicit from the use of "Church" and "Body" in a parallelism.

31 Cerfaux, p. 259. "To say that the Church is the Body of Christ because the life of grace and the life of Christ are alike is not enough. To say that there is an identity of life and therefore an identity of the Church and the Body is too much." (*Ibid.*, p. 258, note 4)

32 Benoit, "Corps, Tête . . . ," p. 21.

33 I Corinthians 3:16; 16:19; II Corinthians 6:16.

34 Cerfaux, p. 260.

35 Ephesians 1:23. Cf. Benoit, "Corps, Tête . . . ," pp. 40-44. For a different interpretation see J. A. T. Robinson, pp. 67-70. Confer also A. Feuillet, "L'Église, Plérôme du Christ d'après Éph.," *Nouvelle Revue Théologique* 78 (1956), pp. 446-472; 593-610.

36 Benoit, "Corps, Tête . . . ," p. 28.

37 II Corinthians 11:2 is explicit; I Corinthians 6:16-17 and Romans 7:4 are implicit.

38 Cerfaux, pp. 263-264.

39 Benoit, "L'Horizon Paulinien . . . ," pp. 517-518.

PART **2** *The Nature of the Church*

CHAPTER 4 *The Church—The Continuation of Christ**

by JOHN VODOPIVEC

AUTHOR: John Vodopivec is professor of Fundamental Theology at Rome's Pontifical University for the Propagation of the Faith and editor of the distinguished journal of that university, *Euntes Docete.* He is a consultant to the Secretariat for the Promotion of Christian Unity and otherwise active in ecumenical work.

ARTICLE: "The Church—The Continuation of Christ" examines the Scriptural and Patristic data on the Church and finds a unifying theme in these sources in the notion of the Church as a continuation of Christ and Christ's historical mission in the world. This theme harmonizes well with the doctrine of Pius XII's classic encyclical on the Church, *Mystici Corporis.* Msgr. Vodopivec recapitulates his research into the Scriptural and Patristic doctrine on the Church with a ten-point summary of that doctrine, built around the theme of the Church as a continuation of Christ.

READINGS: Three penetrating and highly personal summaries of Catholic doctrine on the Church are Karl Adam, *The Spirit of Catholicism* (Image Paperback, $.85); Roger Hasseveldt, *The Church, A Divine Mystery* (Fides Publishers, 1954); and Louis Lochet, *Son of the Church* (Fides Paperback, $1.50). The most useful single tool for keeping abreast of current work on the Church is *Theology Digest* (4 issues a year; $3.00

* "The Church—The Continuation of Christ" is a translation of "L'Église—continuation du Christ," originally published in *Euntes Docete* 7 (1954), pp. 312-325.

annual subscription; St. Mary's College, St. Marys, Kansas), which is packed with highly readable digests of the best current literature in this and most other areas of Catholic theology.

AT THE BEGINNING of this century theological discussion in ecclesiology was especially concerned with the question: Did Christ really found a Church, a "society of the faithful"? The negative solutions, determined primarily by the prejudices of a rationalistic and liberal philosophy blind to the supernatural element in the Gospel, now appear outmoded. But still at issue is another question of even greater importance: What is the essence or true nature of the Church instituted by Christ? The differences which divide the Christian confessions on this point are very marked and at times would appear almost insuperable.

A preliminary remark on the method of this chapter is in order here. It is necessary to set aside all a priori ideas which would only distort the true Christian perspective. It is absolutely necessary to take as our only positive basis revealed truth, especially the teaching of the Gospels and the rest of the Bible, in all their integrity and breadth. Our own favorite ideas ought not direct our inquiry. The sole path to fruitful understanding (in any interconfessional discussions as well) is to recognize the sovereignty of Christ the eternal King, first in our theological reasoning and then in our daily Christian life. If we were to push aside or leave in the shadows in our theological synthesis certain positive biblical conceptions, then we would be fundamentally disobedient to Christ and guilty of an irreparable fault. We are dealing with supernatural realities where the principal response of the human soul is to listen, to accept, and to be joyfully open to the divine gifts and charisms.

The Church: As Institution, as Body of Christ

It is significant that the Church is presented in the Gospels under two aspects which are constantly interwoven. It is, at the same time, an historical and a transhistorical reality, the society of the faithful and the communion of saints, an institution and the Body of Christ Jesus, animated by charity and grace. But also established in a juridical form. These two aspects appear mutually related and complementary. One recalls the other, so that one without the other remains incomplete and incapable of realization. Both serve equally well as starting points for an equally justified synthesis in ecclesiology. But it seems preferable to begin our discussion with the strictly spiritual and supernatural element, for a clearer presentation of the more specific and characteristic elements of the Christian Church will result from this. In this perspective, moreover, the juridical, sociological, and hierarchical elements will acquire an unsuspected depth and meaning.

First we must emphasize that the Church is absolutely unique in the history of both secular and religious institutions. Certainly we can normally say that the spirit of the founder lives on in his work: the genius of Napoleon watches over France; the spirituality of St. Basil or St. Benedict extends into Christian monasticism. Likewise, we can rightly say that the spirit of Jesus, his teaching, his moral code, and his counsels of perfection continue to live in the Church.

But there is also something more. The very personality of Jesus extends into his work in a very real way and to such an extent that we can assert that the Church is the *Body of Jesus,* whereas there would be no real meaning in saying that France is the body of Napoleon or the

Basilian monks are the body of St. Basil. Thus it is clear that an enormous distance separates the Church as institution and Body of Christ from every other institution, secular or religious, comparable to it in some particular aspect. Even as an institution the Church appears incomparably richer and more perfect than all other possible organizations.

We all know the wonderful description of the Church given by Bossuet: "What is the Church? It is the assembly of the children of God, the army of the living God, his kingdom, his city, his temple, his throne, his sanctuary, his tabernacle. More profoundly, the Church is Jesus Christ, *but Jesus Christ poured out and communicated.*" [1] And Bossuet is not alone in looking on the Church in this manner. J. A. Moehler joins him when he defines the Church (in his fundamental work, *Symbolik*) as "the Son of God manifesting himself ceaselessly among men in his human form, eternally renewing and refreshing himself: his perpetual Incarnation, because of which the faithful are called in Holy Scripture the Body of Christ." [2] Many modern authors would also deserve mention here; Karl Adam, for example: "The true Ego of the Church is Christ Jesus." [3] And recent writers are even more explicit. [4]

Christ's Mission: The Message of Scripture

The newborn Christian Church knew clearly that she was the definitive realization of the messianic promises which abound in the Old Testament. She was the heir of the Faith of the patriarchs, the true Israel of God, the faithful "remnant" around the Messias in his eschatological days.

In the prophetic visions, particularly in Daniel's nocturnal vision of the Son of Man, the figures of the Messias and his messianic community—"the Son of Man" and "the people of the saints of the Most High"—are not only closely linked to one another but are often superimposed, with the result that they appear almost identified and interchangeable. [Cf. Dan 7:13 and 7:27.]

But here, as always, the fulfillment is far clearer than the prophecy. In the teaching and deeds of Jesus the great structural outlines of his Church gradually appear. Each time Jesus defines some feature of this institution, he insists with great clarity on the true spiritual nature of its structure. He chooses the Twelve and entrusts to them an apostolic mission; this mission, as presented in the Gospels, is the very mission Christ has received from his Father. "Just as you, Father, sent me to the world, I have sent them to the world. And it is for their sake that I consecrate myself, that they also may be consecrated by the truth" (Jo 17:18-19). Thus the mission of the Twelve appears as the prolongation and direct continuation of the divine mission of Christ.[5] They are witnesses of the risen Jesus, his representatives. Properly speaking, there is but one single mission, that of the Son of Man, prolonged in the apostles and their successors to the end of time. "Whoever welcomes you welcomes me, and whoever welcomes me welcomes him who has sent me" (Mt 10:40; cf. Jo 13:20). Again: "Whoever listens to you listens to me, and whoever disregards you disregards me, and whoever disregards me disregards him who sent me" (Lk 10:16).

In a very special way the unity of the apostles and of the entire Church is a participation in the unity of Christ with the Father. Christ prays "that they may be one, just as we are, I in union with them and you with me, so that they may be perfectly unified, and the world may recognize that you sent me and that you love them just as you loved me" (Jo 17:22-23). Over and over again Jesus declares his mysterious immanence in his apostles: "When that day comes you will know that I am in union with my Father and you are with me and I am with you" (Jo 14:20). It is easy to see here the idea expounded in the discourse on the bread of life: "Whoever lives on my flesh and drinks my blood remains united to me and I remain united to him. Just as the living Father has sent me, and I live because of the Father, so he who lives on me will live because of me" (Jo 6:57). Likewise the parable of the vine and its branches: "You must remain united to me and I will remain united to you" (Jo 15:4). If it is true of each Christian that he is in Christ Jesus, then with even greater reason and in a higher degree is this mystical immanence realized in the apostles as the official representatives of Christ.

⌊Furthermore, the marks of preferment which Jesus showed the apostle Peter and the prerogatives consequent upon this preferment all depend on the special communion and participation of Peter in the mission of Christ⌊ Indeed, it is this mission of Christ which is manifested, exercised, and realized in the ministry of Peter. Peter could not be the rock on which Jesus intends to build his Church if he did not find his support in Christ. He receives the keys from Jesus and will only be his majordomo, while Jesus remains the true son in the house of God: "I will give you the keys of the kingdom of heaven" (Mt 16:19). The keys are obviously not an inheritance, a natural human quality of Peter, but rather a gift from Jesus. It is also Christ who watches over the faith of Peter. ⌊Peter will be able to strengthen his brothers because he himself was strengthened and confirmed by the prayer of Jesus, whose prayer will always be heard: "I have prayed that your own faith may not fail. And afterwards you yourself must turn and strengthen your brothers" (Lk 22:32). Likewise, the investing of Peter with the pastoral office, "Feed my sheep," serves only to emphasize the continual dependence of Peter on Christ, the true head and supreme model of all pastors, the pastor par excellence and, in this sense, the one and only pastor (Jo 10:1-16; I Pet 5:2-4).

The sheep under Peter's direction remain the flock of Jesus.] A most disinterested love for Jesus is the condition for worthy reception and exercise of this task.

In conclusion let us note once more that in the Gospels hierarchical organization and spiritual and charismatic elements, far from being in opposition, are homogeneous: the one implies and completes the other.

The heads of the ancient Church were fully conscious of exercising their authority in virtue of the mission of Christ and under the direction of the Holy Spirit. The most serious and decisive moments for the history of the Church manifest a special activity on the part of the Spirit.[6] This is certainly evident at Pentecost. When there was question of realizing the full catholicity of the Church by opening the doors to gentiles and pagans, Peter seemed quite hesitant when confronted with the case of the centurion Cornelius, and it was a miraculous intervention of the Holy Spirit that decided everything (Acts 10:1-11, 18). At the so-called apostolic council in the year 49-50, the Apostles and presbyters deliberated as true members of the hierarchy, but their decree proclaimed: "The Holy Spirit and we have decided . . ." (Acts 15:28).

The same awareness is seen even more clearly, if possible, in the categorical affirmation of St. Paul, who envisages the Church "in Christ Jesus" and ceaselessly exhorts all the faithful to participation in Christ and the Holy Spirit (cf. II Cor 13:13; Phil 2:1). Paul is only putting into different words the fundamental insight which he received on the road to Damascus and which remained the springboard of his whole apostolate, i.e., the mysterious identification of Christ and his Church: "I am Jesus whom you are persecuting" (Acts 9:5). For St. Paul the Church is the Body of Christ, i.e., the Church makes Christ manifest and visible. The incorporation of the faithful into the Body of Christ is effected primarily

through Faith and the sacrament of Baptism and is perfected through the Eucharist and the continual communication of the Holy Spirit, who is the Spirit of Christ.

Christ's Mission through the Church:
The Message of the Fathers

With regard to the Patristic period, which was so close
and faithful to the teachings of the Apostles, our purpose
is not to cull a few notable phrases but to capture what
could be termed the central religious experience of the
Fathers. As the juridical and hierarchical structure of the
Church was then in a state of evolution and less fixed than
it is today, the Fathers from the beginning preferred to
center their attention on the presence of Christ and the
Holy Spirit in the Church.

The first vigorous affirmation of the monarchical episcopate, which we meet at the beginning of the second century in St. Ignatius of Antioch, is completely impregnated
with a spiritual, charismatic, and mystical consciousness.
The episcopate is imposed by the Spirit and in the Spirit.
Perfect obedience to the bishop is absolutely necessary
and essential for anyone who desires to conform himself
to Christ and live according to God and in communion
with the Holy Trinity. St. Ignatius is not worried about
distinguishing two levels, juridical and spiritual, within
the Church, because he considers them in their concrete
unity and interpenetration.

The same attitude is found in St. Clement of Rome
some years earlier, and again a century later in Tertullian
and St. Irenaeus, engaged in a struggle against gnostic
heresies. The Church is irresistibly drawn into conflict
with all such heresies because she is the sole guardian of
Truth, the living receptacle of the Holy Spirit. "Where
the Church is, there is the Holy Spirit" (Irenaeus, *Adv.*

[88]

Haer. 2, 24, 1). It was St. Irenaeus who described the Church so well as both a system spread throughout the world and the Body of Christ marked by episcopal succession.

From St. Cyprian, another champion of episcopal discipline, we have a completely spiritual definition of the Church: "the redeemed people who are gathered together in the unity of the Father, Son, and Holy Spirit" (*De Oratione Domini,* 23). The teaching of St. Augustine on the Church, the Mystical Body of Christ and the total Christ, is too well known to repeat here. Let us only remark that it was precisely this mystical conception which furnished Augustine with the best arguments for the often repeated and often misunderstood statement, "Outside the Church there is no salvation."

Finally, to clarify another important point in the evolution of patristic thought, we will conclude with St. Leo the Great. St. Leo's demonstration of the primacy of the bishop of Rome is based on the communication that obtains between Christ, Peter, and the current pope: Christ who acted in Peter still acts in his successors. Leo's ideas have remained valid and alive in the whole tradition of Roman Catholicism and are reflected in the teaching of Vatican Council I. In its dogmatic constitution on the Church, the Council introduced its dogmatic definition of the primacy and infallibility of Peter and his successors with the indisputable assertion that the Church is the continuation of the Redemption and herself perpetuates the salutary work of redemption: "The eternal Shepherd and Guardian of our souls, in order to render the saving work of redemption lasting, decided to establish his holy Church that in it, as in the house of the living God, all the faithful might be held together by the bond of one Faith and one love."

Furthermore, Pius XII's *Mystici Corporis* (1943) is in

its entirety an authentic and wonderfully rich presentation of the idea of the Church as the Mystical Body of Christ.

General Perspective of Scriptural and Patristic Doctrine on the Church

Perhaps it will be useful, especially in view of our ecumenical discussions, to gather the biblical and patristic data on the Church into a general sketch which will present the most significant points in the light of the great fundamental principle: *The Church is the continuation of Christ.*

We are concerned here not so much with any application or theological deduction as with the statement of certain facts which are more or less explicitly involved in this general principle.

(1) In the Christian Church, the Mystical Body, Christ himself is prolonged by the continuation of his redemptive mission and, in some manner, by the growth of his mystical personality. The Church not only acts in virtue of powers received from Christ but also *is* Christ, the total Christ, Christ poured forth and imparted, Christ in his communal, social, and collective personality: "Christ and the Church, the total Christ, one person," says St. Augustine. The hierarchical and institutional Church is Christ, the living Redeemer, still living and acting among us down through the centuries. This interpretation is so perfect and essential that no institutional element can be adequately explained without taking it into account.

(2) Through Christ, the Church is reunited with the Trinity and shares, in its divine life as the Body of the Incarnate Word. She enters into intimate union with the three Divine Persons. The Christian Church is the unique Temple of the Holy Trinity. In a very special manner the Holy Spirit is called the soul of the Church.

(3) In Christ "all the fullness of God's nature lives embodied" (Col 2:9), and through Christ this fullness reaches the Church, which thus becomes the *pleroma,* the fullness, of Christ. She is the perfect receptacle for his highest graces and at the same time his completion, since only in the Church with her divinely established organs and institutions does Jesus as Head of the Mystical Body normally exercise and fully disclose his sacred striving for our complete redemption.

In this respect the Church is always perfect, in each age and under all earthly conditions, even in periods of apparent humiliation, as long as she is the true Church of Christ. Even when she is persecuted and humiliated by enemies and the weakness of her own children, as spouse of Christ the Church always remains the *pleroma* of Christ. The Church is the complement of him who is completely perfected only in all his members (cf. Eph 1:23). The spiritual riches of the Church are inexhaustible.

(4) Under the continual influence of Christ the Head, "the whole system, adjusted and united by each ligament of its equipment, develops in proportion to the functioning of each particular part, and so builds itself up through love" (Eph 4:16). The immanent vital law of the Church demands growth to the full and perfect age of Christ. It produces in the entire Body a marvelous and magnificent dynamism which expresses itself, in varying degrees, in all the vital actions of the Church. The Church is marching towards her eschatological goal and her encounter with Christ, the supreme Judge who will lead her, transfigured, into eternal beatitude. The Church is already the Body of Christ the Redeemer. But she is still waiting for the full blossoming of the glory which has been sowed in the Body but has at present matured only in the Head. This Head, Christ, is constantly drawing all the other members towards his glorious state. All the hierarchical

and social apparatus of the Church is at the service of this progressive transfiguration of the entire Body through grace and glory.

(5) The unity of the Church is the vital, organic, and harmonious unity of the Body of Christ. "One Body and one Spirit . . . one Lord, one Faith, one baptism, one God and Father of all . . ." (Eph 4:4-5). Certainly differences are necessary, but only within an organic harmony which admits no contradictions. We can only regret the fact that some theologians have abandoned the idea of the Body of Christ and have sought to justify as permissible in the Church doctrinal antitheses and organizational divisions which are mutually exclusive. The thought of St. Paul was quite the opposite. Can Christ be in opposition to himself?

(6) The unity of the Body of Christ is universal and catholic, because Christ is the sole Redeemer of all. St. Paul supported his universalism with the idea that there is only one God and only one Christ. "Does God belong to the Jews alone? Does he not belong to the heathen too?" (Rom 3:29). Universal monotheism finds its concrete realization in the Body of Christ, in which the parts, previously divided, are united to God in one single organism, through the Cross (cf. Eph 2:16). The ecumenical movement is inspired by this universal unity in the Catholic sense and is tending toward it. But we must emphasize that, according to the thought of St. Paul, this unity is a unity *given in Christ* through his Cross rather than a *unity to be achieved* through human effort. The Body of Christ is one and is meant for all men in the whole of human history; human divisions cannot destroy it since its existence is founded essentially on a divine and not on a human act and since the human institutions of the Church are always assisted by the Spirit of Christ. Therefore in itself this Body is an indefectible and permanent unity. Otherwise our ecumenical efforts would be doomed

to an agonizing despair. Our human strength would not be capable of constructing and re-creating the unity of this divine-human order if, unhappily, it had been destroyed. The task of men is to incorporate themselves into this pre-established order, which has always existed because it has always been sustained by Christ himself. It follows that the ecumenical movement ought to be carried out with perfect obedience to Christ, in a search for the existing unity given in Christ Jesus and his Church.

(7) Like the natural organic body, the Mystical Body acts through its members so that each fulfills its own proper function. As Head, Jesus is, through the Holy Spirit, the unique source of all the activity of the entire Body, but in different ways in different parts. Repeatedly St. Paul returns to this teaching. "Each one is given his spiritual illumination for the common good" (I Cor 12:7). Christ, the Head of the Mystical Body, is the only sovereign master of this distribution. He makes use of the cooperation of men in accordance with his own free choice, wisdom, and goodness. In the sacraments he acts with such direct effectiveness that St. Augustine can say: "Whether Peter baptizes or Judas baptizes, it is really Christ baptizing." Christ makes use of the hierarchical functions in a different way: "Whoever listens to you listens to me" (Lk 10:16). Though the Church's authority to govern involves real jurisdiction over the faithful, it is still an instrument of Christ the Head and serves the common good of the entire Body.

(8) Thus Christ acts in the simple faithful differently than he acts in the college of bishops who are the successors of the apostles and so witnesses, representatives, and ministers of Christ. Their teaching, when unanimously proclaimed as revealed, is not subject to error because it is protected by the special assistance of Christ and his Spirit. Otherwise the whole Body of Christ would fall into error. Moreover, Christ is perfectly free to establish the condi-

tions for such assistance. It is not each bishop who personally enjoys this charism of infallibility but only the college of bishops.

(9) By saying this we do not mean to restrict Christ's freedom by an obligation to act in all the bishops in exactly the same manner. It was the decision of his sovereign will to give the apostolic college and the episcopal college a guide and head who is invested with powers and exceptional charisms for the good of the whole Body. Of course he enjoys these powers not in virtue of his natural qualities or because of a general sociological postulate, but only because Christ himself chose this manner of making his presence in his Body the Church visible and efficacious.

The position of the Roman Pontiff is explained *only* by the fact that in his quality as vicar of Christ and in spiritual union with St. Peter he is the permanent foundation of an indefectible Church, a foundation constituted by the free choice of Christ, the Founder of that Church. Thus the sole explanation for his infallibility (exercised under well defined conditions) is the soverign decision of Christ to act in this manner in his human vicar. The possibility of such a decision is beyond dispute; likewise its usefulness and suitability appear strongly indicated. Indeed, why should not Christ so manifest his infallible guidance in human form in moments of extreme importance for his entire Body?

(10) There is no question here of a substitution of the human for the divine, but rather of a complete confirmation and manifestation of the divine in the human. Every other perspective would be a distortion. If the Church is the continuation and prolongation of the Incarnation of the Divine Word, the possibility of such an invasion of the divine into our human sphere is a necessary consequence of this central fact of Christianity. Far from nullifying or weakening the sovereignty of Christ, it represents a su-

preme manifestation of the primacy of the spiritual and supernatural order over human weakness.

Conclusion

We have tried to understand and define the Church as the Body of the Living Christ, poured forth and communicated among us. To be a Christian does not merely mean adherence to a more or less extensive body of doctrines; it means incorporation and insertion into the living and organic unity of the Mystical Body of Christ, which is at one and the same time both spiritual and visible. One will be fully a Christian only by belonging to the Church, the total Christ.[7] The only place for our total encounter with the total Christ is the Church of Christ, his only true Spouse. By accepting this Church with all her divinely established structures, we simply render a homage of complete obedience and genuine love to Christ, our Head.

Notes

1 Bossuet, *Notes sur l'Église, tirées d'une allocution aux nouvelles Catholiques, d'avant son épiscopat.*

2 J. A. Moehler, *Symbolik*, no. 23.

3 K. Adam, *Das Wesen des Katholizismus* (4th ed., 1927), p. 24.

4 Cf. Charles Journet, *Primauté de Pierre* (Paris, 1953); Roger Hasseveldt, *Le mystère de l'Eglise* (Paris, 1953), p. 204; Yves M. J. Congar, "Dogme christologique et ecclésiologie," *Das Konzil von Chalkedon* (Würzburg, 1954), III, pp. 239-268, esp. 262-263.

5 In connection with this argument it would be interesting to compare two studies, one by the Orthodox theologian Georges Florovsky and the other by the Dominican Ceslaus Spicq. Both papers appeared in the volume of ecumenical studies, *La Sainte Eglise Universelle* (Paris, 1948), pp. 2-57 and 175-219. The two viewpoints overlap and somewhat approach our own.

6 For a more detailed study, cf. the searching essay by Yves Congar, written in 1952, which comprises chapter 13 of this volume, "The Holy Spirit and the Apostolic Body, Continuators of the Work of the Church."

7 Cf. Ch. Moehler, "Orientations doctrinales et perspectives catéchetiques," *Lumen Vitae* 8 (1953), 377-409. The third issue of this volume of *Lumen Vitae* is entirely devoted to the theme, "The Meaning of the Church."

Translated by JOHN J. MAWHINNEY S.J.

CHAPTER 5 *The Church as a Communion**

by M. J. LE GUILLOU, O.P.

AUTHOR: M. J. Le Guillou is prominent in the work of Istina, the center established by the Dominicans of Paris for ecumenical work with Orthodox Christians, and is a frequent contributor to that center's journal, also called *Istina.*

ARTICLE: "The Church as a Communion" is an attempt to present the Church in categories which were common to the East and the West before the schism and which constitute a common heritage for both today. The central notion of the Church as a Eucharistic communion emphasizes the dynamic inner life of communion with the Trinity through the Eucharist and the communion of the individual local churches with one another and with their center, the church of Rome, in the unity of their common apostolic tradition, common apostolic mission, and common Eucharistic celebration. Around this central notion Father Le Guillou constructs a harmonious summary of Catholic doctrine on the Church.

READINGS: This seems an appropriate place to mention two books which everyone really ought to read sometime during the course of a study of the Church. The first is an anthology of eminently Catholic writings on eminently catholic realities: *The Idea of Catholicism* (edited by W. J. Burghardt, S.J., and W. F. Lynch, S.J.; Meridian Books, 1960). The second is a penetrating analysis of the essential nature of Protestantism, by a former Calvinist divine now a Catholic priest and world-

* "The Church as a Communion" is a selection translated from Father Le Guillou's *Mission et Unité* (Éditions du Cerf, 1960), vol. 2, pp. 155-170. It is reprinted here with the kind permission of Helicon Press (Baltimore), who will publish an English edition in 1964.

famous scholar: Louis Bouyer, *The Spirit and Forms of Protestantism* (Newman, 1956).

The Notion of "Communion"

THE TRADITIONAL ecclesiology common to the West and to the East before the schism can be summed up in this phrase: the Church is a catholic *communion* whose center is the Church of Rome.[1]

For the New Testament as for the fathers, the Church is constituted by a communion, a *koinonia*, a *communio*. The consciousness of this is so prevalent in the first centuries that St. Augustine can declare: "The testimony of the canonical writings demonstrates, without having need of an interpreter, that the Church consists in a communion of the entire universe." [2]

So too the Catholic Church, in her very visibility, is constituted by the communion of local churches represented by their bishop and identified with him, a communion which has its center and head in the Church of Rome. In other words, the Catholic Church is not a simple communion in the Faith but a communion in the Eucharist which is expressed by the mediation of the bishops in union with one another and with the first of the bishops, the Pope.

Let us briefly try to make these various points a little clearer.

A COMMUNION OF FAITH

All the terms expressive of communion, whether they be Greek terms like *koinonia, koinonia kai agape, symphonia kai eirene,* or Latin terms like *communio, communicatio, societas, pax,* or even such a phrase as "the communion of saints," [3] designate, beyond the particular

[98]

nuances each of them implies, *the Church in her visibility*. They never designate a community founded on a simple communion of thought or even a simple communion in the faith. It is not that the early Church did not have an extremely acute sense of unanimity and harmony in the faith. If there were need of them, texts such as those of Irenaeus are there to attest it: "This faith, although it be disseminated throughout the entire world, the Church guards as carefully as if it dwelt in a single house; she believes in these things as if she had a single heart and a single soul; she preaches them with the same agreement, she teaches them and transmits them as if she had but a single mouth." [4] Born in response to the apostolic preaching, the Church is well aware that she lives only by her confession of the kingship of Christ. Is she not the community of the last days which has for its special mission the spreading of the Word by the proclamation of the "mighty deeds of God?" [5]

But this communion in the faith does not suffice to constitute the Church, unless one includes the Church's sacramental structure and the charity she expresses in relations of reciprocal service. Excommunicated sinners who keep the faith, schismatics such as the Novatians who have always had the same faith as the Catholic Church, are nevertheless cut off from this communion. Agreement in the faith, a condition *sine qua non* of communion, is not this communion itself.

A SACRAMENTAL COMMUNION

It is in the Eucharist, efficacious sign of the unique sacrifice of Christ, expressive of the death and return to the Father of that Body whose Head is Christ, that the communion of the Church is constituted and expressed. Here, too, the union of the baptized among themselves and with the glorified Christ is confirmed and intensified. Here is revealed, in the recollection of the Lord's death,

[99]

the Church as Body giving witness by her unity to the life of Christ made manifest in mortal bodies. So also the local church manifests its nature in the liturgical assembly presided over by the bishop, "sacrament" of the celestial High Priest: it is a communion, and a communion so profound that the bishop is identified in some way with his people. The texts of St. Ignatius and St. Cyprian come to mind:

> May that Eucharist alone be regarded as legitimate which is made under the direction of the bishop or his delegate. Have care to do all things in holy agreement under the direction of the bishop.[6]

> One must do nothing without the bishop in that which concerns the Church.[7]

> The Church is the people united to their bishop and the flock devoted to its shepherd.[8]

> Know it well: the bishop is in the Church and the Church is in the bishop. Those who are not with the bishop are not with the Church.[9]

The bishop *is*, in a way, the Church; he personifies it; he is the living expression of its communion.

The local community is in communion with all the other churches spread throughout the world. According to St. Irenaeus, the custom was to send the Eucharist as a sign of communion; the popes had the Eucharist sent to the bishops of Asia.[10] In a more regular fashion, in the fifth century the custom was introduced (in the East especially) of naming in the anaphora the bishops with whom one was in communion.[11] This communion between local churches allowed a bishop passing through a city to be admitted to concelebration with the bishop of that city and similarly allowed a travelling member of the faithful to attend communion services with the faithful of the city. In the beginning of the third century the epitaph of Abercius assures us that he found brothers everywhere, with whom he partook of "the large fish" (that is, the Christ).[12]

The Christians of the various local churches thus form a single people, the Church, because they belong to the same communion whose Sacrament is the Eucharist. They do not have to choose between local church and universal church: the adhesion to both is made in the same movement.[13]

A COMMUNION OF SERVICES

This communion is also expressed, on the local level, in the reciprocal services that the charismatic gifts and the diverse hierarchical functions imply and, on the universal level, in the network of relations and services which the churches perform for one another. Evidence for this includes the exchange of letters on the occasion of episcopal consecrations or important events like persecutions, etc., as well as collections, reciprocal aid, and voyages specially made to Rome.[14]

Communion, then, expresses the *mutual organization of the Church in love,* its plenitude of life as Body, in which the members encourage one another in a unified diversity of the charisms given by the Spirit.

This *corporate* aspect of the Church seems to have been perceived in all the activities of the Church and particularly in the liturgy. Does not the word *leitourgia* evoke precisely the corporate note of an action which is that of all the people but realized in the person of its head or representative? Better still, are not the life and common work of the entire Church a liturgy? So also, even in the action where the bishop as minister of Christ remits sins, he is aware that he does it with the praying participation of the entire body of the faithful.[15]

A COMMUNION STRUCTURED BY THE MEDIATION
OF THE BISHOPS

This communion of the various local churches is expressed in the communion of the bishops among themselves: they are the ones who, as joint guardians of the

Faith and unity of the Church and official representatives of Christ, have the power to grant or refuse the right to participate in this communion. "He who has a bishop," says Optatus, "communicates through him with the other bishops and through the bishops with the other churches." [16] They alone have power to grant letters of communion.[17]

The Church thus appears as a communion determined by an element of authority (which necessarily assumes a juridical character, namely, the power of the bishops).[18] It is useless to wish to discover in the Church of the first centuries a Church which would be only the expression of a charity conceived in modern terms of purely affective ties. Communion always includes a juridical element, without which it is inconceivable, namely, the authority of the bishop as sole judge of entry into or continuance in the communion. Moreover, the bishop can make decisions only in as much as he represents the universal Church for his flock and dwells in communion with the other bishops.[19] He is not the head of a community which he can model according to the whim of his own desires or fantasies. He knows—indeed, it is the very condition of communion—that he is joined by a corporate act [20] to a college which, by succession, draws its origin from the apostles and, in assuring the continuity of the Church in time, has the care of the Lord's flock. In nourishing the part of the flock which has been entrusted to him, he is acting in communion with this college; in case of difficulty, he has an ultimate criterion of this communion in the bishop of Rome.

It is, in fact, the college presided over by the Pope of Rome which is the principle of unity of the Church, because there is present there, in the visible sign of Christ the King guiding it by his Spirit, the principle of authority. Thanks to the gift of the Spirit, communicated to the apostles and transmitted from age to age by the imposi-

tion of hands, the bishops participate in the priestly kingship of Christ. This participated kingship admits of two
aspects: one of government, the other of sanctification.
The bishops are the leaders who succeed the apostles in
their mission of leadership, with the charge of speaking
with authority in Christ's name to guide the people by the
Word. They have received by this title "the Spirit of sovereignty" and their first function is to spread the Word of
God, "their essential mission being to govern the Church
and feed the flock" as true pastors and doctors.[21] By their
priesthood, centered in the Eucharist, they are to sanctify
the faithful in their personal relationship with Christ.
They are the "images" and the "sacraments" of Christ.[22]
In other words, the bishops—by reason of their consecration—participate in the mediation of Christ the King and
are the administrators of the mysteries. They have the
function of transmitting to the faithful sacred things—the
mysteries of Scripture and of the liturgy: i.e., the faith
and the sacraments—and of taking the place of Christ in
the midst of the faithful in order to govern them. They
have power to perpetuate and fortify the Church of Christ
sacramentally and, according to the extremely strong formula of St. Thomas, they represent Christ as founder of
the Church and instituter of her ministries.[23] They possess
a sacramental power which they cannot lose; this establishes a new link between the bishop and the Church,
analogous to the conjugal bond.[24] The ensemble of categories which designate bishops is also common to East and
West: the expressions which the medieval theologians
used in reference to bishops (*supremum ultimum in ecclesiastica hierarchia, princeps totius ecclesiastici ordinis,
dux exercitus christiani*) go back to the Eastern Fathers,
certainly as far back as Origen; [25] and the notion of hierarchy as title of a harmonious system of mediation between God and men, expressive of the thearchy or divine
kingship, derives from Dionysius.[26]

Lastly, the college of bishops is, as such, responsible for the evangelization of the entire world, because it has received *ex officio* the deposit of the New Law.[27]

This communion of the bishops among themselves around the successor of Peter explains and expresses visibly the communion of the entire Church. The communion of the bishops is thus like the visible splendor and the symbolic expression of the communion which is the Church in her profundity. It somehow portrays in itself the corporate nature of the entire *catholic* body. The communion of the episcopal body sums up and condenses— or, rather, recapitulates—the communion of all the churches with one another. The Church is a communion, a body of charity in which are made exchanges of life, energy, and services; and particular churches are not at all independent of one another or closed in upon themselves: they exist only in proportion to their exchanges of charity with the other churches.

This communion of the bishops is not limited to space; it also has a temporal dimension. The bishops, in effect, are conscious of a transmission, along with the deposit of Tradition, of a charism which comes to them from the apostles and, through the apostles, from Christ. Their power and their authority do not have their principle and norm in themselves; these powers have never been conceived as an autocratic and irresponsible despotism; they are, on the contrary, completely governed by communion with the primitive Church and with the Apostolic Church in particular. The point is that Christianity is a gift received from God in Christ through the mediation of the apostles; until the end of time, the bishops have no other role than to transmit this deposit, that is, what was given in the very foundation of the primitive Church, what is first and last at the same time, and forever unsurpassable, what St. Paul and Tradition call "the Mystery." This Mystery is both an act and a truth to be believed; in other words, it is both the redemptive action, the gathering together by God himself of the children of God who were dispersed (a gathering accomplished in the Body of God's only Son who died and rose again), and the revelation of this redemptive action.[28]

The corporate structure of the episcopate has as its purpose the maintenance of communion with the Apostolic Church, which has a normative and constitutive function with regard to the post-apostolic Church. It is not simply the primitive Church in the purely chronological sense of the word; it is a permanent foundation, an unchangeable norm of the entire future Church, the permanent law of all its future development.[29] Here again the corporate nature of the episcopacy is expressive of the communion of the entire Church: it is to the people of God *in assembly* that the Spirit, as guarantee of continual presence and fidelity, gives the intimate knowledge of God, extolled by St. John in his first epistle. This knowledge preserves the faith left by the apostles to the primitive community; the directive impetus of the episcopate serves as the decisive criterion for it.

This communal unity of the Church is entirely at the service of the affirmation of the kingship of Christ. The bishops are only stewards of Christ. They are his image or his vicars. "They take the place of Christ; they are God's representatives in the government of the Church," say the theologians.[30] It is not their job to constitute the Church or to build it; this is the work of the one and only Savior and Lord. Their work is simply to permit Christ to perpetuate to the end of the world the exercise of his royal power.

Thus the Catholic Church is one whose unity is guaranteed by the communion of the bishops. "This numerous body of bishops," says St. Cyprian, "is bound by the cement of mutual harmony and the bond of unity in such a way that, if one of our college should try to preach heresy, to separate the flock of Christ and devastate it, the others would come to the rescue. . . . For although we are many pastors, we feed a single flock and we must assemble and care for all the lambs that Christ has won by his blood and passion." [31] "The Catholic Church is one; it is organized and united by the cement of the bishops who are bound to one another." [32]

This consciousness of communion gave birth to the ecumenical councils, which are nothing else but the episcopal college, the *ordo episcoporum*, assembled to exercise with common accord the joint charge they have of governing the Church of God, while preserving the deposit under the guidance of the Spirit. [33]

A CATHOLIC COMMUNION CENTERED IN THE CHURCH OF ROME

The Church is conscious of being not only one but also catholic: it knows that it is both universal and (in contrast to heresy) true and orthodox, because the bishops united to one another form a communion. [34]

The word *catholic* often does nothing more than express this consciousness of communion. It is enough to recall the text of St. Augustine cited at the beginning of our study. Augustine opposes the Church as a transcendent whole to its particular realizations; he contrasts the power of its internal cohesion with the diversity of its local churches. [35] He distinguishes the Church from dissident sects, emphasizing its organic totality in opposition to all particularisms. His statement is the solemn proclamation of the corporate nature of Catholicism. [36]

An essential element in this communion, however, would be missing if one failed to note that it is centered in the bishop of Rome. In considering the history of the first centuries, it is evident that Rome made herself known by serving as the center and head of this communion rather than by frequently and directly intervening in the affairs of individual churches. It suffices to be in communion with the church of Rome in order to be assured of being in communion with all the catholic churches spread throughout the world.[37] Also, in case of conflict, the judgment which Rome pronounces is binding; Rome is the ultimate criterion of communion in its catholicity.[38] It is truly the one which presides over charity, i.e., over the communion of the churches.[39]

Elements of Traditional Ecclesiology

The Church is a communion of faith, sacramental life, and discipline. It appears as the people of God, gathered together by the Word in the sacrifice of the Alliance, the Eucharist. The Word is proclaimed and the sacrifice is realized by the presence of the episcopate, the principle of the Church's apostolicity and unity as well as of its growth and organization. The Church can also be defined as the communion of the bishops assembling their local communions in the unity of the Catholic Church, whose center is the bishop of Rome. This visible communion opens into an infinitely greater reality: it is the sign and foundation of communion with the Trinitarian mystery.

TRINITARIAN ECCLESIOLOGY

This communion with the bishops and, through them, with the apostles is the basis of a communion in Christ with the Father, according to the text of the first epistle of St. John (which is so often felt present behind all the texts which speak of communion): "That which we have seen and heard we announce to you, in order that you may be in communion with us. As to our communion, it is with the Father and with his son, Jesus Christ" (I John 1:3).

The visible communion of the Church is thus the sign and basis of communion with the Trinitarian mystery. "The communion of the Father, Son, and Holy Spirit is present in the place where the faithful are supposed to communicate on Sundays." [40] An admirable text, frequently cited, of Nicetas of Remesiana, states this lyrically:

> After having professed belief in the Blessed Trinity, you confess belief in the holy catholic Church. Is the Church anything else but the congregation of all the saints? Since the beginning of the world, the patriarchs Abraham, Isaac, and Jacob, the prophets, the apostles, the martyrs, all the just who were, are, or shall be, form a single Church, because sanctified by the same faith and the same life, marked by the same Spirit, they become a single body. Of this body Christ is the head. I say still more: even the angels, even the powers and heavenly beings are included in this single Church, according to the revelation of the apostle: "In it have been reconciled all things, those which are on the earth and those which are in the heavens" (Col 1:20). Therefore believe that it is this single Church that you will obtain the communion of the saints. Know that it is the one catholic Church, diffused throughout the world, whose communion you profess to cling to so firmly. [41]

Thus it is a communion with the life of the Trinity which is brought about for the people of God, the Body of Christ which is the Church, by means of the bishops who give the people Eucharistic communion. The Church is the people whose bond is God himself, through his Spirit.

The Church is the image of the Trinity in its very communion, if one accepts the formula of St. Gregory of Nyssa that Christianity is an "imitation of the divine nature." [42] And catholicity is a reflection of the Trinitarian life. Does not canon thirty-four of the Apostolic Rules institute the synodal administration of metropolitan provinces in order to "glorify the Father, Son, and Spirit in the very order of ecclesiastical life"? [43]

ECCLESIOLOGY OF WORD AND SPIRIT

The ecclesiology of communion is also and indissolubly an ecclesiology of the Word and of the Spirit. If the successors of the apostles, the bishops, are the instruments of communion, it is because they have in their capacity as leaders the charge of both announcing the Word which convokes the Church and celebrating the Eucharist which effects what the Word announces, i.e., incorporation into this Church.

The Word of God and the Church are, for the entire ancient Christian tradition, correlative realities: the *Sacramentum Verbi* always has priority over the sacraments, because it is the cause of faith.[44] The Word of God Incarnate, Christ, has taken hold of humanity in its misery in order to communicate to it, through the cross, by the glory of his exaltation, the vivifying Spirit. Henceforth the Word Incarnate reaches different generations by the preaching of the Word and by the Eucharistic celebration which flows from this preaching and makes real what the preaching announces. He gives us in Scripture the key to the sacramental symbol which presents to us the very object of revelation and which is finally realized in us.

This ecclesiology is also an ecclesiology of the Spirit. The entire Church appeared as a communion animated by the Spirit. Every hierarchical or prophetic function appeared as an operation of the Spirit working for the sanctification of the community, serving its growth towards the eschatological era.

In all its visible being the Church is the manifestation and witness of this presence in it of the glory of God in the Spirit. It is in its very visibility the Body of Christ because the Spirit lives within it. The Spirit remains faithful to the gift which he has given, and it is he who rouses the fidelity of his Church. He watches over the hierarchy as a corporate body to make of it a channel of communication of Christ to his own, to build the people of God. He remains in the entire Body to nourish within its interior the knowledge of God of which St. John speaks and to guide it towards glory, where the full interiority of the Beatific Vision will be achieved.

Thus, because it is the Body of Christ, the Church cannot cease to be under the vivifying influence of the Spirit who is given to it by the risen Christ. It lives the promise of the Spirit's indefectible assistance which Christ has made to his body in its visible structure as a communion. Also, it is in this Body that the authentic Christian liberty of those who are led by the Spirit as true sons of God is manifested.[45]

ECCLESIOLOGY OF TRADITION AND MISSION

Here we have an ecclesiology of the accomplishment of the divine promises in the reality of the visible Church. It is an ecclesiology of a revelation which is always identical, unsurpassable, received in faith. In other words, it is an ecclesiology of a *tradition,* i.e., of a Church, a reality instituted by Christ and transmitted by the communion of the bishops in his Word and his Spirit. Since communion has a double dimension, spatial as well as temporal, it is at the same time an ecclesiology of mission, for this communion is by nature called to include all men in itself.[46] As a communion the Church is an open society and, even if only in germ, the gathering together of humanity reconciled with God, itself, and nature. It is a guarantee of the definitive triumph over evil, division, and death.

The Church is thus defined as an essentially dynamic unity, entirely bent on its missionary accomplishment. Yet by this same dynamism it is drawn towards the eschatological era, since its missionary accomplishment is the image and prefiguration of its eschatological accomplishment. By her very presence the Church visibly signifies the universal salvation which she proceeds to make actual.

And her real action infinitely surpasses her apparent efficacy. Indeed, her entire role is to construct in the world a sign of catholic salvation; in each generation she is destined to confront men with the apostolic testimony. She is charged with preserving the deposit of Tradition (or, if one prefers, of the kerygma) in order to be able to proclaim the Gospel untiringly and thus lead non-Christians to find Christ in it. She hastens the day when all will be one in the charity of Christ. Thus, as a communion created by divine charity flowing from the Trinitarian life, the Church, in order to be an instrument which communicates salvation to the world, lives out her participation in the apostolic mission. It is the entire Church which is a mission, as we have already said; the Church is definitively charged with assuring the visible unfolding of the missions of the Son and the Spirit by announcing the death and resurrection of Christ and by renewing his Pasch in the Spirit of Pentecost.

APOSTOLIC ECCLESIOLOGY

To define the Church as communion is to define it as the people assembled together by the apostolic Word, since the Church's object in her exterior communion is to bring us into contact with the testimony of the apostles communicating with the Word of life.

Moreover, if the Church is the cause and sign of an invisible communion with the mystery of God in her sacramental, Eucharistic visibility and in the presence of the corporate episcopate with its center in the successor of Peter—both of which constitute her as a visible communion—she clearly comprises several interconnected levels, in the full sense of the word: (1) communion in the faith; (2) communion in charity realized by the sacraments, particularly the Eucharist; (3) organization in charity bound to an authoritative, and jurisdictional level which controls admission to and continued membership in the ecclesiastical communion, and at the same time protects the faith. This last level is a guarantee of the preceding levels.

The authoritative and jurisdictional level of admission to and continued membership in the Eucharistic communion and in the plenitude of the faith is the domain of the bishops, but only in as much as they are members of the apostolic college grouped together around the successor of St. Peter.

Such an ecclesiology never perceived an opposition (which was to arise constantly under the influence of Protestantism and then of modernist subjectivism) between *the Church as a community of life* under the immediate direction of Christ in the Spirit and *the hierarchical Church*. Far from separating them, it always perceived their fundamental and indissoluble unity. It is impossible to discover at this level the least difference between East and West: both agreed on the authority of the bishops, the respective position of priesthood and laity, the "inspiration" of the Councils by the Holy Spirit, the place and significance of canon law, the role of Christ as sole priest in the celebration of the mysteries, and of the Holy Spirit as the one who makes real all the sacred actions. Both recognized the sacramental and hierarchical character of the Church as well as her mystical and eschatological aspects.[47]

Communion: Common Heritage of East and West

This theology of the Church as a communion is the common heritage of both the Eastern and the Western Church. It is a theology which presents the Church as both a visible institution and a hidden mystery, or rather as a visible sign manifesting a hidden reality. It transcends any oppositions one can discover between the Latin and the Greek Fathers. It is the Catholic ecclesiology par excellence in as much as it presents "Orthodox" and "Catholic" ecclesiologies in their basic harmony. It is the ecclesiology of a holy Church which, while extending itself to the ends of the earth, still maintains unity of faith[48] by means of its apostolicity. It is the ecclesiology of a living Church which, in the communion of its bishops centered in the church of Rome, is aware of its duty to constitute a visible society which has the same faith, hope, and charity, in a communion of one and the same Eucharist. This ecclesiology expresses what the Fathers, following the lead of the apostles, have unanimously understood by the Word of God. Thus it is normative in its essential lines; it constitutes a fundamental ecclesiology which cannot be questioned. If it has known development as it certainly has in the Catholic Church, it has developed only by remaining fundamentally identical with itself, in unfailing fidelity.

Notes

1 On this question see the fundamental article of Ludwig Hertling, "Communio und Primat," in *Xenia Piana* (*Miscellanea Historiae Pontificae*) VII-9 (Rome, 1943), pp. 4-48, which inspired the first part of this study. See also Dom Botte, "Presbyterium et Ordo Episcoporum," *Irénikon* 29 (1956), pp. 5-27; and, indirectly, P. M. Gy, "Les rites de la communion eucharistique," *La Maison-Dieu*, #24, pp. 154-164.

2 *De unitate Ecclesiae contra Donat.*, 20, 56; PL 43, 434.

3 On this notion of *communio sanctorum* see Badcock, "Sanctorum Communio as an Article in the Creed," *Journal of Theological Studies* 21 (1919-20), p. 110 ff. See also P.-A. Liégé, "*Communio sanctorum*," in *Catholicisme* II, col. 1391-1393.

4 Irenaeus, *Adv. Haer.* 1, 3.

5 Cf. Acts 2:10 and 10:46.

6 Ignatius of Antioch, *Magn.* 6, 1.

7 Ignatius of Antioch, *Smyrn.* 8, 1.

8 Cyprian, *Epis.* 66, 9.

9 Cyprian, *Epis.* 14, 4.

10 Eusebius, *Hist. eccl.* 5, 24.

11 These are the "eulogies" which have remained vigorous for so long. We still have one in the Roman canon: *Una cum papa nostro et omnibus orthodoxis (episcopis)*.

12 Quasten, *Monumenta eucharistica et liturgica vetustissima,* p. 23.

13 It seems, however, that the adhesion was made by right first of all to the universal Church.

14 See Battifol, *Cathedra Petri: Études d'histoire ancienne de l'Église* (Paris, 1938) and the works cited in note 1.

15 This is undoubtedly the most essential element in the ancient perspective.

16 Optatus, 2, 6; PL 11, 959.

17 See Hertling, *op. cit.,* p. 11 ff.; Botte, *op. cit.,* p. 19.

18 We mean the word "juridical" in its largest sense. It is impossible to avoid it, for it answers to an authentic reality.

19 See Hertling, *op. cit.,* p. 20.

20 The consecration was made by the bishops. See *Traditio Apostolica* 2 and Cyprian, *Epis.* 67, 5.

21 See J. Lécuyer, *Le sacerdoce dans le mystère du Christ* (Paris, 1957), p. 257.

22 *Ibid.,* p. 257.

23 Cf. *In IV Sent.,* d. 24, q. 3, a. 2, qa. 1; *Suppl.* q. 40, a. 4.

24 Remember that the episcopal ring, from a simple seal, gradually became a wedding ring. Cf. the reference in the Pontifical d'Aurillac in the year 900: "By this ring of the Faith we entrust to you the spouse of Christ. Keep her holy and immaculate before his face."

25 See P. Battifol, *L'Église naissante et le catholicisme,* pp. 360-369.

26 Cf. L. M. Orrieux, "Fonctions et pouvoirs hiérarchiques," *Revue Thomiste* 59 (1959), pp. 654-674, esp. 655-657.

27 J. Lécuyer, *loc. cit.*

28 H. de Lubac, "Le problème du développement du dogme," *Recherches de Science Religieuse* 35 (1948), pp. 130-160.

29 Karl Rahner, *Über die Schriftinspiration* (Herder, 1958), p. 87.

30 On the notion of bishops as vicars of Christ, see Tromp, *Corpus Christi quod est Ecclesia* (Rome, 1946), p. 143.

31 *Epis.,* 68, 3-4.

32 *Epis.,* 66, 8.

33 We do not deny that historical factors have had their importance in the convocation of councils. But their significance, as Dom Botte has shown so well, does not lie in these factors.

34 It should be noted that the word "catholic" signifies a Church which is both "orthodox" and "universal." Cf. Ignatius of Antioch, *Smyrn.,* 8, 2, and Cyril of Jerusalem, *Catechesis* 18, 23 & 26.

35 The title "Catholic Church" came into use during the third and fourth centuries and rapidly became the Church's official designation. It expressed the institutional state of the Church which, as a totality, localizes itself here and there without any fragmentation. With all its vital forces the Church strives to constitute itself as a totality.

36 This totality is automatically opposed to that which causes divisions, namely, heresies and sects.

37 One can pass, in a sort of regressive analysis, from fourth and fifth century texts to those of the first centuries. The continuity of theme is then much more noticeable.

38 It is not necessary here to review the Roman interventions. But we should note behind these interventions—which are of the order of action and often depend on a series of rather accidental circumstances—the reality from which they originate: the role of the Pope as the principal unifier of the Church.

39 This is, of course, the actual formula of Irenaeus.

40 Cf. Morin, *Revue Bénédictine* 14 (1897), p. 481.

41 Nicetus de Remesiana, *Explanatio Symboli*, PL 52, 871.

42 This formula is wisely taken up again by W. Lossky, in his *Essai sur la Théologie Spirituelle de l'Église d'Orient*.

43 *Ibid.*

44 See Delehaye, *Die Kirche als Heilsvermittlerin bei den altchristlichen Vätern* (unpublished thesis; University of Tübingen, 1951).

45 One could multiply texts on the bond of the Spirit and the Church as a communion. See Tromp, *De Spiritu sancto anima corporis mystici testimonia selecta* (Rome, 1932).

46 We use the word "missionary" in its broad sense, referring to the expansive dynamism of the Church.

47 Protestant authors also admit these facts.

48 L. Bouyer, "Ce qui change et ce qui demeure," *La Maison-Dieu,* #32, p. 117.

Translated by DAVID F. STOKES, S.J.

CHAPTER **6** *The Church and the Trinity**

by PETER FRANSEN, S.J.

AUTHOR: Peter Fransen is professor of Dogmatic Theology at the Jesuit theologate in Heverlee, Belgium. He is the editor of the Flemish research journal, *Bijdragen,* and the author of numerous articles. His book, *God's Grace and Man,* appeared in English in 1962.

ARTICLE: Father Fransen sees the Church as the sacramental manifestation of the work of the Holy Trinity in salvation history and around this concept unifies all the characteristics of the Church presented in the symbols of the Church as the New Israel, the People of God, the Lord's Vineyard, the Body of Christ, and the Bride of Christ. The Church is indeed the "primordial sacrament," the visible symbol of the presence of the three Persons of the Trinity in the midst of men and human history. Christ, the incarnate Word of the Father, is the living Head of his Body the Church, which carries on the trinitarian work of salvation under the inspiration of the Holy Spirit, the Paraclete sent by Christ and his Father. Fransen's insights into the deepest nature of the Church incorporate the views presented by Monsignor Vodopivec and Father Le Guillou into a larger synthesis of great breadth and power.

READINGS: Chapter six of *The Splendor of the Church* (Sheed & Ward, 1956), by Henri de Lubac, S.J., also examines the sacramental nature of the Church. Every chapter of this brilliant work on the Church is worthwhile, as is the whole of

* "The Church and the Trinity" was previously published in *Thought* 38 (1963), 68-88. It is reprinted with permission.

Father de Lubac's earlier book, *Catholicism* (Sheed & Ward, 1950 & 1958). A good analysis of the Church as the Body of Christ is found in chapter four of *The Mystery of the Church* (Helicon Press, 1960), by Yves Congar, O.P.

CHRIST HAS ENTRUSTED his revelation and his Salvation to his Church, and he has promised that he himself and his Spirit would never forsake this Church.

This promise does not, however, mean that the Church, as a community of actual and historical people, cannot be affected by the particular sociological, cultural, and philosophical structures and tendencies of any particular age, In other words, the essential idea of what the Church is, which has been given by Christ himself, has always been lived and realized in the concrete in terms of particular human conceptions about the nature of community and of authority which in any particular period have belonged to the inheritance of the dominant culture. It is, for example, undeniable that the Constantinian conception of the State, Germanic feudalism, the autocracy of the *ancien régime,* and the modern centralizing conception of the State have, each in its turn, exercised their influence on the concrete historical forms in which the Church's life has been expressed. There is even fear that the strong economical structures of our modern society could infect the mentality of our great episcopal curias and our large parishes with the technical outlook of modern business.

Because this holy Church of God is also a Church of Sinners, it is not impossible that these various influences, acting through particular historical forms and customs, should have obscured Christ's own essential idea of the Church and brought it into danger. The Church has therefore the obligation, in every period of its history, to reflect again on Christ's original message, and to purify itself from the various accretions that may have been accepted in a previous generation.

To this end, the surest way must always be to reflect upon the original message of Christ as it has been preserved and handed down in Holy Scripture, provided that this is not done in any spirit of utopian longing for the renewal of the Church simply after the model of the primitive Church of apostolic times. This idea, which has been that of many sects from the third century onward, is an illusion which cannot be realized. Not only is such an idea philosophically and psychologically impossible, since it is impossible for us to turn our backs on history and the inevitable developments which it brings, it is an illusion to think that we can live today just as they did in the first century after Christ. But also this idea involves a denial of one of the most fundamental facts of Revelation itself: Revelation is, as such, history. In other words, the Church was founded by Christ as a historical reality, and for the Church, faithfulness to her Lord cannot mean a static immobilism but rather dynamic growth and development.

We must begin by emphasizing that the Church is both a human and a divine reality, and for this very reason its essential nature can never be fully expressed in our human concepts. It is neither a democracy, nor yet a dictatorship; neither an aristocracy nor yet, as one might sometimes be tempted to think, a gerontocracy; and still less is it a purely spiritual and hidden thing. It is, on the contrary, a clearly visible and historical reality, but one that extends far beyond the historical forms in which it is manifested, as far as the very throne of the all-holy Trinity.

Thus the Church is and must always remain a mystery, which does not mean, as some people still sometimes think, an incomprehensible paradox to be accepted once for all and then set aside, but something so full of richness and depth, of meaning and of reality—that our limited human understanding can never fully and worthily penetrate and express it.

There cannot be any ready-made definitions of the Church, but only descriptions, among which some will be better than others in the measure that the deeper and richer aspects of the Church are more or less well expressed and described in their right relationships and in their true meaning.

We propose, therefore, to consider the principal aspects of the Church, as they are witnessed to in Holy Scripture, and to try then to test against them our present-day conceptions and practice of Church life.

The New Israel

The first thing that the Bible tells us about the Church is that it is the New Israel—the "Israel according to the Spirit and not according to the flesh," the definitive people of God. We know how Israel came into being: how two thousand years before Christ, God called Abraham to be the father of a great people, the people of God's election and promise (Gen 12:1-13, 18). This people he delivered from slavery in Egypt, and it is this deliverance, called *Pasha* in Aramaic, together with the giving of the Law on Mount Sinai, that became the archetype of all God's redemptive acts in history, in the first place for the Jews, and then later for the Church. This is why Easter and Pentecost are still for us the central celebrations of our faith.

This redemptive election by God, as a result of which Israel became what it did in history, is often expressed in the Old Testament as follows: God has acquired for himself a people, appropriated a people, gathered a people together for himself, made a people to be his own inheritance. And in the New Testament these expressions come back continuously as a means of expressing the essence of our Redemption, so that we can never separate the Redemption which was brought to us in Christ from the Church itself in which this Redemption has taken place.

The supreme expression of this saving activity of God in the history of Redemption is the covenant that God made with Abraham, that he renewed with Moses on Mount Sinai, and to which the prophets appeal continually in their efforts to bring Israel back to its God. And the most perfect expression of the covenant which we can find, from the very beginning of Israel's history to the last chapters of the Apocalypse, is the following promise: And I shall be their God, and they shall be my people.

When Israel showed itself again and again to be unfaithful, and persisted obstinately in its apostasy in spite of the prophets, God promised through them that he would preserve and appropriate to himself a small remnant of faithful ones, the "poor of Yahweh," the insignificant and the weak, who would remain faithful to the very end. It was this remnant that was to become the people of the Messias; it would be these, little and of no account as they were, who should be saved in the great Day of Yahweh. To them, and to all among them, the Spirit of Yahweh would be given as a messianic gift.

It is obvious that these themes which are used to describe Israel in the Old Testament are themes which at the same time equally belong to the New Testament. When Christ gathered around himself the 'little flock' of the apostles, he found the Church, the creation of which in the messianic time had been foretold by the prophets. He thus deliberately set his little community in line with the thousand years of Israel's history. This is the New Israel, the true Israel of the Promises, of the true covenant, that "was not sealed with the blood of bulls and goats, but in his blood." He referred to this "blood of the New Covenant" at the most important moment of his life, at the Last Supper, which became therefore the highest sacramental expression of our unity with Christ in the Church.

Moreover, we must not forget that for the Jews and in the language of the Old Testament the symbolism of the blood indicates sanctification, purification, consecration by God and therefore appropriation by God. The blood was regarded by the Jews as something holy because it contained the life, which was the greatest of God's gifts and the most characteristically divine. The whole purpose of the rites of sprinkling with the blood of sacrificial animals was to indicate in a symbolic manner that God had appropriated to himself a people by delivering it from its sins and so purifying and sanctifying it. Thus the New Covenant, too, was sealed with the blood of Christ, and the Church became the New Israel which God had appropriated to himself, a people which he had once again and this time definitively *acquired* and made to be his own possession.

This is the fundamental idea which we find stated even more clearly by Christ. Just as the Old Testament recognized the sons of Jacob as the twelve Patriarchs, who had dispersed themselves in twelve provinces over the Promised Land, so now the Church accepted the twelve apostles as its leaders and fathers in the faith, who would be dispersed "from Jerusalem to Samaria and from there to the very ends of the earth" (Acts 1:8). These twelve are a community of 'little ones,' and it is they who form the original nucleus of the Church, the 'remnant' foretold by the prophets, to whom the Spirit of God would be assured as a messianic gift.

When after Christ's ascension, on the day of Pentecost, the Holy Spirit, "the Promised One of the Father," reveals himself to them and descends upon them, it is then that the New Israel is founded: the Israel that from now on shall be open to all peoples—symbolized by the various languages and peoples assembled about the cenacle—that possesses a new Law, engraved henceforth in their hearts in fulfillment of the prophecy of Ezechial, and that therefore stands under the direct guidance of the Spirit.

The apostles did not understand immediately the full meaning of Pentecost. They continued, as Luke tells us, to live individually as pious Jews, and most of them probably continued thus until the end of their lives. For them it went without saying that one could not follow Christ without first having been taken up into the Jewish people through circumcision and the acceptance of the laws of the Old Israel.

It was only as a result of a new and miraculous revelation of the Holy Spirit which was given to the heathen centurion Cornelius and his family, and this in the presence of Peter himself (Acts 10-11), that the "freedom" of the Gentiles in regard to the Jewish laws became apparent to them. This event is rightly referred to as the "Pentecost of the Gentiles," and Luke devotes a number of chapters of Acts to it and to the effect which it produced upon the preaching of the apostles. And we may particularly notice in this account how, in answer to the scandalized or doubting brethren of Jerusalem, Peter continually repeats the same argument: "The Holy Spirit has fallen on them, as on us at the beginning." This crisis came to a head at the Council of Jerusalem (Acts 15), at which Peter again came back to the same argument.

The last struggle for "the freedom of the children of God," and thus of the New Israel, from the obligation of the Jewish Torah, and from every legalistic and rabbinic conception of religious life for that matter, was fought by Paul, on occasions with great vehemence and intensity, as when he opposed certain of Peter's timid compromises (Gal 2:11-21), and when in his two epistles to the Romans and to the Galatians he set himself against the judaizing tendencies of the Pharisees who had become Christians.

When we remember that for the rabbis slaves and gentiles stood outside the Law, and that even the Jewish woman could not benefit from the Law except through her husband, Paul pronounced the final words in this controversy when he wrote: "All you who have been baptized in Christ's name have put on the person of Christ; no more Jew or Gentile, no more slaves and freemen, no more male and female; you are all one person in Jesus Christ. And if you belong to Christ, then you are indeed Abraham's children; the promised inheritance is yours" (Gal 3:27-29).

The People of God on Earth

Now if the Church is in fact the New Israel, we cannot but regard it as the visible people of God on earth. This aspect of the Church is an extension of what we have said up to now.

It is of course in this aspect that we see the Church's characteristic of visibility. For the Church is by no means a purely spiritual brotherhood of like-minded people, or an assembly of true believers who are known only to God. It is not a hidden reality, eluding our human sight completely. Faced with the practical difficulties of life, man is all too ready to take refuge in some kind or other of vague spiritualism, a fact which is well known to the psychologists. That this is true is clear from the history of the Church. There have always been sects which have taken refuge in spiritualism from the problems created by the historical reality of the visible Church. All that offends or stands in the way is devalued to the level of purely human and secondary realities, and the Church is safely put away in an unreachable and invisible world of grace.

But in reality, the Church is indeed a visible people among the human community of peoples—a special kind of people, of course, since it is not limited by the ties of race, language, and cultural history, or by those of national and civil community in matters of law, civil obligations, and privileges, in the forms which these take in a modern state.

It is, nevertheless, a Church of visible people, with its own authority, its own customs and way of life, its own structures and organizations, with a clearly established manner of being made a member of this community in Baptism, Confirmation, and the Eucharist, and with established forms of exclusion from this community by excommunication, schism, and heresy.

It is a people that is to be found visibly gathered around its pastors in every parish, and the parishes in turn united together under a single bishop. All these bishops together constitute, since they are truly the successors of the apostles, a holy college, the supreme consecrating and authoritative leadership of the Church. Within this episcopal college—not above it—there is the Pope of Rome, and thus as the successor of Peter, he possesses his first and fundamental title and function, the task of visibly and effectively bearing witness to the true unity of this visible people of God on earth.

(It is obvious that this charismatic function of the primacy of Peter has been expressed concretely in various ways in the course of history, a fact which professors of systematic theology are prone to ignore. It upsets their handy little systems.)

This charismatic function, which contains also a primacy of jurisdiction, may also be expressed in various juridical forms, and indeed when one thinks of the complex variety of the life of a worldwide Church, it is normal and likely that it will be so in the future.

Yet there is a much deeper level at which this witness for the unity must be realized, that of *communion*—the living, conscious, and therefore also visibly expressed unity of faith and sacramental life, which finds its highest expression in the common celebration of the Eucharist, the sacrament of unity. And this visible "communion" of the whole episcopate within itself, with the Chair of Peter, and last but not least with the people, finds its most concrete and tangible expression in an ecumenical council.

Thus everything which this visibility of the Church implies, and which in ordinary human terms may be presupposed as needful for the existence of a people on this earth, belongs to the Church, and indeed by the same token, to the grace and the mystery of the Church—for God has founded a people composed of and intended for human beings, who must necessarily live together according to the laws of human existence on earth.

We may not, therefore, allow ourselves to devaluate the Church's authority and its principal structures to the level of purely human and secondary realities. In saying this, we do not mean that all these various forms of Church life which have developed in the course of history are perfect and of divine origin, and therefore unalterable in themselves. History proves the contrary. The great majority of the laws and visible structures by means of which the Church is visibly manifested on earth are on the contrary susceptible of improvement, and thus capable of being altered, because in the last resort they are of purely ecclesiastical origin, and not of divine institution.

We also want to avoid the conception of the Church which developed after the Council of Trent in reaction against the Reformation and the various attacks against the Church in the last centuries, that the Church's nucleus, or essence, or elite, is constituted by her hierarchy and her priests. On the contrary, it is obvious from the doctrine of the Scriptures and the saints that the ministry, as the word itself implies, is a *diakonia,* a service within the Church. Not above it. The ecclesiastical and sacerdotal ministry is indeed a sacral function of authority given to some members of the Church—for the service of God, Christ, and his people.

As a conclusion we may express this in the following way: the concrete details of most ecclesiastical structures are alterable and susceptible of constant change and adaptation, but they are nevertheless necessary and indispensable to the Church's existence in history. She must be constantly reconstructing and re-expressing herself through them, and that she should do so belongs to her very nature, by the fact that Christ has founded her as a "visible people of God on earth." It is necessary to emphasize this point, for it is something that is very easily pushed into the background of the conception which even deeply believing Catholics have of the Church, when they are confronted with the reality of sin and human imperfection in the Church, when they are, as is necessary today, reacting against the conception of a Church which became too clerical, too exclusively hierarchical, and in some places too exclusively papal. But it is precisely this fundamental idea of the Church as identically the people of God on earth, and not primarily a community of consecrated priests, which could restore the proper balance in our vision of the deepest nature of the Church as a visible community of God on this earth and in this human history.

The Primordial Sacrament

By saying that the Church is visible in her deepest nature, with all that this implies in the human dimension, we have not yet expressed the full mystery of what the Church is. For this visibility is not something that stands by itself, like a splendid Gothic arch over an empty and ruined house. It is, on the contrary, full of meaning and significance, supported and held together by the interior reality, and can have no possible meaning without this profound inwardness. We must therefore go on to say that the Church's visibility is a *symbol*—in the deepest meaning of this word, and not simply a certain sign or token—of the fullness of this inward reality. It is for this reason that the Church is sometimes called *Ursakrament*—the Primordial Sacrament. A sacrament contains the fullness of grace which it manifests. So does the Church.

THE LORD'S VINEYARD

Holy Scripture bears witness to this truth in various ways. St. John, for example, uses the very ancient biblical image of the Lord's vineyard.

The prophets often describe Israel as "Yahweh's vineyard" (Jer 2:21, and in the prophecy of Isaiah, 6:1-11). The liturgy of Good Friday reminds us during the ceremony of the veneration of the Cross, of Isaiah's moving Canticle of Israel as the vineyard that brings forth nothing but bitter fruits (Is 5:1-7).

We can only understand the full meaning of this symbolism when we think of the care and the love which an oriental peasant will lavish on his vineyard from morning to evening, the way he protects it from weeds and wild animals and from thieves, prunes it and keeps it free from every kind of impurity, and then in the evening, when the heat of the day is past, irrigates it with 'living water.'

For John, it is Christ who is the vine, and his Father the husbandman. "Each of my branches," he says, referring to us who have heard the Word of Faith in the Church, "that bears no fruit, he cuts off; and every branch that does bear fruit, he purifies, that it may bear yet more fruit." And there follows the conclusion, which is in fact a constant theme of the Last Discourse: "Abide in me, and I in you" (Jo 15:1-11).

[128]

The Church and the Trinity

St. Paul on the other hand chooses another image, one of which we have generally become more conscious in the years since the first World War. He speaks of the Church as the Body of Christ.

In his first letter to the Corinthians and in his letter to the Romans he uses this comparison in a way that was fairly common in his time. The idea of a 'body' expresses the unity and diversity of an organized community that has many aspects, but that is striving after a single end, such as the Roman and Greek city-state or *polis*. So Paul writes in I Cor 12:12-31: "For just as the body is one and has many members, and all the members of the body, though many, are one body—Jews or Greeks, slaves or free —and all were made to drink of one Spirit. . . . Now you are the body of Christ and individually members of it." And he says the same thing in the epistle to the Romans: "For as in one body we have many members, and all the members do not have the same function, so we, though many, are one body in Christ, and individually members of one another" (Rom 12:4-14; see also I Cor 6:12-20 and 10:14-22).

Paul is simply saying that in the Church we form all together one single people and community, and that this Christian people, notwithstanding the diversities of origin and manner of life, notwithstanding also the diversities of function which exist within the Church itself, belongs all together to the one Christ, is led and guided by him and is filled by his one Spirit. This is brought out especially in I Cor 12:4-11: "Now there are varieties of gifts, but the same Spirit; and there are varieties of services, but the same Lord, that is the risen Lord, Christ Jesus; and there are varieties of working, but it is the same God, that is the Father, who inspires them all in every one. To each is given the manifestation of the Spirit for the com-

[129]

mon good. To one is given through the Spirit the utter-
ance of wisdom," etc. Paul then enumerates the different
gifts of the Spirit, ending with the conclusion: "All these
are inspired by one and the same Spirit, who apportions
to each one individually as he wills."

In his later letters, and especially in the epistles to the
Ephesians and to the Colossians, Paul goes a step further.
He begins explicitly to describe Christ as the Head of the
Body, and at the same time clearly to identify this Body
with the Church as such, or with what he also calls "the
Christ." Thus, for example, in the ancient hymn which
he refers to in the epistle to the Colossians: "He (Christ)
is before all things, and in him all things hold together.
He is the head of the body, the church; he is the beginning, the first-born from the dead, that in everything he
might be pre-eminent" (Col 1:17-18).

Behind this development in Paul's language, there lies
a deepening of his theology, as he reflects on the deepest
mysteries of the Church's being and existence. Just as in
Christ "there dwells the fullness of the Godhead," so in
the epistle to the Ephesians the Church is called "the
fullness of Christ." This is Paul's way of expressing the
same mystery which will later be expressed by John in
more personal terms in the Last Discourse: "As the Father
is in me, and I in him, so am I in you and you in me."
Paul continues: "And he (that is, the Father) has put all
things under his feet (that is, under Christ's feet), and has
made him the head over all things for the Church, which
is his body, the fullness of him who fills all in all" (Eph
1:22-23). We may also turn to chapter 4 of the same epistle, where this vision is brought together with the teaching
of Romans and Corinthians in a wide vision of true catholicity: "And his gifts were that some should be apostles,
some prophets, some evangelists, some pastors and teachers, in order to perfect the saints for the work of the ministry, for building up the body of Christ, until we all

attain to the unity of the faith and of the knowledge of the Son of God, to mature manhood, to the measure of the stature of the fullness of Christ. . . . Rather, speaking the truth in love, we must grow into perfect union with him who is the head, into Christ, from whom the whole body, joined and knit together by every joint with which it is supplied, when each part is working properly, develops and builds itself up in love" (Eph 4:11-16).

THE BRIDE OF CHRIST

There is yet another image of Paul's which further enriches that of the Body and in so far as might be necessary corrects it by rethinking the physical symbolism into a personalistic symbolism; it is that of the Church as the Bride of Christ.

In the Old Testament we often find the covenant between God and Israel described in terms of the love relationship of marriage. The Song of Songs, which is in fact a poetic bridal song, has always been thus understood both by the rabbis and by the Church. For Ezechiel, the covenant is like a kind of fairy story about a king who finds a child abandoned in the desert, and brings her up to be his wife, notwithstanding her sinfulness and unfaithfulness. We find also that the most scandalous sin of all in the Old Testament, that of idolatry, is constantly compared to that of adultery.

Both St. Paul and St. John apply this theme to the Church. We shall have occasion to quote the relevant text of St. John in another connection. That of Paul, like so many of his texts about the Church, is from Ephesians. Speaking about marriage, he proposes to Christian husbands and wives, in a very daring comparison, that they take the love of Christ for his Church as an example: "Wives be subject to your husbands, as to the Lord. For the husband is the head of the wife as Christ is the head of the Church, his body, and is himself its Savior. As the

Church is subject to Christ, so let wives also be subject in everything to their husbands. Husbands, love your wives, as Christ loved the Church and gave himself up for her, that he might sanctify her, having cleansed her by the washing of water with the word (a reference to Baptism and the preparatory preaching of the message of faith), that the Church might be presented before him in splendor, without spot or wrinkle or any such thing, that she might be holy and without blemish. Even so husbands should love their wives as their own bodies . . . as Christ does the Church, because we are members of his Body. . . . This is a great mystery, and I take it to mean Christ and the Church" (Eph 5:22-32).

The danger with this text is that with our modern ideas about marriage we may let our attention be deflected by a certain reaction against what St. Paul says about the position of women from the real meaning of this important text. In this matter Paul could hardly think otherwise than with the ideas of his time and of his Judaic upbringing and tradition: for him, the inequality of the sexes, at least in marriage, goes without saying. But this is not at all the main point, which is that within the terms of a historically contingent view of marriage he sets as the highest law and example of married love the very love of Christ, in the line of the whole tradition of the Old and the New Covenant: "Be you perfect, as my heavenly Father is perfect." Moreover, with him the emphasis lies not on this contingent conception of the relationship of marriage but on the living archetype of it all, the love of Christ for his Body which is the Church.

If the Church is thus truly the loving Bride of Christ, then we are all with her and in her personally united to Christ as the bride is to her bridegroom, "even as he (the Father) chose us in him before the foundation of the world, that we should be holy and blameless before him" (Eph 1:4), and still more clearly in II Corinthians, where

Paul says, speaking in the name of Christ: "I feel a divine jealously for you, for I betrothed you to Christ to present you as a pure bride to her husband. But I am afraid that as the serpent deceived Eve by its cunning, your thoughts will be led astray from a sincere and pure devotion to Christ" (II Cor 11:2-5).

These words are not specifically addressed to the women of the community as the liturgical use of this text may tend to suggest, although it is clear from the history of Christian mysticism that it is for these that the many forms of the so-called bridal mysticism can have a more direct application. Nevertheless, this aspect of the Church as the Bride of Christ has a meaning for us all, both men and women, because it is this symbolism which recalls the fact that the Church does not exist apart from our personal self-giving in faith and love. Any idea according to which we could, as it were, be automatically and magically saved or sanctified in the Church is simply an illusion.

The Church as the Temple of the Holy Trinity

There is, lastly, yet another scriptural image to which we have not yet referred: that the Church is the Temple of the Trinity.

We have already seen that the Redemption is not something that was achieved by Christ as it were by a great superfluity of sufferings, but rather by his obedience "unto death, even the death of the Cross" (Phil 2:8). It is by this obedience and love of Christ, made fully and utterly visible on the Cross, that the Father has acquired for himself a people, sanctified it, and made it his inheritance. Or we could express it more existentially by saying that Christ, by his obedience and love, has merited for us that together with him, and in him, and through him—in the solemn words of the conclusion of the Canon of the Mass—we as servants in the Servant, as children in the

Son, should return to the Father in the same obedience and love, and this through the power of the Holy Spirit. The only true redemption from sin is the conversion of the heart: such is the age-old teaching of the prophets, which was repeated over and over again by Christ and the apostles. Against this there is our constant human tendency to want to express everything in quantitative and juridical terms, to measure the Redemption in terms of quantity of suffering, and to see it as a kind of compensation for the evil that we have done by our sinfulness. Behind this lies a deeper and often unconscious tendency. which is the fundamental danger of every religion, to divert the personal obligation to devotion and love to so-called ontological, but often quasi-magical rites and accomplishments.

This sort of correction and purification of our way of looking at the Redemption may also help us better to understand another way of describing it which we find in Paul, Peter, and John, and in the epistle to the Hebrews. By sin we were before far away from God, and now by the sanctifying and purifying blood of Christ, and by his love and obedience, we are once more close to him. He lives once more in our midst. Paul writes: "For he has created in himself one new man in place of the two (that is, the Jews and the Gentiles), so making peace, and by reconciling both to God in one body through the Cross, has brought the hostility (that is, between Jews and Gentiles, but also with God) to an end. And he came and preached peace to you who were far off (the Gentiles) and peace to those who were near (the Jews). For in him we both have access in one Spirit to the Father" (Eph 2:15-18).

We find the same idea with Peter, but now associated with the charming image of the shepherd: "Till then, you had been like sheep going astray; now, you have been brought back to him, your shepherd, who keeps watch

over your souls" (I Pet 2:25). "You are no longer exiles,
then, or aliens; the saints are your fellow citizens, you belong to God's household" (Eph 2:19). It is easy to see from
this passage why the New Testament frequently emphasizes that we all, each of us in himself and again all of us
together, by our Baptism and Confirmation, have become
a Temple of God, that we must constantly allow ourselves
to be built up into a Temple upon the cornerstone that
is Christ, and that on the foundations that Christ himself
has set, in other words, the apostles (Eph 2:20-22).

If we are to understand the full significance of this age-
old image, we must remember that for the Jews the Temple was the holiest of all places. They believed that in the
Holy of Holies, in the very heart of the magnificent Temple at Jerusalem, above the golden plate of propitiation
and between the wings of the golden cherubim in the
room where the Ark of the Covenant was kept, God's majesty and glory were present in the midst of his people in a
highly special way. This was the Tabernacle—the Latin
word for Tent of the Covenant—which represented the
Holy Tent in which God had followed the wanderings of
his people in the wilderness.

There is no idea from the Old Testament that is taken
up again with more power in the New Testament than
this, that God himself now lives in the midst of his people. Now, however, it is no longer in a temple of stone
and gold that he dwells, but in living people in the Holy
Church, which is the dwelling place of the Holy Trinity.
We find this in I Cor 3:10-17; II Cor 6:16-18 (here explicitly in connection with the Promises) and Eph 2:11-22
and 4:15-16; I Timothy 3:15; and in the baptismal text,
I Peter 2:4-10.

John returns again to this fundamental truth in the
Apocalypse, where he describes the heavenly Church in
symbolic language, seeing it "coming down from God"

triumphantly at the end of time, thus as a divine grace and gift. It is described here as the Temple, as the Tabernacle of God's glory, as the Holy City, as a "bride adorned for her bridegroom," as the definitive Paradise—here we should remember that it was the particular characteristic of Paradise to live in the immediate presence of God—and as the heavenly garden from the midst of which flows the eternal stream, none other than the Holy Spirit, which flows out like the clearest crystal from the throne of God the Father and of the Lamb (Apoc 21:1, 22).

Notice again how in this prophecy all the ancient themes which we have already mentioned come together in a final vision of glory and joy: the twelve apostles as the foundation of the Holy City, the words of the Covenant, God as our light, God in his living presence, the perfection of the Church expressed by the number twelve and its multiples, and so on. It is like a marvelous summary of all the biblical themes about the Church.

The Church and the Holy Trinity

We have now progressed from the consideration of the Church in its visible and historical form to stand before the very throne of the Holy Trinity. We might, indeed, sum up the whole theme of this study as follows: the Church is the place and the holy sphere in which the Holy Trinity dwells in our midst. The deepest meaning and the fullness of the Church consists in the very life of the triune God.

It may well be admitted that Roman Catholics probably do not think enough about the Church in this way. In the Oriental Church, however, such an approach is perfectly normal, and it is from the starting point of such a living belief that the Holy Liturgy is seen as a kind of reflection of heaven, which forms the basis of the East-

ern theology of grace and of the sacraments, of the episcopate and of the priesthood—in short, it is upon this sort
of vision that is based the whole Oriental theology of the
Church as the Temple of the Holy Trinity.

Our starting point must be the Redemption. We have
been redeemed by the Father, who "has so loved us that
he sent his only-begotten son, that we might live." This
Son, "became like unto us in everything except sin." That
is to say, he has come into this sinful world, where he has
redeemed us by his obedience and his love, and has thus
made us to be God's people. He has come here in this very
world of ours as the Servant, who has fulfilled the will of
the Father in filial love to the very end "unto death, even
unto the death of Cross." Thus it is that he has merited
for us that we should now with him, in him, and through
him return to the Father in obedience and love, and in
doing so become God's possession and inheritance, because we are thus consecrated to God as his people.

The mystery of the Redemption is thus at the same
time the mystery of grace. What this implies is manifested
fundamentally in the Incarnation—in other words, it is not
a purely invisible mystery, but it comes to us in the visibility of the divine Witness of the Word in our human
history.

This principle of the Incarnation is not superseded by
the fact of the Resurrection. On the contrary, through
his Resurrection, Christ, as the risen Lord, lives nearer to
us than in the time of his earthly life. The invisible Word,
sitting henceforth at the right hand of the Father, his
image and his Anointed One in the Spirit, remains visibly
in our midst in his Body, which is the Church. Thus the
Church has in our own day rightly come to be called the
Primordial Sacrament, and rightly, too, the Eucharist has
come to be seen as the central sacrament in which the
Church is ever and again edified and vivified. The Risen

Lord is the living Head of his Body, which is the Church; and yet, as a divine Person, he cannot be separated from the Father, nor the Holy Spirit from the Father who sends him and with whom he is one in the divine nature, nor yet the Son from the Holy Spirit, who is sent by the Father and the Son to bring the unique work of the Trinity to its perfect consummation.

We should like especially to emphasize this living unity of the three divine Persons, not only in themselves—which is clear enough—but also in their work, which is the Church. For the work of the Redemption and of grace, which is visibly made present in the one Church, is also truly one. And each of the divine Persons has his part in this one divine work, according to his own deepest property: the Father as the unique origin and end of all grace, the Son as the sole image and unique form of all grace, and the Holy Spirit as the one and only realization and perfection of all grace.

The Holy Spirit is not subordinated to any man, not even to the Pope. On the contrary, even within the Trinity, he retains his full and complete originality, even if this is in full and entire unity with the Father and the Son, a unity which is unthinkable apart from the fullest consubstantiality and therefore apart from the fullest originality or property. He it is who from the deepest property of his personal Being brings the one work of the Father in the Son to its perfection. The pneumatic element in the Church can therefore be nothing other than the bringing to life precisely of the grace of the Father in the Son through the Holy Spirit. This one work of the Father is the Church, which is why the Holy Spirit is also often called the Soul of the Body which is the Church, and of which the Son is the Head.

It is for the same reason that we think it mistaken to make a separation between the Church as a pneumatic community and as a juridical institution. Such an exaggerated distinction between order and charism is not to be found either in Scripture or in the Fathers, and is rather an invention of the liberalism of the nineteenth century. This is not to say that tensions cannot arise between the two, tragic tensions sometimes, but in so far as they do, this is never to be attributed to the Trinity itself, but rather to our human limitations and sinfulness.

So too we must not try to separate the activity of the Holy Spirit from the efficacy of the sacraments. For, if it is true that we receive grace by the sacraments in the Church, it is because in them and by them the Holy Trinity give us Its love, that is to say Its grace, which comes to us from the Father in the Son and by the power and activity of the Holy Spirit. The ultimate basis of sacramental efficacy is thus the Holy Spirit, and it is this alone that gives meaning and value to that somewhat unwieldy concept known as *ex opere operato*.

It should be clear from this kind of sacramental theology that, also in the Roman Catholic view, the Church, which is realized in the sacraments, and which is indeed sacramental in its deepest nature, must be seen as the visible manifestation of the living Trinity on this earth. To say that in the West the Church has been reduced to a merely juridical institution is a classical objection which one hears repeated often enough, but which does not correspond to the actual living reality which we find in the Roman Catholic Church. We do not at all deny that the juridical aspect has been given exaggerated emphasis in the West. Nor do we deny that this juridicism is a permanent temptation for the West. But we would maintain that the living tradition of the Roman Church, as it is preserved in her liturgy and in the best of her theologians and in the practice of the saints, and above all in the living Magisterium, in no way reduces the Church to such a conception.

Conclusion

No doubt it is true that the West must constantly be prepared to reflect even upon its dearest traditions, if they are to be purified from this special temptation which has assailed them, especially in recent centuries. There is a real danger of a kind of rabbinic Christianity in which only the *Law* would remain as the life principle. Indeed, we are all faced with a very urgent program and challenge. Laity and clergy, together, we have a great responsibility at this time to reflect upon our understanding of the Church's deepest nature, that by a better knowledge of the riches of our faith we may be enabled to live our faithfulness and attachment to the Church more purely and truly, less according to the characteristics of our particular national or continental traditions, more according to the fullness of the teaching of Christ. Only the truth can make us free. It alone can make us *one*—the truth which is Christ Jesus.

PART 3 *Authority in the Life of the Church*

CHAPTER 7 *The Authority of the Councils**

by PETER FRANSEN, S.J.

AUTHOR: Peter Fransen is author of the preceding article "The Church and the Trinity," and professor of dogmatic theology at the Jesuit theologate in Heverlee, Belgium.

ARTICLE: "The Authority of the Councils" is actually two articles in one. *Part I* is a carefully nuanced and sensitive analysis of the role of authority in the Church. Only after he has painstakingly sketched the functions and defined the limits of Church authority in general does Father Fransen go on, in *Part II,* to examine in detail the authority of the councils, its characteristics, limitations, and general purpose within the life of the Church.

READINGS: An excellent sketch of the history of the significant Church councils is *The Ecumenical Council, the Church, and Christendom* (Kenedy, 1961), by Lorenz Jaeger, archbishop of Paderborn. The author is an outstanding German prelate, a member of the Secretariat for the Promotion of Christian Unity, and a leader in German ecumenical activities. A brief but perceptive survey of conciliar history is now available in *Ecumenical Councils of the Catholic Church* (Herder & Herder, 1960), by Hubert Jedin, the world's leading authority on the subject.

---

* "The Authority of the Councils" is a selection from an essay originally published in *Problems of Authority* (Helicon, 1962). It is reprinted here with permission.

Dogmatic Foundation of Religious Authority

IF WE WANT to deepen our grasp of the divine mystery which operates through the authority of the Church, we must above all remind ourselves of certain essential truths, for they have a profoundly religious value and alone make genuine ecumenical work possible since they deliver us once and for all from any clerical pride and from our sectarian complacency.

In matters of faith, no man, not even the Pope or the bishops, *possesses* the truth. Faith is a divine truth. Christ himself, the Word of the Father and the only way, truth and life, continually gives himself to his Church in the outpouring of his Spirit. This divine truth *possesses us.* And it possesses us in three ways. It commands our acceptance with the very authority of Christ and of God. It gives itself to us as lifegiving truth, and therefore not as abstract or speculative. And finally, it always remains itself, that is, a divine truth which of necessity transcends our powers of understanding and our capacity to express it in human language. All our human thoughts and formulae will always fall short of God's fullness. But since the truth possesses us in this way, we must go on to recognize at the level of our own action, that any reflection on the data of faith—and such reflection occurs whenever a Council is held—involves an authority which is not ours, involves too the need for a living witness and a deep sense of humility and of our unworthiness. All reflection on the data of faith is, in a word, a *diaconia,* a ministry (or in the old sense of the word, *service*) of the Word. To this point we will return shortly.

Truth takes possession of us. But we must go a step further. It does not take possession of us individually, for this truth is *entrusted* before all to *the Church.* Similarly, at the level of the Church as a whole, we cannot strictly say: "The Church is in possession of the truth, of the true faith." Yet the true faith is unfailingly entrusted to the Church, the Body of Christ and the Bride of the Lord. It is entrusted to her as a sacred heritage which never becomes her own property. In other words, the sum total of her teaching will never exhaust all its wealth. The Church, too, necessarily lives a life of *diaconia,* and that is why she is called our Lord's Bride.

This religious view of the mystery of the Church alone makes it possible for us to understand the words of John XXIII who so frequently called on us to see the Second Vatican Council as an invitation to our separated brethren to join us in seeking the unity which Christ is preparing for us. If the Church were simply in possession of the truth in the over-simplified and commonly held sense, all she would have to do would be to wait benevolently for the heretics to return.

But if this truth is entrusted to her as a sacred heritage, she too must ceaselessly purify herself in adoration and faith, and by a renewal of Christian life bear witness before the world to this truth which, while it gives her life, yet transcends her. Only then will she be able to begin the ecumenical dialogue with that deep sense of humility and charity which alone makes it possible.

The Word of the Father became incarnate in the Son, God's Word, and continues *to become incarnate* in the Church. To become incarnate means to adopt the human condition in all its fullness, and while doing so to recreate it from within, according to the rhythm of the Trinitarian life. Here lies the noblest of Christian paradoxes, the paradox of divine love. We must hold that in a certain sense Christ *made his own human nature divine in the very process of making it human.* In other words, only God could so completely regenerate humanity. This mystery of love was expressed in its absolute perfection in the union of the eternal Son with his own human nature. But through his Spirit the Father united the whole of humanity to Christ in the Church. In both cases, this mystery of grace does not destroy our human situation; it purifies it from sin and makes it new in Christ.

We have now to ask what this human condition is in relation to the preservation of truth. Every human truth is acquired, elaborated and developed within a community. None of us can think without using a language, without using words. So true is this that the discovery of certain aspects of truth is sometimes impeded by the fact that some languages do not possess words or the grammatical constructions which are found in others. In order to think we need not only words that correspond to abstract concepts, but also—and this to a far greater extent—we need symbols. It is only too clear that all this linguistic and symbolical and rational and poetical heritage is the particular possession of a given people, a given race, a given human community.

The most inspired thinker can only become a philosopher or a poet if his education in the family and at school has made it possible for him to share in this national heritage. But even then, no progress can be made by thought except through the dialogue between man and man, through the strange dance of question and answer that develops when complementary points of view are brought face to face. There is a dialogue between individual persons, between groups, between periods of time. We are all aware of the swing of the pendulum which takes the thought of a nation from one extreme to the other and so makes it possible to progress in the discovery of truth. The human race thinks somewhat in the same way it walks. It is its state of unstable equilibrium which makes it able to move forward. Thought at rest is dead thought.

We may go even further; sometimes we have the impression that the human race has a kind of communitarian soul, for at certain moments in history considerations that are strangely similar to one another arise unexpectedly in different areas of a given continent among persons who have never seen one another and never read one another's writings. The solitary thinker is an illusion. To think in solitude is in fact the risk of old age because it is to shut oneself up alone with one's memories and so to lose life-giving contact with the community.

Application of These Principles to the Church

When Christ entrusted his truth to his Church, he showed the respect of the Creator for his work by respecting the communitarian fabric of our thought. His word is to be preserved by the Christian community, by the people of God. And the Christian community cannot preserve the Word by fixing it once and for all in static formulae, for this would involve the death of our faith. It must preserve it by living this truth in the Liturgy, in its public and private life, by defending it against heresies within and attacks from without, by preserving the Word 'in its heart,' as did the Blessed Virgin, and not merely in its head; and so it will discover throughout its long history new meanings, ever wider and more rewarding relationships and horizons.

This is the process known as the evolution of Christian dogma. The only difference between the Church's thought and that of any other people on earth lies in the fact that her thought is still less isolated than secular thought. It is the thought of the Bride of Christ, to whom Christ has granted his Spirit to remain with her until the end of time. This is why the Church cannot err. This is why she is infallible, for she meditates on the Word of her Bridegroom, in this constantly renewing dialogue with his Spirit.

It is above all important in connection with our subject to note that this sacred deposit is entrusted primarily to the Church as a whole, to the *catholica,* as St. Augustine readily called her. She alone is unable to err, for she alone is the Bride of Christ. This *catholica* is the Church as the Body of the Lord, as the people of God throughout time and space, according to the apt phrase of Vincent of Lerins: *quod ubique, quod semper, quod ab omnibus*— what is believed everywhere, always, and by all. Here again, we find that the laity have a vocation which cannot be taken from them, anointed as they are as living members of the Church by Baptism and Confirmation. And we should not forget that the Pope and the bishops, before receiving their office, were (and *still remain*) members of the body of the faithful, baptized and confirmed believers.

But *in the community of God's people,* as St. Paul says, "there are different kinds of service, though it is the same Lord we serve, and different manifestations of power, though it is the same God who manifests his power everywhere in all of us" (I Cor 12:4-6). In a word, there are various charisms and so also various missions within the Church, but all are manifestations of the one power of the Trinity. We can never forget these two complementary aspects of the Church, this diversity of ministries in the unity of the Trinitarian grace. The diversity is therefore a real one, it is holy and thus hierarchic. But it is also *organic* since it is constantly renewed by grace and so never loses its fundamental unity. St. Paul continues: "The revelation of the Spirit is imparted to each, to make the best advantage of it," for the common good which is the building up of the Church of Christ, a theme which runs right through the next chapter of I Corinthians (14:3, 4, 5, 17, 26).

There are different charisms and ministries. First of all there is the *Ordo Episcoporum,* the Order of Bishops, successor to the College of the Apostles. There is the *Presbyterion,* the priestly Order, destined to be auxiliary to the episcopate, and through its rite of Ordination sharing in several of the liturgical, pastoral, and governing functions of the episcopate. There is the *People of God,* which, under the guidance of its religious leaders, and one with them in faith, is to bear its witness as a body of believers before the world.

As we have already said, all are baptized and confirmed. Since this is so, all have received the strictly common vocation of witnesses to the truth and grace within them, and this witness they are to bear both within and without the Church. From this standpoint, the Pope, the bishops, priests and laity all have the same responsibilities. From this fundamental point of view there is a similarity between the Church and our democratic institutions. It is even true to say that this aspect of the Church gave rise to the democracies of today. True democracy is only possible in Christendom.

But the Church is not a democracy on the Western model. The Church is a hierarchy, which according to the etymological sense of the Greek word means a community governed by a sacred authority. She is also a people with a hierarchical organization, that is, a people in which each individual has received a place corresponding to his vocation.

Now that we have established this fundamental point of view, without which all that we are about to say would run the risk of complete distortion, we can now apply ourselves solely to the study of the nature and work of this charismatic authority which has been given by Christ to the Church.

And here we meet at once another axiom already alluded to. Since authority is divine, it is never the private possession of any man. It is divine and was given by the Father to his Son, our Risen Lord, who is the one and only High Priest just as he alone is our King. Every other exercise of authority becomes by the same token, and in a very real sense, a *diaconia,* a ministry. 'Minister' means 'servant.' We have already seen that we do not possess truth, it possesses us. So too, we do not possess authority, authority possesses us. I must apologize for insisting so much on this basic principle, but history shows that unfortunately few truths are so easily forgotten as this one. How many times did our Lord have to return to it as he taught the apostles! Its neglect in practice leads to clericalism in all its forms, a great cause of scandal to our separated brethren. It is tragic that it is this particular abuse of authority which so easily arises in fervent Christian communities. It is true to say that the respect shown by the faithful towards their pastors becomes a dangerous temptation for the pastors to fail to recognize the profound religious and christocentric nature of every form of the exercise of authority in the Church.

If we insist on the aspect of service (*diaconia*) in the ministry of authority, it is not with the idea that we ought to diminish the majesty of this authority of the Church, as did the Reformation. On the contrary we are convinced that in reality the Church of Christ, which is the apostolic and Roman Church, speaks to us in the name of God. No authority in the world possesses any power like it. No secular power can bind men's conscience as she does. None of them can demand such sacrifices. None deserves that devoted obedience which is characteristic of the Catholic attitude.

This hierarchical authority is in fact unique. It cannot be compared to any authority known to us in the various societies of men. That is why it is difficult to exercise it with great purity of heart. It is unique from different points of view. No human authority demands such renunciation from the men who are invested with it.

It is never identified with a person, and this for three reasons. We have already mentioned two of them. God is the only source of this authority and that is why its ministry is a holy *diaconia.* In addition this authority cannot dispense with the light that emanates from the Body of Christ, the light she possesses in the witness of her faithful. For if the divine Spirit inspires the Hierarchy, it is the same spirit who prays and bears witness in the life of the faithful. It is the same Spirit who guides the former in its mission of authority and inspires the latter in its mission of witness and obedience. It is therefore the same Spirit who maintains and gives life to this charismatic and 'pneumatic' dialogue, who maintains the life of faith within the Church. Hence the authority of the Hierarchy is never purely identical with the person of the bishop or priest.

There is a third reason for this and it is more clearly evident when a Council is held. No bishop possesses personal infallibility—and even that of the Pope has to be properly understood. The First Vatican Council did not condemn the need for a dialogue of faith between the Pope on the one hand and the bishops together with their faithful on the other. The Vatican definition was directed solely against the remains of Gallican and conciliar teaching when held that the authority of a pontifical definition depended on the subsequent approval of a Council or of the College of Bishops.[1]

Hence in a Council it is the Episcopate in communion with the Pope which pronounces on truths of faith or which decrees reforms. Episcopal infallibility is therefore a charism *possessed in common* by the episcopal order. At the same time it remains one *particular* aspect of the basic infallibility of the whole Church, of the *catholica,* an ultimate and particular specific characteristic determined by the authoritative function of the bishops in the body of the Church. It is moreover noteworthy that the First Vatican Council decided to define the personal infallibility of the Pope by firmly linking it to the infallibility of the whole Church. We are continually meeting this communitarian view of the Church and not the atomistic stand-point to which our rationalist individualism has accustomed us.

We have just used the word *communion*. Communion is a concept which unfortunately has scarcely any further interest for us in the West. Yet it has remained quite universal and central in the East, known as "koinonia" or, in Russian, as "sobornost." We must not forget that it is precisely this primal conviction that the bishops cannot exercise their authority fully in the Church unless they remain 'in communion' with their brethren in the Episcopate which has given rise to the institution of Councils. Hence the 'communion' between large or small local churches in the person of their bishop preceded the appearance of Councils and was one of the basic reasons for their inauguration.[2]

What then is meant by living in communion? Above all else, it is communion in the same faith, that is, a constant care to compare the way faith is expressed in the Creeds and in Christian life with the *sensus fidei*, the way the faith is understood, judged by the expression given to it in the other churches. It is therefore a constant care not to lose touch with the living witness of the *catholica* (or the *oekoumene*, as it was then called). This anxiety was composed of different elements; it was expressed above all in the awareness of the bishops as successors of the apostles, that they possessed a certain jurisdiction over the Church as a whole. This aspect is still always in evidence whenever a Council is held, although it must be admitted that theology has hardly even begun to concern itself with it. This anxiety also revealed the bishops' sense of their responsibility in the Church. The forms in which they gave expression to their faith could not be a matter of indifference to the Church as a whole. If they condemned heretics, this was of great importance for the life of the Church beyond the limits of their own episcopal or patriarchal jurisdiction. In other words, they felt they were under an obligation to invite the other Churches to share in the witness of their own community. Thirdly, this anxiety arose from a need to bring their own particular ideas to the bar of the *catholica*. No bishop thought that he could be the ultimate court of appeal in a matter of faith or even in a matter of discipline which (like the date of Easter) concerned the whole Church.

This communion was brought about by frequent journeys, by exchanges of letters or delegations between one Church and another, and by communicating information as to disciplinary decrees, liturgical texts, definitions of faith and creeds used at baptism. Its highest expression was found in the common participation in "the sacraments of faith," and especially in the Eucharist. In the ancient basilica, the bishop celebrated with his priests around him. When it became necessary in Rome to increase the number of churches and services, the officiating priests received from the Pope during Mass the *fermentum*, that is, a particle of the bread consecrated at the pontifical Mass. They thus showed that they were in communion with the pontifical Eucharist.

All this has ceased to be customary and has disappeared from our consciousness of the Church. We may even venture to say that our bishops are only very rarely interested in religious questions outside their own diocesan jurisdiction. This is a tragic fact in our times when unbelievers and pagans are anxious to unify the world by means of intensive international collaboration, while it is difficult to bring Catholics together on the international plane and to make them forget their barriers of race, language, nationality, and their religious ghetto. We are accustomed to leave this kind of work to the Roman Congregations and to the Pope and it is no longer considered a matter of life and death for each local Church.

We might add a fourth reason to prove that episcopal

authority is not identified with the bishop as a person. It is dogmatic in character and will at the same time make it possible a little later to describe the nature of this hierarchical authority which is *unique* because instituted by Christ and brought into the world by his Spirit.

When Protestants consider the infallibility which Catholics acknowledge in the Pope and in their bishops, they are prone to think of this charism as a particular revelation on God's part. God tells the bishops in a vision or in a dream, as he did with the ancient prophets, what he eventually wishes to reveal to the Roman Church.

This idea is obviously false. Revelation was closed after Christ's preaching on earth and the foundation of the apostolic Church by the Holy Spirit. In this respect there is an essential difference between the bishops and the apostles. The latter were the founders of the Church because they were the privileged witnesses of Christ's Resurrection and the mouthpieces of the Holy Spirit who was given to them so that Christ's work in them might be completed. The bishops are in no sense founders. The Church is "guardian and mistress of the Word." *They preserve the deposit of revelation.* Their infallibility and so also their authority is limited to interpreting in new ways adapted to the circumstances and needs of the time the truths revealed to the apostolic Church by Christ and confirmed by his Spirit. And this they must do without falsifying them.

Thus the charism of the Episcopate does not rest on a particular revelation. When the Pope or the bishops speak or write to us, they are not inspired in the exact sense of the word as applied to the authors of Scripture. The Biblical writers possessed the charism of inspiration, that is, the efficacious assistance of the Holy Spirit which makes their writings at the same time the Word of God himself. God speaks to us in the Holy Spirit through the instrumentality of the sacred writers. God does not speak to us in the same way through the instrumentality of the Pope, the bishops or the Councils. It is therefore very important to note that there is an essential difference between a text in Holy Scripture and a conciliar text. It must be admitted that a spirituality of obedience, a certain form of papolatry due to reactions following on the First Vatican Council, has sometimes made us forget these important distinctions.

What then is the nature of this episcopal or conciliar authority? Theology has a precise term for it. Neither revelation nor inspiration, it is the *assistance* of the Holy Spirit. This concept of assistance has two aspects. Before all else, it implies the need for study of the sources of our faith: scripture and tradition. The bishops must consult the Bible and the life of the Church. This study which is, at the same time, a form of prayer, they undertake themselves, or else entrust it to their theologians, canonists or other specialists. As we have already seen, the witness of the Church as a whole is important. In this reflection on the data of revelation, the bishops are assisted by the Holy Spirit, that is, the *conclusions* they reach do not falsify the data of revelation. The *conclusions*, be it noted, since the arguments used at a Council do not possess the same guarantees of infallibility as the conclusions. In fact only the conclusions involve the bishops' hierarchical authority and belong to their authoritative mission. As we shall see later, this statement imposes very clear rules for the interpretation of conciliar texts, as well as for the interpretation of every episcopal or pontifical declaration.

Nor is this assistance of the same character under all conditions; as we have seen, Councils define the faith or decree reforms or attempt to solve practical problems of Christian living that affect the Church as a whole.

Theologians speak of a *positive assistance,* whenever a Council defines a truth of faith or a central point of Christian morals. This positive assistance guarantees that conciliar definitions genuinely express a revealed truth in matters of faith or morals.

Since it is a question of *assistance* granted to human study, it is easy to understand that these conciliar formulae are not necessarily the best possible, the only possible, or the most complete. It is possible for the Church to fall short on all these points because, for instance, theology at any given time may be defective because the bishops allow themselves to be carried away by partisan considerations, etc. Yet the assistance we are speaking of is a *positive* one. This means that, in spite of human weaknesses at a given period or among a group of men, the Holy Spirit himself guarantees that *what is asserted is irrevocably true from God's point of view* because divine truth is eternal. Hence what a Council asserts really expresses the divine mystery although in a human and therefore always imperfect manner. This is why these definitions are called dogmas of faith; they bind our conscience and are binding on our faith.

The assistance of the Holy Spirit is of quite a different character when ecclesiastical reforms are in question. In this field our human situation prevents us from achieving permanent results, for the conditions of our life are in constant evolution. At a still deeper level, all concrete legislation, including that of the Church, inevitably involves advantages and serious disadvantages. The Church will often have to choose the lesser of two evils. Hence, we only use the term *negative assistance* in such cases, which means that conciliar or pontifical decrees cannot run counter to faith or offer any grave threat to any of the Church's constituent factors, for example, in matters concerning the sacraments. The guarantee is negative, for these practical problems do not belong directly to the domain of faith. Here in their connection we do not speak of dogmas of faith, but of conciliar decrees, canon law, ecclesiastical reform. It is no longer a matter of revealed truth, but of ecclesiastical truth or certitude, that is, in fact, truth whose authenticity is guaranteed by the negative assistance of the Holy Spirit. This latter point is still a subject of theological controversy, and we are not attempting here to advance proofs to justify our point of view; we confine ourselves to stating it. In our opinion, it is of great importance for the formation of a more adult religious consciousness in priests and people.

It could be objected that all these distinctions may well occupy the leisure hours of a theologian, but that they are of no interest at all for priests in their apostolic work or for laymen. We are convinced that the opposite is the case. At this present time especially in the history of the Church, when she finds herself facing a new world of continental dimensions, laymen can no longer do without an adult and instructed faith. If so many priests and laymen have found themselves upset, scandalized or anxious in the presence of the liturgical and canonical reforms of recent Popes, or the enormous work which is being done in theology and Biblical exegesis (and this work has its echoes in preaching and catechetical instruction), it is because they put everything to do with their religion on the same absolute and eternal level—the Trinity and the eucharistic fast, the nature of the Episcopate and the wearing of cassocks, the unity of the Church and the use of Latin, the creation and the origin of Eve in Adam's rib, original sin and the apple of the terrestrial paradise, etc., etc.

There are in our faith certain realities or truths that are absolute and irrevocable and which come to us from God; there are theological explanations of these same realities or truths, whose content is divine but whose mode of presentation is human—and *so* relative; there are the opinions of the schools; there is canon law which repeats certain principles of natural law as well as laws directly promulgated by God and laws which, since they are promulgated by the Church are therefore reformable; finally, there are our Western and national customs and habits of thought, which are only the concrete form in which the white race or a given Western people lives its Catholic faith. All these realities and truths involve varying degrees of certitude, of sanctity, and of religious value. They are often made obligatory upon us by ecclesiastical authority, but this act of authority also implies different degrees of obligation. It is high time people realized this.

So far, we have been studying the nature of hierarchical authority, its limits and its greatness. Above all, we have emphasized its character as a *diaconia,* a service done to God, Christ and his Spirit, a service done to men, to the Church. "The Son of Man did not come to have service done him; he came to serve others" (Mt 20:28). The Greek Matthew here uses the word *diakonein,* 'to serve.' It is this 'ministry' which confers upon ecclesiastical authority all its strength, majesty, and sanctity.

The Authority of Councils

We have come to the second part of our discussion. Now we may study the concrete exercise of this hierarchical authority in a Council. As we said a moment ago, hierarchical authority is above all a *diaconia.* All the Councils have met in the name of the Holy Spirit. The First Council of Jerusalem in the year 51 already wrote in its apostolic letter to the Churches of Asia: "It is the Holy Spirit's pleasure and ours that no burden should be laid upon you beyond these . . ." (Acts 15:28). This is why conciliar decrees today still have the following solemn heading (I quote the First Vatican formula):

Thus therefore, while there sit and judge with Us the bishops of the whole world, met at this Ecumenical Council in the Holy Spirit and by Our authority, taking Our stand upon the Word of God in scripture and tradition as we have received it preserved in the Catholic Church and expounded by her according to the truth, We decree before all men from this Chair of Peter that this saving doctrine must be confessed and declared against the contrary errors which we prohibit and condemn by the authority which God has given to Us (Denzinger 1781).

It would be difficult to find a better summary of all that we have said in the first part of this study. The conciliar ministry is a *diaconia* of the Holy Spirit and so also of divine truth. This truth possesses the Church but we do not possess it. From this profound sense of the transcendence of revealed truth there has arisen a whole *conciliar tradition*.

The Councils, for instance, have always avoided the introduction of technical terms forming an essential element in a given, enclosed philosophical system, even when such a system is a Catholic one. Thus the Tridentine definition of transubstantiation—in any case the word itself is not strictly speaking defined—disregards the Aristotelian and Thomistic cosmology, as the formula in which the canon is couched makes abundantly clear (canon two of the 13th session), as do also the Acts of the Council.[3] At the Council of Nicaea, there was even a conflict of conscience in the case of several bishops when they found they were obliged by the very objections of Arius to look for terms which were not to be found in the Bible.

More recently it has been noted that for the most part Councils refuse to explain a revealed truth but content themselves with condemning obvious errors arising from all quarters. It is as though they are defining *the limits within which the outlook of our faith remains orthodox,* by simply excluding views which have no future. This long conciliar tradition remains much more respectful of the divine mystery than do the theologians who, during the Council or after it, have tried in their efforts at interpretation to find warrant for their own personal little systems. Thus the Council of Trent defined that the Mass is a sacrifice but did not attempt to explain this term except again in so far as it barred the garbled assertions of the Reformers. The first ecumenical Councils all returned by diverse ways to the same truth, namely that Christ is true God and true man, but we will find nowhere any explanation of this mystery. The Church leaves this work to the theologians.

This attitude is of very great importance. It shows that the Fathers are acutely conscious of the profound inadequacy of language by comparison with the abundance of divine truth. If our priests in their catechetical instruction and their preaching, and our laymen in their thinking about religion, had a greater respect for the divine mystery, they would come nearer to sharing the theological understanding of their Fathers in the faith, the bishops assembled in Council. Every expression of divine truth, even in a dogma defined during a general council, even in Scripture, even in the sacred words of Christ, determines the correct *perspective,* the orthodox direction in which we are to attempt to contemplate the Truth which is God himself. No human word, however sacred, can be identified with the Word of God. Though it is true that Christ's human word is at the same time the word of the Son, it is equally true that this human word is included in our Savior's state of kenosis. Hence a defined dogma is always a *starting-point,* which makes it possible for our prayer, contemplation and theological reflection to set off on the right path and to move securely *in the direction* of the Truth whole and entire. These considerations are only one application of the principle we have previously stated: *we* are not in possession of the truth, not even in a Council. It is the Truth which possesses us in the Spirit and which leads our minds and hearts towards itself. The Councils have never forgotten this fundamental law of all religious thought within a religion which is fundamentally a *revealed* religion.

This is why the Councils—and here we find another fairly common tradition—avoid as far as possible the condemnation of opinions formerly defended by the Fathers of the Church, the great Catholic Doctors and the chief theological schools that have flourished in the Church. There is in this attitude not only a respect for the witness of the great saints in matters of faith, but also a refusal to enter into theological discussion within the area of Catholic dogma. As we have shown in our studies on the canons of the Council of Trent in regard to marriage, the work of the Fathers often consisted, especially during the sessions devoted to the sacraments, of a laborious effort to find a formula so carefully worded and delicately balanced that it avoided condemning a Catholic author and dealt only with Lutheran errors or heresies. Anxiety to achieve this has sometimes made the formulation of the canons extraordinarily complicated.

We have seen that the authority of the Church is never identified with the person of the bishop or the Pope, b must normally be exercised in a living communion the Body of the Church, with the *oikoumene*. This a of ecclesiastical authority is also more obvious durin holding of a Council. It is from this same concept Oikoumene, that the whole world, the whole Cl that the technical term "Ecumenical Council," me General Council, is derived. In this connection we our times a widespread error which confuses Ecun Council with the ecumenical *movement*. While 'ec cal' in the ancient and canonical sense of the wo essentially based on the unity of the whole Churc out in a full communion of faith and sacrament, th ern meaning necessarily presupposes a state of and indicates any movement or current of though seeks to restore unity. In drawing attention to this laying our finger on the regrettable fact that we have lost the sense of the primordial value, in every manifestation of the life of the Church, of visible and spiritual unity and communion.

In any case a Council is one of the most solemn forms of communion in one and the same faith and in one and the same charity. The bishops of the whole world, who moreover bear the names of their episcopal sees and so of their dioceses rather than their own as persons, gather round the same altar and round the same Vicar of Christ.

Although Councils have always been meetings of bishops in the sense that final authority has always lain in their hands, history proves that priests and laymen have not been absent from them. From the dogmatic standpoint, their presence gives rise to no difficulty. The only thing which can change, and has in fact done so, is the concrete manner in which their presence has been accepted. And this necessarily depends on the modes of thought and the way of life at given moments in history, although it is fundamentally inspired by the essential structure of the Church given to her by Christ. The same is true of Conciliar procedure. The first eight Councils under the Empire were largely indebted for their own procedure to that inherited from the procedure of the Roman Senate. The General Councils in the Middle Ages up to those of Constance and Basle were very similar from a procedural point of view to the imperial and royal diets. Hubert Jedin has shown that the influence of parliamentary methods is observable at the last Council of the Vatican.

Laymen then have always been present at Councils, ne exception being the First Council of the Vatican. co were formally represented at the earliest provincial he's. Under Byzantine rule they were represented by C ror who was considered by all to be the Patron of ch. the "temporal bishop by divine right." He was either present in person or represented by the Empress, his ministers or his generals. During the Middle Ages, the Emperor of the West attended, as did also the other Christian princes or their ambassadors. Towards the end of the Middle Ages they were joined by representatives of the universities and of certain public bodies. Jedin has rightly pointed out that previous to our own period the question of the responsibility of laymen in the Church arose in a very different manner from that in which it presents itself today. Our ancestors inherited the clan-concept of society from the Germanic peoples, and quite naturally entrusted a part of their civil, political and therefore also their religious responsibilities to the former chiefs of the clans, who were now their princes. The Church did likewise by admitting to her Councils the natural representatives of the faithful, the princes, the kings, and the Emperor. After the French Revolution and the disappearance of the Ancien Régime this social framework was irrevocably destroyed. Hence the last Council of the Vatican was unable to find an immediate solution suited to a new type of society. It found itself face to face with laymen deprived of their age-old corporate ties, face to face with an amorphous mass of individuals. A century later we have to admit that the solution has still not been found although the problem presents itself much more clearly now than it did in 1870.

It should be obvious that conciliar authority does not do away with the necessity for a dialogue between the hierarchy and the laity.

Notes

[1] R. Aubert, "Documents concernant le tiers parti au Concile du Vatican," in *Abhandlungen über Theologie und Kirche, Festschrift für Karl Adam* (Düsseldorf, 1952), pp. 241-259, and "L'ecclésiologie au Concile du Vatican," in *Le Concile et les Conciles* (Paris, 1960), pp. 245-284.

2 Dom H. Marot, "Conciles antinicéens et conciles oecuméniques," in *Le Concile et les Conciles, op. cit.,* pp. 19-43.

3 Denzinger 884. See G. Ghysens, "Présence réelle et transsubstantia-tion," *Irénikon* 32 (1959), pp. 420-435. The Council of Trent not only placed the term 'transubstantiation' in a secondary position, namely, in a relative clause referring to the customary terminology of the schools, but also preserved, in spite of the opposition of some of the Fathers, the ancient terminology, which is less philosophical: "change of the entire sub-stance, though the appearances remain." The Council's commission refused to alter this term 'appearances' in favor of the one in common use at the time, "accidents." See S. Merkle & Th. Freudenberger, *Concilium Tridenti-num, Acta et Diaria,* Vol. VI (Freiburg im Br., 1950), pp. 160-161.

CHAPTER 8 *The Episcopacy and the Papal Primacy in the Life of the Church**

by CARLO COLOMBO

AUTHOR: Carlo Colombo is a member of the faculty of the Archdiocesan Seminary of Milan, Italy, and a frequent contributor to its research journal, *La Scuola Cattolica*.

ARTICLE: Father Colombo's study outlines the history of the functions of the episcopal college as the successor of the Apostolic College, compares these functions to the functions of the papal primacy as these have evolved over the course of centuries to our own day, and then draws some apposite conclusions. In view of the historic importance of the charism of episcopacy in the life of the Church, Father Colombo suggests a number of ways of (1) utilizing the energy and talent of local bishops to the full without undue interference from above, (2) achieving maximum cooperation between local bishops and regional groups of bishops and the central authority of the Church in Rome, and (3) drawing on the wisdom and charisms of the individual local bishops for the good of the universal Church.

READINGS: *The* book to read on this question is a brief volume by Karl Rahner, S.J., and Joseph Ratzinger, *The Episcopate and the Primacy* (Herder and Herder, 1962). Its authors are brilliant, balanced, and bold; the problem of centralization

* "The Episcopacy and the Papal Primacy in the Life of the Church" is a translation of "Episcopato e Primato pontificio nella vita della Chiesa," originally published in *La Scuola Cattolica* 88 (1960), pp. 401-434.

vs. local autonomy is important and keenly argued in the contemporary Church.

R ATHER THAN present a fully developed treatment of the doctrine of the episcopacy and the papal primacy in mutual relationship, it seems better here * to inquire into the necessary and permanent elements, and then into the variable elements, as they all pertain to the one Church of Christ.

Obviously one cannot examine the immutable and variable aspects of this relationship without sketching in broad lines the doctrinal basis of the two revealed truths of the episcopacy and the papal primacy. Here a question of method arises. This should be clarified immediately.

Speaking abstractly, a subject such as this could be treated in two ways: *historically,* a method which would consider the facts as they occurred, insofar as we can reconstruct them, and then attempt to derive from these facts the doctrines which they inspired; or *theologically,* a method which would begin with the defintions of Vatican Council I and the clarifications of later papal pronounce-

* This article is a reworked version of a paper read at a study session of the "Catholic Conference on Ecumenical Questions" held at the Villa Cagnola in Gazzada, Italy, on September 19-23, 1960.

The general theme of the meeting was research into the necessary and immutable aspects of the life of the Church, which are of divine origin, and the variable aspects, which are of historical origin. The aim was to extend research into the diversity of traditions compatible with the unity of Catholic faith and thus to discover possible patterns of contact with separated Christians.

The aim and method of the meeting, which required that a synthetic presentation of the subject selected be submitted for discussion by the participants, explains and justifies the content of this paper, which does not attempt an exhaustive treatment, undertaken from an historical point of view, but endeavors to engage in theological reflection on the problem of the relationship between the episcopacy and the papal primacy.

ments [1] and would then set about deducing from these sources the doctrine of the relationship between these two essential functions in the constitution and life of the Church.

In this area, however, a purely theological study is impossible for two reasons: first, because we do not possess an adequate, detailed dogmatic presentation of the nature of the episcopacy; second, because the Vatican I definition of the primacy and infallibility is incomplete.

Many authors have pointed out the unfinished state of the Constitution *De Ecclesia Christi,* which is due to the fact that the Constitution defines the particular, proper powers of the bishop of Rome without specifying the proper powers and functions of all the bishops of the Church; neither does it specify the relationship of the bishop of Rome, the successor of St. Peter, to the episcopal college, the successor of the apostolic college, and thus it creates the impression that the pope is somehow outside the episcopal college.[2] Unless I am mistaken, the reason for this incompleteness lies in the fact that at the First Vatican the papal primacy was considered more as a revealed juridical principle than as an historical supernatural reality, positively instituted and determined by our Lord Jesus Christ. From the very beginning the Church had a certain consciousness of the content and meaning of this reality, but it has grown and been clarified in the course of centuries, so that perhaps even today the Church's understanding of this reality is not complete. This lack of historical view in the consciousness of the primacy has restricted the theological definition of its meaning.[3]

With all the more reason can this be said of the doctrine of the episcopacy. And here I understand this doctrine with reference to the episcopal college as such as well as to each bishop in particular, his supernatural reality, his function, his supernatural charisms for his own diocese

[167]

and for the universal Church. The episcopacy is not an abstraction, but a real supernatural institution, positively willed by our Lord; the Church has been conscious of this from the beginning. This awareness is manifested in doctrinal affirmations, through historical events, by means of juridical decisions; it has grown and continues to grow and be clarified in the interplay of many factors. The historical inquiry into this awareness of the function of the episcopacy in the Church is just as necessary for the study of our subject as an exact analysis of the definition of Vatican I. Here is a concrete example. If we were to prove theologically, by means of historical research, that episcopal consecration is the sacrament by which the charisms communicated by Jesus to the apostles for the continuous building up of the Church until the end of the world are conserved and transmitted in the Church, then the problem of the nature and function of the episcopacy and its relationship to the papal primacy would be presented in a manner entirely different from the approach which views them solely as a juridical function.[4]

For these reasons a study of the doctrine of the episcopacy and its relations to the papal primacy should be solidly based above all on historical view of the Church's awareness of the episcopal function, in order to draw from this awareness as far as possible its dogmatic content. Moreover, it is necessary to remember that, since the constitution of the Church has not changed, the dogmatic tradition of the patristic period on the episcopacy still has value today, after the definitions of Vatican I, in determining the divine constitution of the Church.

Then again, the doctrine of papal primacy has had a doctrinal development down through the centuries and has resulted in certain conclusions at Vatican I. These were almost certainly not clearly present in the thought of the Fathers of the third to the sixth century, not even in the thought of the Fathers at Chalcedon and the bishops to whom Leo the Great spoke. Yet this doctrine of the Vatican (more recently specified in the encyclical *Mystici Corporis*) gives us the creative will and thought of our Lord on the constitution of the Church in a manner more precise and clear, corresponding more fully to reality, than did the ideas of the bishops of those early centuries, which were only partly determined and still uncertain. This doctrine helps us to understand more precisely and penetrate more deeply their own Faith and doctrine on the episcopacy and its relationship to the primacy. It also obliges us to rethink this relationship as they would have viewed it today, knowing and believing present Catholic doctrine on the primacy now more clearly defined.

This is why a treatment of this subject seems to me to comprise three sections: (1) an historical sketch of the awareness of the function of the episcopacy in the Church in order to bring out its dogmatic elements; (2) a determination of the relations between the episcopacy and the primacy in the light of the preceding conclusions and current Catholic teaching on the primacy; and (3) some conclusions on the immutable elements and the variable elements in this concrete relationship.

It is scarcely necessary to state that these three sections intend to present synthetically some conclusions for reflection and common discussion, rather than develop the subject fully in a scientific way. The historical treatment, especially, must be merely a suggestive summary because of the lack of sufficient research in this area.[5]

Awareness of the Function of the Episcopacy in Church Tradition

What is the fundamental concept of the episcopacy in the tradition and teaching of the Church? Without question, it is the concept of the bishops as successors of the apostles. Here we must investigate the meaning of this phrase.

In the thought of the early Church, the proclamation of a bishop as a successor of the apostles signified two things: first, that the bishop possessed apostolic powers; second, that he possessed the Holy Spirit communicated by Jesus to his apostles for the building up of the Church.

Apostolic Powers

The consciousness of the bishop's apostolic powers is revealed in various ways. First it is seen in his possession of apostolic truth. The same function which the apostles had with respect to Jesus Christ, i.e., authentically preserving his doctrine, is found in the bishops with respect to the doctrine of the apostles; they are the ones who have the apostolic truth and present it authentically, each bishop in his own diocese and the united episcopacy in the universal Church. Their teaching is not based on scientific competence, but on a legitimate possession of the apostolic doctrine entrusted to them. It is because of an awareness of their legitimate possession of this apostolic doctrine that the bishops are recognized and accorded the right of judging doctrinal questions which arise in the Church.[6]

The second fact that manifests the presence of apostolic powers in the bishops is their sacramental function (or 'sacerdotal' function, to use the term current in the early Church). In his own church the bishop possesses all the sacramental powers which the apostles possessed in their time; he possesses them as the source from which his priests draw in order to participate in them and as the sovereign agent on whom his helpers depend in their own activities. The principle of Ignatius, "Let no one do anything which pertains to the Church without the bishop"

(*Smyr.* 8, 1), is a basic principle in the sacramental life of Christian antiquity. There is so because the bishop was the faithful administrator of the sacramental life of his own church, and as such he assumed the right to determine (at least within certain limits, specified below) the method of administering the sacraments in his church. These different decisions of bishops are the sources not only of diverse liturgical traditions but also of the diversity in the ministers of the sacraments themselves and in their matter and form in the East and the West.[7]

Possessors of apostolic truth and faithful administrators, masters of sacramental gifts in their own communities, the bishops were successors of the apostles in yet another function, that of feeding their flock and leading it to salvation. For this they had to be able to judge what was suitable or unsuitable for the Christian spirit. This involved, among other things, the power of admonishing, prescribing, disciplining the lives of the faithful and the community: in a word, the ability to govern, which rendered them pastors and heads of the Church in "filling the role of Christ" as Paul did with the Christians of Corinth (I Cor 5:4-5).[8]

Great Distance from the Apostles

The difference rests in this, that the apostles were witnesses of Christ and founders of the Church, while the bishops are those who preserve and authenticate the apostolic tradition in their church and thus propagate the work of salvation whose foundation was laid by the apostles.[9]

However, in order to fulfill these offices the bishops are truly successors of the apostles, i.e., they possess the powers of the apostles. They possess apostolic truth, all the gifts of grace for the sacramental building up of the Church, and the ability to govern.[10]

The foundation of their apostolic powers is the Holy

Spirit received by the imposition of hands by other bishops who, by a similar imposition of hands, had become successors of the apostles before them.

Bishops: Possessors of Apostolic Charisms

One thing above all stands out in the consciousness of the early Church concerning the episcopacy: the episcopacy is not just a power of jurisdiction but rather it is also a charism which is transmitted from the apostles to their successors by the imposition of hands. It carries with it a special gift of the Holy Spirit and places the bishop in a new supernatural state, ontologically superior to the other members of the community (priests included).

First we shall consider separately each of these essential affirmations in order to understand more fully the traditional concept of the episcopacy; then we will inquire whether all this supposes that episcopal consecration is a real sacrament.

APOSTOLIC CHARISMS

The doctrine of Irenaeus on the subject of the magisterium of bishops is well known. It is not based on human competence or on the simple fact that bishops are "heads of churches" (i.e., in modern terms, endowed with the power of jurisdiction) but rather on the fact that bishops possess "the unfailing charism of truth" (*Adv. Haer.* 4, 26, 2). The charism of truth about which Irenaeus is speaking in this famous text is the true apostolic doctrine which the duly consecrated bishops transmit to one another in apostolic succession according to the will of the Father. But if we bear in mind that for Irenaeus the source and guarantee of truth in the Church is the presence and charismatic action of the Holy Spirit,[11] we will readily see that for him the firm possession of apostolic truth by the bishops cannot be simply a juridical fact but is the effect of a special gift and indwelling of the Holy Spirit, i.e., of a charism proper to bishops.

Bishops, then, in order to guarantee and faithfully preserve apostolic truth, must possess a special gift of the Spirit of Truth, who is the principle in them of the higher knowledge necessary to carry out their task. The identity of the Spirit of Truth, working through the bishops in the various local churches, ontologically guarantees the identity of faith in the whole Church (*Adv. Haer.* 1, 10, 2; 5, 20, 1). Moreover, the identity of the Spirit communicated by the apostles to their successors ontologically guarantees the identical apostolic truth in the Church.

The possession of apostolic truth is not a purely juridical fact but a supernatural reality founded on and caused by the possession of an ontological gift (charism) of the Spirit of Truth.[12]

Irenaeus does not say how the bishops possess this charism of truth nor whether their charism is limited to this task or extends to others. But what Irenaeus does not say is clearly taught in liturgical testimonies; the importance of these testimonies will never be sufficiently emphasized, inasmuch as in them the living awareness of the Church is expressed.

CHARISM EXPRESSED IN LITURGICAL TRADITIONS

It is not possible here to present an analysis of the Eastern and Western liturgical traditions on the episcopacy; indeed, I have not the competence for such a task.[13] I will limit myself to a few observations which I believe will suffice to justify the statements made above.

First, it is known that the *Traditio Apostolica* of Hippolytus presents the totality of gifts and powers transmitted by the imposition of hands from the consecrating bishop to the new bishop as extending to all the tasks of governing and building up the Church. Their foundation is the transmission of the Spirit possessed by Jesus and communicated by him to the apostles.[14]

Second, all liturgies clearly distinguish the gifts communicated to bishops from those communicated to other ministers; this is not a quantitative but a qualitative distinction. One who receives the gift of episcopacy possesses a fullness of charisms which renders him the prime source in his church of every other principle of supernatural life. The other ministers partake of his fullness, which sanctifies the whole Christian community.[15]

Third, Christian thought clearly distinguishes the *possession* of episcopal charisms from their *exercise*. It knows that the bishops, each in his own right, though they possess the charism of truth, are not infallible and are not always faithful to apostolic truth; it knows that while they have been consecrated as builders of the Church and shepherds of the flock they do not always fulfill this role and feed their flock as they should. It knows, in a word, that the episcopal charisms received with the imposition of hands have a double content: a permanent and inalienable content which constitutes the foundation of the different functions or episcopal powers, and a content whose purpose is the successful accomplishment of these functions and which can be spoiled or lost by human fault. (In current terminology, one could say that the early Church knew how to distinguish between an inalienable episcopal *character* and a *sacramental grace*, although their thought did not allow the distinction to be expressed as clearly as it is today.) [16]

THE EPISCOPAL STATE AS SACRAMENTAL

The testimony of liturgy and tradition compels us to hold that episcopal consecration puts the recipient in a proper supernatural state inside the Christian community; this is the supreme supernatural state in each particular community, characterized by the possession of a particular charism (or a body of charisms if one looks at it with respect to each function).

Was this a sacramental state which had at its root a sacramental act analogous and parallel in nature and efficacy to the sacramental acts which confer the state of being a Christian (Baptism) or the priestly state (Orders, the ability to offer prayer and sacrifice for the community)? This is not an idle question, for Christian tradition knew supernatural states which were not of sacramental origin, such as consecrated virginity.

From an historical and liturgical point of view there is no doubt about the answer: if the priestly state in general is based upon a sacramental act, the episcopal state, which is its highest and fullest form, it is perforce a sacramental state. For this is the state of Christians consecrated by a sacramental act (imposition of hands) to be successors of the apostles, i.e., possessors of apostolic powers and apostolic charisms for the full building up of both the local and the universal Church.[17]

Local and Universal Functions of the Episcopacy

We already know the functions which tradition accords to bishops: authentic preservation and interpretation of apostolic truth, ministering from the fullness of the gifts Jesus left to his Church, shepherding the flock of Christ.

Were these functions they could and should exercise only for the particular church for which they had been consecrated, or did each bishop have a function which reached beyond his local church and extended to the Church as a whole?

(1) Ancient discipline stressed the bond of each bishop with the church for which he had been consecrated; it was at pains to determine the governing powers of each bishop

and to prevent invasion and interference in the life of one church by another.[18]

But history also shows that certain bishops in practice exercised a directive function, recognized as legitimate, with respect to the churches of their region. The example of the bishops of Alexandria and the institution of *chorepiscopoi* ['place-bishops' in outlying districts, dependent on a metropolitan] come to mind. These facts reveal an awareness that episcopal power is not delimited territorially on geographical lines. On the contrary, it is designated by a juridical prescription of the Church, that is, by the will of the bishops who agree to impose a certain discipline on the exercise of their own powers. But this still does not mean that there was awareness of a function in any way universal.

(2) There are other facts, however, which clearly indicate that the bishops were aware that their charisms involved not only a local function but a universal one as well. First there were sporadic but significant events; then, more importantly, came the councils. It is significant that Dionysius of Corinth wrote to the churches of Asia to warn them against error and confirm them in the true apostolic faith,[19] just as later Cyprian concerned himself with the problems of the churches of Spain and Arles.[20] More significant still is the exchange of letters among bishops, especially letters of communion announcing elections and consecrations. These expressed the belief that the Church was not the sum of many independent, self-contained units, but rather a communion, a sacramental community, in which each bishop had the duty and right of judging authoritatively in matters of doctrine and discipline and admission to communion with the Church.[21]

Conscious of being successors of the apostles and possessors of apostolic charisms, the bishops knew that they could and should, in some way, be concerned with "the care of all the churches." Of course, each one retained his special local responsibility; but while feeling obliged to respect this local authority, the bishops were aware of being co-responsible for the universal Church and endowed with a charism which enabled them to work for the good of the universal Church.

Their thought-process must have been along these lines: the truth which they possessed and taught was the apostolic truth; it was the truth of all the churches, of the Church universal; the gifts of grace which they conferred were the gifts of Christ, left by him for all the Church; as shepherds they represented Christ, his mind and will with respect to his flock, the Christian people. The consequence of all this was that, wherever in the Church because of deficiency or human fault the apostolic powers and charisms should be wanting or badly administered, there the bishops could and in practice did feel authorized to extend the exercise of their own apostolic powers beyond the ordinary frontiers of their own church.

(3) The surest expression of this awareness of a function in some way universal occurs in the councils. I am not insisting here on the manifestation of this awareness of a universal function which the bishops possessed and exercised in the councils, especially in the ecumenical councils, convoked as such and immediately recognized as such. This is well known.

Rather it is essential to bring to light the basis of this awareness: i.e., the presence in the bishops of the Holy Spirit, the Spirit communicated by Jesus to the apostles and transmitted by them to their successors for the full building up of the Church in truth and holiness. The universal value of conciliar decisions resulted not from numbers or from an accord of human minds and wills, but from the presence and exercise of a charism of a universal nature which, according to the consensus of that age, found its highest form of manifestation in a council. Each bishop, in communion with the *catholica* and with its center at Rome, knew that he was the co-possessor of the Spirit.[22]

Another indication of an awareness in the bishops of a responsibility not limited to the care of local churches could be claimed in the missionary activity sometimes undertaken by bishops to extend Christianity in areas bordering on the territory of their own church. Important in this regard, however, is the different type of awareness and action found in the bishops of Rome, who felt the responsibility of a universal missionary power.[23]

This consciousness of different functions and powers on the part of the bishop of Rome and the other bishops leads us to probe more deeply the relations between the functions of all the bishops and those proper to the bishop of Rome—between the episcopacy and the papal primacy.

Relationship Between the Episcopacy and the Papal Primacy

An adequate study of the relationship between the episcopacy and the papal primacy would require a recapitulation of the historical development of the primacy as well as a consideration of the theological significance of this development for the understanding of the doctrine of the primacy. Here we can only sketch these two elements in a general way.

Primacy: Historical Function and Doctrine

The first function which is explicitly acknowledged in the church of Rome and in her bishop is that of authentically preserving apostolic tradition. This is the teaching of Irenaeus and is what Pope Victor claimed in the Easter controversy.

This is the function which each bishop fulfills in his

own church and which all together fulfill in the universal Church. But there is this difference: the apostolic tradition of Rome, being the tradition of the first Apostle, "the Rock" (Mt 10:2), is the one to which the other apostolic traditions must necessarily conform. If there should be divergences between the apostolic traditions of the various churches, that of Rome should prevail, and de facto it did prevail. For this reason the bishop of Rome authentically preserves apostolic tradition, both in doctrine and in discipline, for the universal Church and not simply for his own church. He is the center of communion,[24] the keystone of the episcopal body, who authentically preserves apostolic tradition in its entirety.

Clearly this function of the bishop of Rome is not completely independent of the function of the other bishops. Since the Church is one and teaches one and the same truth wherever she is found, the apostolic traditions agree among themselves; they sustain and guarantee one another. Indeed, the church of Rome herself inquires into the traditions of other churches and reinforces the value of her own tradition with their authority. It is only when important divergences which concern the 'heritage of tradition' (i.e., the deposit of Faith) arise that the bishop of Rome takes cognizance of his role of acting for the apostolic tradition and takes his stand for the authentic tradition, the true doctrine with which the other bishops must agree. In this regard he replies and decides authoritatively numerous questions submitted to him.[25]

Next, the role of authentically preserving the apostolic tradition leads the bishop of Rome to exercise a twofold function with respect to the other churches: (a) a certain control over the legitimacy of their apostolic succession and (b) a surveillance over their fidelity to the apostolic tradition of the Church (and consequently some exercise of judgment over their bishops).

The duty of guaranteeing the apostolic tradition nec-

[179]

essarily involves the ability to judge the legitimacy of the instrument by which the apostolic tradition is preserved and transmitted in each church (i.e., the bishop), and to make judgments on how this local authority is exercised. This is the justification of recourse to Rome in cases of doubtful succession and deposition and in controversies over doctrine.

The surveillance over the legitimacy of the apostolic succession and the exercise of apostolic powers in each of the churches was originally exercised after the manner of a college, that is, by exchanging letters of communion and by the ordinary relations between each bishop and each church, and later on by means of both local and universal councils. We have already noted that the bishops considered themselves to be bishops in the universal Church and not merely in their own local church. Nonetheless, they were not aware of possessing any authority over other churches and other bishops. The bishops of Rome, on the other hand, increasingly act to affirm their exercise of "concern for all the churches." They also affirm their power to intervene authoritatively in the life of any church to ensure fidelity to apostolic tradition in all areas: teaching, discipline, the Christian spirit, rites, and juridical norms which concern the sacraments or actions basic to the life of the Church. This awareness of the bishops of Rome, based on their full appreciation of being the successors of Peter, the foundation stone of the Church, and shepherds of the whole flock, is the traditional basis of the universal and "truly episcopal" power of jurisdiction which will later be defined at Vatican I.

And lastly, this awareness, present even in the early centuries, is translated into concrete acts of government through a long process in history which is characterized by three factors: (a) an awareness and assertion of a power of jurisdiction which is universal in principle, justified in terms of Petrine succession; (b) initially sporadic intervention in the life of the other churches, whether because of respect for traditional powers of jurisdiction mutually agreed upon among the bishops or because of the whole complexus of historical causes which sometimes favored and sometimes hindered the bishop of Rome in his exercise of authority, particularly in the East; (c) decisive intervention, growing more regular and normal, when serious problems in the life of the Church made obvious the need for a single seat of authority which was not merely common or corporate; an authority was required which was supreme and independent of the will of each bishop, supra-national and truly universal, one which would definitely guarantee the Church's unity, holiness, capacity for reform, catholicity, and independence of local or national interests.[26] The conclusion of this long and complicated historical process, which has shown diverse characteristics in East and West, is the present Catholic teaching on the papal primacy as contained in the doctrine of the First Vatican Council.

Present Teaching on Primacy

I believe this teaching can be summarized under three headings.

(1) A double function of magisterium and a twofold jurisdiction belong to the Roman Pontiff, the bishop of Rome. One is episcopal, common to every bishop; it pertains to the pope's own diocese and contributes to the formation of Christian faith and discipline in the whole Church in common with the other bishops through the pope's pastoral care for the diocese of Rome. The other is primatial, the pope's alone, and looks to the whole Church; it makes the pope the one center of truth and the one depository of all authority for the whole Church; this authority is exercised according to the divergent needs of the Church's life.

✓ (2) The primatial function of the Roman Pontiff makes him the *authentic teacher* (in certain determined cases, the infallible teacher) of truth, not only for the whole Church in general but for each and every diocese and for each of the faithful. This is joined to the power of teaching proper to each bishop, in order to constitute one complete teaching authority whose purpose is to preserve revealed truth faithfully and to present it in a way which fully answers the needs of the Church as a whole and of each Christian community in particular.

This primatial function also makes the Roman Pontiff the universal pastor, endowed with full authority of pastoral jurisdiction, a "truly episcopal" power not only towards the Church in general but also for each and every diocese and each of the faithful. This is joined to the pastoral authority and function of each bishop to constitute with it a single adequate seat of authority for pastoral government. The purpose of this authority is to maintain necessary unity in the Church and at the same time to preserve and promote in each local church the true Christian spirit and life in order to lead every soul to salvation and to the holiness assigned it by Christ.

The primatial function of the Roman Pontiff does not, then, contradict the authority and functions proper to the bishops; rather, it is intended to reinforce them and render the exercise of the bishops' teaching office and pastoral care more effective by strengthening the value of their teaching and their decisions with the added weight of approval from the supreme authority with which they are in communion. And this communion with the supreme authority renders the mutual assistance of the individual churches for the building up of the Body of Christ more certain and efficacious, simpler, and more truly universal.[27]

(3) The diverse functions of the individual bishops,

successors of the apostles, and of the bishop of Rome, the successor of St. Peter, are based upon a diversity of gifts and powers communicated by Jesus to the apostolic college (and to St. Peter as a member of it) and to Peter personally as distinct from the other apostles. These gifts and powers are transmitted by the legitimate episcopal succession by which the body of bishops in its entirety succeeds the apostolic college and prolongs its powers of teaching and governing, but only the bishop of Rome succeeds Peter and prolongs his personal, exclusive powers of teaching and governing the whole Church.

This diversity of powers and functions determines a double line of apostolic succession in the Church: (a) by the sacrament of orders all the bishops are equal among themselves, possess a relationship of direct and immediate succession to the apostolic college (that is, without the intervention of any other authority), and enjoy powers of sanctification which are valid for the whole Church and destined for the building up of the whole Church; but the legitimate exercise of their powers is had only in communion with the whole Church and above all with the bishop of Rome who is the center of the Catholic communion; (b) this is so because there is no immediate, autonomous transmission of authority to govern from each apostle to each bishop, but only from Peter to the bishop of Rome: all the other bishops participate in the apostolic powers in the Church insofar as they legitimately form part of the episcopal college and persevere in union with it; they receive their powers from Jesus Christ through that college; because the college is not acephalous but has a head which of itself possesses the fullness of apostolic power required for the life of the whole Church, all the powers of each of the bishops are already contained in this power as in their source and foundation.[28]

Most particularly, under this aspect the primatial

power of the Roman Pontiff is distinct from the episcopal power of all the other bishops individually and collectively, but it is not for this reason separated or opposed to theirs.

The *truth* which the Roman Pontiff teaches is the same truth that the episcopal college teaches. The discipline in Christian life which the Pontiff wants to preserve is the same discipline which the whole episcopal college is bound to preserve in the universal Church and in each diocese. The goals of salvation and sanctification, of spreading the kingdom of God, which the Pontiff wants to set in motion, are the same ends which the episcopal college has in view.

The difference exists in the choice possible regarding the means to be used in reaching these goals. The Roman Pontiff has an autonomous power of decision in his choice of means, while all the other bishops, whether in their teaching or in their government, both individually and collectively, are bound by the decisions of the Roman Pontiff.

The *result* of this diverse authority and power is doubtless a diminished capacity on the part of the bishops for exercising direct and immediate influence in the life of the whole Church as well as diminished liberty of personal action in their own dioceses.

However, the unity of the Church, its independence from external pressure, vital exchange among all the Christian communities, and the faithful preservation of doctrine and discipline have been more surely strengthened and promoted since this awareness of the papal primacy became explicit and fully effective.

Yet one might reflect whether it would not be possible to conceive some form of collaboration between the papal primacy and the episcopacy which would further enhance the function of the bishop, not only in his own diocese but also with respect to the whole Church. This was the case, at least to some degree, in the early Church through its use of letters of communion. Certainly this is a situation especially desired today by the Orthodox.

Some Preliminary Conclusions

The basic difference between the organization and life of the Church in the period of union with the East and after the separation appears to me to rest in a certain predominance which has developed in the West of the power of jurisdiction over the power of Orders. This development was necessary and beneficial, as is evidenced by the almost complete disappearance of schism in the West,[29] but it has not allowed the bishops' power of Orders to exercise its full influence for the good of the whole Church. A subordinate factor in this historical situation, but an important one, has been a lessening of our consciousness of the sacramental value of episcopal consecration and its importance for the preservation and communication of the apostolic powers, which are not only juridical powers but powers and gifts of grace for the building up of the Church, i.e., charisms. Our first task is to explore more thoroughly the meaning and value of the charism of episcopacy in the Church.

The Charism of Episcopacy and Its Action

If one accepts the doctrine of the sacramental value of episcopal consecration, which seems traditional and indisputable to me, it is a further question to determine what gifts of grace or, better, what charisms this consecration confers. According to the traditional teaching, episcopal consecration transmits in the Church and thus confers on the recipient the apostolic charisms, the Holy Spirit communicated by Jesus to his apostles and destined to remain in the Church to the end of the world for the complete building up of the Church.

Traditionally these charisms consist of: (a) a fullness of the powers of sanctification, i.e., fullness of the power of orders; (b) a gift of knowledge of revealed truth which makes bishops able to teach the truths of faith authentically and, under certain determined conditions, even infallibly; and (c) a gift of governing which enables the bishops to fulfill the office of good shepherds, both individually in their own diocese and collectively in council for the whole Church.

These powers and gifts make the bishop an instrument for the action of the Holy Spirit, a personal, responsible instrument whose powers and capacity for action are conditioned by factors of three different orders: juridical decisions of divine and ecclesiastical law which condition the exercise of these gifts; personal holiness; and personal human qualities which enable the instrument to meet responsibility more or less effectively. Undoubtedly each bishop in the Church is, to some degree, a principle of the supernatural knowledge of revealed truth, of sanctification, and of pastoral care: a true image of Christ—Teacher, Shepherd, and High Priest.

This real supernatural state of a bishop, which is destined to operate effectively in the Church and not remain inactive, acquires its full capacity for action and influence when the bishop, designated by legitimate authority (legitimate succession according to the canons or appointment to a diocese by the Roman Pontiff), assumes the functions of episcopal responsibility for a definite Christian community. The office of a bishop in his own church is not only to preserve the Faith, the true Christian spirit and life, but to incarnate the truth and the ideal Christian life according to the needs and spirit of his community: to resolve its problems, promote the spiritual life, and see to it that human development serves this supernatural life. Certainly the natural and supernatural characteristics of a bishop's personality in his pastoral activities have an important influence on the spirit which he communicates to his community. Because of this, different spiritual traditions arise in the Church, created and fostered by outstanding bishops of whom history furnishes many examples. . . . As a citizen of Milan, may I be allowed to cite the influence of St. Ambrose and St. Charles Borromeo on the Milanese church.

The primary function proper to a bishop in his church and the irreplaceable effect of the charism of episcopacy is to promote in the community the formation and development of this spiritual tradition, understood in an ecclesiastical and not merely an ascetical sense. It is immediately evident that this influence does not benefit only one particular church but helps in the great work of building up the universal Church, the Mystical Body of Christ, whose life is enriched by the many members who compose it.

Charism of the Episcopacy and the Charism of Primacy

In the light of this treatment of the proper function and nature of the charism of episcopacy. I think its relation to the charism of primary becomes clearer. They can be studied in the life of both a particular church and the universal Church.

With respect to a particular church, the *bishop's charism* gives him the power and the office of applying to his local conditions the apostolic tradition of the universal Church. The *charism of primacy* involves the duty of guaranteeing, even in the local church, the faithful preservation of the apostolic tradition and maintenance of a solid catholic communion among the different churches through their communion with the church of Rome.

But what is required to have this preservation of apostolic tradition and catholic communion, without at the same time fostering enforced uniformity and failing to respect the variety of gifts which the Holy Spirit can communicate to the Church through the spiritual traditions formed in each individual church? And who is to be judge in these questions?

It is here that the second form of the collaboration of the bishops for the good of the universal Church appears. This collaboration is fully realized in a council.

The proper and primary judge of the conditions necessary for the preservation of apostolic tradition and catholic communion is the bishop of Rome, the Roman Pontiff. He is also the highest and final judge. The doctrinal infallibility of the entire episcopal college in union with him is no greater that the infallibility he personally possesses, nor is its authority more extensive or complete than his personal authority.[30]

But in the united episcopal college there is a *richer* charism for the building up of the Church than is found in the bishop of Rome, the universal pontiff, taken alone. This is true both in the realm of doctrine and in the area of pastoral care.

In the realm of doctrine, because each bishop individually has a charism of teaching which is proper to himself and matches the needs of his own community, the sum of all these charisms united with the charism of the bishop of Rome makes the episcopal college a most suitable instrument for the deep penetration and presentation of Christian truth according to the needs of the entire Church at any given time. For the primacy confers the charism of personal *infallibility*—but not *omniscience*—in teaching revealed truth.

In the same way, because the bishop has a pastoral charism for the full "building up of the Church in love," the sum total of all these charisms united with the charism of the Roman Pontiff makes the episcopal college a true image and fitting instrument of the Good Shepherd. It is appropriate here to recall that the characteristic of the Good Shepherd is a pure personal knowledge not only of his field of labor but also of his flock, his Christians and their special needs: "I am the Good Shepherd; I know mine and mine know me" (Jo 10:14). This personal contact or relationship with the needs of souls, which is an essential element in the picture of the Good Shepherd, is what explains and demands the multiplication of bishops in the Church according to the needs of souls. And it also explains why in the united episcopal college, although its authority is no greater, there is a capacity for judgment more surely adequate to the pastoral needs of the Church than in the Roman Pontiff alone. The picture of the Good Shepherd of the Church is not represented by one pastor alone but by a body of pastors, with diverse offices, gifts, and powers.

Finally, a consequence of these relations between the charism of episcopacy and that of the primacy is the necessity for harmonious cooperation between them, so that the Church may have a capacity to develop more fully into the "complete age of Christ" which Divine Providence has decreed for her at each stage of history.

Cooperation between the Episcopacy and Papal Primacy

Reflecting on the dogmatic principles treated above and adding to these a consideration of history, it seems to me that we may formulate four principles which should be harmonized to bring about fruitful cooperation between the bishop of Rome and the other bishops.

UNITY

The first good of the Church and the first condition of her apostolic activity is unity: unity of Faith, unity of spirit, unity in her hierarchy and sacraments. This unity must not only be juridical and formal but internal and external as well, based upon love and communion of good will with those who possess the charisms of the Holy Spirit in the Church, the first of whom is the Roman Pontiff. For this, the Church must study and put in operation these means which insure the preservation of unity.

PASTORAL CONCERN

The unity of the Church is not an ultimate goal but rather a condition desired by our Lord in order to attain the ultimate goal, the salvation and sanctification of souls, i.e., the salvation and sanctification of the faithful who already belong to the Church and the extension of the Church to all men. The pastoral principle undoubtedly demands of the Church a continual adaptation to the religious history of mankind. As the Word of God was made flesh for our salvation, so the Christian truth of the Church must be made 'all to all' in order to save and re-unite all men in one fold under the one shepherd. This makes it necessary to accept and initiate diverse spiritual traditions in the life of the Church, within the unity of Faith and the sacramental and moral discipline positively desired by our Lord. The most suitable judge of this diversity in unity will be the episcopal college united with and under the guidance of the Roman Pontiff.

CATHOLICITY

The formation of diverse spiritual traditions in the Church is not an end in itself but a means of building up the universal Church, that is, a means of facilitating the salvation and sanctification of each of the local communities and of enriching the community of the Church universal. This demands that each of these spiritual traditions be capable of being communicated from one church to another, as was the case in the early Church. Spiritual traditions (always in an ecclesiastical sense) so opposed to the traditions of the rest of the Church that she could not accept them would be banned from the catholic communion. On the other hand, local traditions are all the more truly Christian and beneficial for the local community and the whole Church as they are more readily communicable.

This means that each bishop in overseeing the traditions of his own diocese must also strive, as far as possible, to remain in touch with other bishops. When there is question of the solution of problems which are common to several dioceses in a certain area or are of considerable historical importance, cooperation between dioceses and their shepherds becomes a necessity, a duty; for then their united search for solutions to common problems will insure a greater probability of success in answering current needs than would purely independent activity by each bishop in isolation.

RESPECT FOR TRADITION

The formation of spiritual traditions in the Church is a providential fact of history. It should be viewed not simply as the basis for historical divergences of human origin but also as the source of a wide variety of supernatural gifts. It is destined to enrich and increase the manifestation of the manifold grace of God. Hence the full growth of the Church requires a respect and concern for these spiritual traditions of the various churches (a concern which is ex officio a duty of the bishops), as far as this is compatible with the unity and catholicity of the Church, through sincere, healthy pastoral activity. Perhaps we do not fully realize the value of this diversity of traditions for the universal Church. Some of these traditions are so ancient that they originated in immediately post-apostolic times. Consideration of these values could easily open up new approaches to the solution of contemporary problems (e.g., liturgical and missionary questions).

Practical Applications

Now, as a result of our treatment, I think certain applications can be drawn in the matter of the relationship of the episcopacy to the papal primacy. I would like to offer these especially for the reflection of those who desire to work together in the Church to seek conditions for fruitful ecumenical encounters.

(1) Since the entire definition of episcopacy depends on whether one's concept of a bishop is purely juridical or basically sacramental, the primary condition for a precise determination of the nature and office of a bishop seems to me to be a dogmatic definition of the charism of episcopate and of the sacramental character of episcopal consecration.

This kind of dogmatic definition would certainly be welcomed by the Orthodox, and I also feel it would be favorably viewed by the Anglicans and the Reformed Churches as an important sign of the Catholic Church's desire to be faithful to an apostolic tradition which is so clearly manifested in her early centuries.

(2) Since the end of the charism and office of a bishop is the spiritual building up of his own local community, I think that greater liberty of action and more power should be left to bishops in juridical, disciplinary, and pastoral matters. In this way they will be truly able to form, preserve, and transmit a spiritual tradition in their churches. And this tradition will be the meeting of the eternal and universal Christianity of the whole Catholic Church with the traits and spiritual needs of this com-

munity of men, whose bishop is truly *their* shepherd through the providential choice and grace of the Holy Spirit.

Obviously these Christian spiritual traditions must be understood in a way which is rigidly faithful to the apostolic tradition preserved in the Catholic Church and to the visible unity of the Church in everything which seems necessary for this end at each moment of history.[31]

To insure the accomplishment of this episcopal duty I feel that the very choice of a bishop should be so determined as to guarantee that in addition to his task of faithful witness and representative of the apostolic tradition of the universal Church, his role as interpreter and molder of Christian spiritual traditions will also be fulfilled. Indeed, the formation of a spiritual tradition demands a certain continuity of direction and communion of spirit which are not easily improvised.[32]

(3) On the other hand, the spiritual life of any one diocese, no matter how large it may be, is not isolated from that of other dioceses, either *de jure* or *de facto*. As a matter of fact, in a world which is becoming increasingly 'one world' sociologically and spiritually, communities of men much larger than a mere diocese are taking shape as peoples, nations, states. They present common spiritual problems, often dependent on one another; their solution demands some unity of direction and active cooperation among the dioceses involved.

This situation provides an opportunity to encourage cooperation among dioceses belonging to the same community of men by means of appropriate, workable juridical forms and institutions. It is the same historical phenomenon which gave rise, in the past, to the founding of ecclesiastical provinces and their councils, as well as to the historical and ecclesiastical role of the patriarchates. One can think of juridical forms which would revive the historical experience of the past with its capacity for adapting to regional problems and for influencing each of the regional communities, while at the same time avoiding the dangers of such institutions. Progress in this direction has already been made through national conferences of bishops, whose powers could be increased even more.

The development of a corporate organization in the life of the Church, based upon the cooperation of bishops responsible for a determined body of men (a people or a state), would not only respond to contemporary pastoral requirements but would also fit in nicely with the tradition of the Church before the Eastern schism. This would be welcomed by all the Churches which are conscious of this tradition, as the Orthodox and Anglicans surely are, nor would it be displeasing to the Reformed bodies as a demonstration of the spiritual fellowship which such organization involves.

The determination of the concrete form of such groupings and corporate activities, while aimed at unity in juridical structure, could also take into account valid historical traditions already existing or traditions which could subsequently be realized on a pastoral and spiritual plane. This is especially true of the patriarchates, which could acquire a contemporary juridical-spiritual significance beyond their present purely historical dignity.

(4) Nonetheless, at this moment in the Church's life, it is surely impossible to return to the forms of juridical organization which existed before the Eastern schism, and this for two reasons: first, the Church's actual experience in history of the dangers for her unity inherent in these forms (dangers which are not all imaginary even today, with the growth of indigenous hierarchies); second, the basic principle involved. The Catholic Church cannot renounce the increased knowledge she has of the primatial functions of the bishop of Rome, nor can she lessen her appreciation of their necessity for the preservation of the Church's unity and faithfulness to apostolic traditions.

This appreciation has grown up over a period of a thousand years. I mean she cannot yield on the basic principles of the personal primatial function of the pope and of his intervention in the life of each church, as these principles have been determined by Vatican I (even if they were not clearly exercised or universally recognized before the schism).

It is a question now of finding out whether other forms of cooperation between the episcopacy and the primacy are possible, forms different from those which have existed till now, which respect not only dogmatic principles but also venerable historic traditions. One such form would be the establishment at Rome of central bodies, convened periodically, composed of bishops, some chosen by the pope, some chosen by national conferences of bishops. To these bodies would be entrusted the task of examining and deciding all emerging problems of a doctrinal, disciplinary, or spiritual nature, in order to reconcile the unity, universality, and apostolicity of the one Church of Christ with respect and concern for the spiritual traditions of the various areas of the one Church and for the pastoral powers proper to the bishops. Obviously these decisions would become valid only through approval and promulgation by the pope.

In this way the judgment of the Catholic episcopacy would be cooperating with that of the Roman Pontiff and, on a deeper level, the charism of episcopacy would cooperate with the charism of primacy, in order to establish an instrument for the Church's life which would meet more adequately both the universal and the local requirements for building up the Body of Christ. Here we would have a visible and meaningful demonstration that the episcopal college, presided over by the bishop of Rome, continues in the Church today the mission and power entrusted by Jesus Christ to the apostolic college, presided over by St. Peter, for building up the Church even to the end of time.

Notes

1 I am thinking particularly of the encyclical *Mystici Corporis,* which proposes in authentic fashion the doctrine of the mediate origin of the power of episcopal jurisdiction. This is the doctrine which Dejaifve calls the Roman theory. However, one should keep in mind the teaching of the encyclical *Fidei Donum* on the universal apostolic responsibility of bishops.

2 A recent author on this subject is G. Dejaifve, "Le premier des évéques," *Nouvelle Revue Théologique* 82 (1960), pp. 561-579.

3 To understand the difference between the *reality* and the *doctrine* of the primacy a useful article is the study of L. Hertling, "Communio und Primat," in *Miscellanea Historiae Pontificiae* VII (Rome, 1943), pp. 1-48.

4 Historically, it seems quite certain that the denial of sacramental value to episcopal consecration by the majority of scholastic theologians from the twelfth to the sixteenth century was due to a lessened awareness of the powers and functions of bishops in the Church. Indeed, for the same reasons the Council of Trent's teaching on this point was relatively uncertain. And Vatican I prepared a long schema on the papal primacy but originally included nothing on the episcopacy. Before 1000 A.D. this would have been unthinkable.

5 The Second Vatican Council will undoubtedly stimulate research into the historical aspects of the question of the episcopacy.

6 In this question the voices of unknown bishops whose anonymous statements have survived show clearly the common belief of the early Church as a whole.

7 For the diversity of sacramental traditions in the West and the powers of bishops in this regard, one should note the tract *De Septem Ordinibus Ecclesiae,* which supposes that bishops can concede to priests more or less ample powers of administering the sacraments, including Confirmation. It explicitly affirms that different churches of the West have different traditions, determined by their bishops. Cf. *PL,* 30, 155-157.

8 A fine example of pastoral awareness on the part of a bishop is the anonymous *De Aleatoribus,* probably by an African bishop of the fourth century. The author lays down rules for the participation of Christians in pagan games, because he is conscious of being the shepherd of the flock of Christ, to whom he must render an account.

9 The bishops' awareness of the duty to be faithful to apostolic tradition helps to explain the incident of the Easter controversy and the resistance of Bishop Polycrates of Ephesus to Pope Victor as narrated in Eusebius.

10 The famous text on the consecration of bishops in the *Traditio Apostolica* attributed to Hippolytus stresses the continuity and equality of the powers communicated by Jesus to his apostles and by them to the bishops for the life of the Church. Cf. Quasten, *Monumenta Eucharistica et Liturgica Vetustissima* (Bonn, 1935), I, pp. 28-29.

Whatever the origin of the *Traditio Apostolica* may have been, it remains a fundamental liturgical and historical document for understanding the faith of the Church in the third century.

11 Cf. *Adv. Haer.* 3, 24, 1.

12 "The Spirit Which Is Truth," whose action constitutes for Irenaeus the basis for the preservation of the true faith in the Church, does not coincide with our notion of sanctifying grace (or with the action of the Spirit as the principle of personal sanctification). Irenaeus does not consider it as proportional to the personal sanctity of each bishop (which is not measurable) but rather as connected with the function exercised in the Church by its possessor; it is a charism.

13 The theological significance of the Eastern and Western liturgical traditions on the sacrament of Orders, including episcopal consecration, has been briefly analyzed and summarized in the study of B. Botte, "L'ordre d'après les prières d'ordination," in *Études sur le Sacrement de l'Ordre* (Paris, 1956), pp. 13-35.

A more profound analysis of the rite of episcopal consecration in the *Leonine Sacramentary* has been made by A. Béraudy, "Les effets de l'Ordre dans les préfaces d'ordination du sacramentaire léonien," in *Tradition Sacerdotale* (Le Puy, 1956), pp. 81-107.

Both authors conclude by affirming the sacramental nature of episcopal consecration and the sacramental distinction between episcopacy and priesthood.

14 The *Tradito Apostolica* was and still is used for episcopal consecrations in the Coptic Church and is at the basis of many Eastern liturgies whose rites of ordination have always been recognized as valid by the Church, that is, as expressing her own Faith and doctrine on the sacrament of Orders.

15 In addition to the recognized formulas of priestly ordination which present the priestly order as a participation in offices and powers which originally belong to the bishop, the concept of the Bishop as the source of the supernatural life of the local church becomes clear from the importance given by the Church of the fourth and fifth centuries to the observance of the anniversary of the bishop's consecration. It was not a feast for a person, but a feast of the Christian community which honored on that day the source of its supernatural life. Many formulas for Masses on this anniversary are found in the *Leonine Sacramentary*.

16 On the twofold content of the liturgical formulas for the consecration of a bishop, see the study of Béraudy cited in note 13.

17 From an historical-theological point of view I think that the sacramental nature of episcopal consecration is certainly definable. About the opportuneness of such a definition we shall speak later on.

18 J. Gaudemet, *L'Église dans l'Empire Romain* (Paris, 1958), pp. 115-117.

19 Cf. Eusebius, *Historia Ecclesiastica*, VI-VII, devoted for the most part to setting forth the career of the "great bishop, Dionysius."

[20] For Cyprian, see G. Bardy, *La Théologie de l'Église de St. Irénée au Concile de Nicée* (Paris, 1947), chapter 4.

[21] Cf the work of Hertling cited in note 3. Certainly each bishop did not have absolute and autonomous power to judge the faith and traditions of other churches and bishops, but they could control membership in the 'Catholic communion' of doctrines and persons. If these did not seem to be in full conformity with the requirements of this communion, they could suspend the admission of suspected bishops to the lists of successors of the apostles. Final judgment belonged to the 'communion of bishops' in a local or general council; however, it was the judgment of Rome which prevailed.

[22] This knowledge is expressed in the well known formulas of the councils, wherein all the bishops present declare that they are "gathered together in the Holy Spirit."

[23] This concern is well expressed by Pope Leo the Great, Sermon 5, on the day of his ordination (*PL*, 54, 153).

[24] This is the expression which Hertling prefers to indicate the function of Rome in the first centuries. Cf. Hertling, *op. cit.*, pp. 43-48.

[25] The historical evidence for this assertion is well known; it includes letters of authoritative decisions (dating from the Easter controversy to the controversy on the baptism of heretics) which the bishops of Rome began sending to other bishops at the beginning of the fourth century, even before Leo the Great.

[26] Yves Congar has shown that the full understanding of the function of the bishop of Rome in the Church has not been brought about by a deepened philological or theological understanding of the biblical texts on the primacy but rather by the needs of the life of the Church. Since Peter and his successors were known as the 'foundation stone' of the Church, and the life of the Church showed the need and opportuneness of determined intervention in authoritative fashion by the Pope, it seemed clear that each such application was included in the Pope's power. Cf. Yves Congar, *Esquisses du Mystère de l'Église* (Paris, 1953), pp. 123-125.

[27] Chapter 3 of the Constitution *Pastor Aeternus* of the First Vatican Council stresses this harmonious relationship of the primatial powers of the pope and the episcopal powers, making reference to the famous statement of Pope Gregory the Great to Eulogius, Bishop of Alexandria: "When I am honored, honor is not denied to each of those to whom it is due."

[28] In this way, I feel, the origin of the powers of jurisdiction of the bishops from the Roman Pontiff, as taught in *Mystici Corporis*, can and should be explained: not as an ever present communication of jurisdiction, which historically did not exist for many centuries, but as a radical derivation of particular power from *full* power—which, according to Catholic teaching, exists fully in the Roman Pontiff even without the cooperation of a council. The actual communication of jurisdiction is a historical fact, now common but not so in antiquity; the radical deriva-

tion, on the other hand, is a relationship which belongs to the original constitution of the Church, which was not built upon a grouping of bishops independent among themselves who derived their power directly from the apostles, but upon the apostolic college presided over by Peter. To this apostolic college the episcopal college, presided over by the Pope, succeeds in its turn. In this way Peter and his successors possess in their own right the fullnes of apostolic power.

29 The schisms which have occurred in the West since the Eastern schism have all involved heresy, at least soon after the initial separation; such is the case with the Anglicans, Jansenists, Old Catholics, Philippine Independent Church.

It has been observed that the schisms of the first millenium led the Western Church to assert more strongly the papal prerogatives; but it should be remembered that the Church encountered an even greater difficulty than schism in the second millenium: i.e., the Reformation, which was not without a causal dependence on the concrete historical forms in which papal primacy was asserted.

This observation has a certain relevance and shows how it is impossible to attribute all the good or all the evil in the life of the Church to any one factor. Nonetheless, it is true that both schism and heresy are evils and to remove the legitimate possibility of them in the Church, Christ instituted a 'center of unity,' endowing it with the requisite powers and charisms. That these have not always been subsequently well used by men is a sad fact which brings us face to face with those elements in Divine Providence to which faith alone can provide an answer.

30 This is the explicit teaching of Vatican I. The pope in the Church possesses "the full power of feeding, ruling, and governing." When he speaks *ex cathedra* he enjoys "that infallibility with which our Divine Redeemer wished his Church to be endowed when defining doctrine concerning faith and morals." Note that the Latin phrase *"plena potestas"* means "fullness of power," and the infallibility of the pope is identical with that of the whole Church, i.e., of the whole episcopal college, joined with the Roman Pontiff.

31 The means taken at a particular point of history to manifest and make effective the visible unity of the Church can be different and can vary at different times: liturgy, law, pious custom, universal traditions, etc.

32 The possibility of forming a spiritual tradition in a diocese is also proportionate to the spiritual and material resources which the diocese has at its disposal and so, indirectly, to the size of the diocese.

Translated by ROBERT G. CREGAN, S.J.

CHAPTER **9** *Our Temptations Concerning the Church**

*the Church**

by HENRI DE LUBAC, S.J.

AUTHOR: Surely one of the outstanding Catholic theologians of our century, at present Henri de Lubac is professor of Church History at the Institut Catholique de Lyon. He has published widely in several fields of scholarship: the Fathers of the Church, medieval theology and exegesis, the life and problems of the contemporary Church. Father de Lubac is known for his solid scholarship, his wide knowledge of current problems and attitudes within the Church, and his courageous efforts to put his scholarship at the service of the contemporary Church. His books are always relevant, often brilliant, and sometimes controversial.

ARTICLE: Father de Lubac here discusses with his usual candor and sympathy the various temptations which can face the contemporary Catholic who is honest enough to see some of the shortcomings of his Church in her great mission of salvation, and zealous enough to be bothered by this situation. He takes up the problem of constructive and destructive criticism in the Church, and shows that loyalty to the Church need not always be blind loyalty, nor adaptation always a betrayal of tradition.

READINGS: The reader is urged to begin with a wise and somewhat dispassionate book, *The Human Element in the Church of Christ* (Newman, 1954), by Paul Simon, but by all means to go on to two equally wise but definitely less dispassionate

* "Our Temptations Concerning the Church" first appeared in English in Father de Lubac's *The Splendor of the Church* (Sheed & Ward, 1956), pp. 208-226. It is reprinted here with permission.

books, *Free Speech in the Church* (Sheed & Ward, 1960), by Karl Rahner, S.J., and *The Council, Reform, and Reunion* (Sheed & Ward, 1961), by Hans Küng.

———————————————————

LOVE SHOULD, of course, be our only reaction to our Mother the Church. Yet in fact there are many temptations which trouble us with regard to her. Some are clear enough, and violent; others are less clear, and all the more insidious. There are some that are perennial, and some that are peculiar to our time, and they are all too varied—even to the point of mutual opposition—for any one of us ever to think himself sheltered from the threat which they constitute.

Identifying the Church with Ourselves

There will always be men who identify their cause with that of the Church so totally that they end by equating the Church's cause with their own, and this in all good faith. It does not occur to them that if they are to be truly faithful servants they may have to mortify much in themselves; in their desire to serve the Church, they press the Church into their own service. It is a "dialectical transition," inside-out from *pro* to *con,* as easy as it is unobtrusive. For them the Church is a certain order of things which is familiar to them and by which they live; a certain state of civilization, a certain number of principles, a certain complex of values which the Church's influence has more or less Christianized but which remains none the less largely human. And anything which disturbs this order or threatens this equilibrium, anything which upsets them or merely startles them, seems to be a crime against a divine institution.

Where there is question of a muddle of this sort, we are not always involved with those crude forms of "clericalism" which estimate the amount of honor paid to God by the privileges accorded to his ministers, or measure the progress of divine rule over souls and the reign of Christ, by the influence (either hidden or open) of the clergy on the course of secular affairs. Here the whole order of thinking may well be on the loftiest plane—as when Bossuet, towards the end of his life, adjusted the whole Catholic order in accordance with a Louis-Quatorze pattern of things, and was unable to see anything but a threat to religion in the mixed forces which began to disintegrate that particular synthesis, which was of course a *brilliant* one but was also matter for questioning, in some aspects at least—a thing contingent, and by essence perishable. Against those forces he made his stand, and that with every ounce of his strength.

Bossuet was as perceptive as he was forthright; yet his perceptiveness did not go the whole way. "Together with an imperious will, he had a spirit by nature timid." [1] He wanted to maintain forever (though courageously condemning certain faults and criticizing certain abuses) the mental and social world in which his genius found a natural ground for its unfolding. He could not imagine how the faith could survive it—rather like those ancient Romans (among whom were even some Fathers of the Church) for whom the collapse of the Empire could not be anything other than the heralding of the end of the world, so great an impression had the Roman power and majesty made upon the mind of the time.[2] But since Bossuet's dream was of something which was in fact impossible, he found himself involving with the moribund world in question the Church, whose business it was to free herself from it in order to bring life to the coming generations. The inadequate defenses he threw up against the oncoming evil buried beyond hope of germination

[203]

the seeds of the future; he was apparently victorious on every field on which he fought, but it was irreligion which profited from the way in which he won his victories.[3]

In the same way, we are sometimes all the more self-confident and strict in the judgments we pass in proportion as the cause we are defending is the more dubious. It is possible that we sometimes forget in practice something we know well enough in principle—that the intransigence of the faith is not a passionate unbendingness in the desire to impose upon others our personal tastes and personal ideas. A tight-clenched hardness of that kind is fatal to the supple firmness of truth, and is no defense to it whatsoever; a Christianity which deliberately takes up its stand in a wholly defensive position, closed to every overture and all assimilation, is no longer Christianity.

Sincere attachment to the Church can never be used for the purpose of canonizing our prejudices, or making our partialities part of the absolute of the universal faith. It may thus be pertinent to recall that a certain confidence and detachment are part of the Catholic spirit. At the right time, the Church can find in the very shrines of the devil things to beautify her own dwelling; that particular miracle is always something new and unforseen, but we know that it will happen again.[4] However rooted in history the Church may be, she is not the slave of any epoch or indeed of anything whatsoever the essence of which is temporal.

The message which she is bound to pass on and the life which she is bound to propagate are never integral parts of "either a political régime or a social polity or a particular form of civilization," and she must forcefully remind people of the fact, in opposition to the illusive evidence to the contrary which in fact derives simply from the bonds of habit.[5] She repeats for us, in their widest possible sense, the words of St. Augustine, "Why are you dismayed when earthly kingdoms pass away?"[6]

For she is founded upon no rock other than that of Peter's faith, which is faith in Jesus Christ; she is neither a party nor a closed society. She cannot resign herself to being cut off from those who do not yet know her simply for the sake of the comfortableness of those who make up her traditional faithful. She does not want to oppose men with their realities, since they are all her sons, at least virtually. On the contrary, she will make it her aim to set them free from all evil by giving them their Savior.

We should therefore ourselves get into this frame of mind, which was that of Christ,[7] and we should if necessary impose on ourselves the often painful adjustments fitted to this end. Far from failing in the intransigence of the faith, we can in this way alone sound its depths. We must not relax in any way our zeal for Catholic truth, but we should learn how to purify it. We must be on our guard against turning into those "carnal men" who have existed since the first generation of Christians and who, turning the Church into their own private property, practically stopped the apostles from announcing the Gospel to the Gentiles.[8] For if we do that we lay ourselves open to something yet more calamitous—collaboration with militant irreligion, by way of making it easier for it to carry out its self-assigned task of relegating the Church and her doctrine to the class of the defunct. We provide irreligion with a clear conscience, as it were, for it has no understanding of the actuality of the eternal. Its attitude is, "Let the Church remain what she is" (and we know what sort of petrifaction that wish implies), and then "she will receive all the appreciation always accorded to historic relics." [9]

An irreligion of this type mixes up at will cases of the most widely differing situations which have ceased to be, and takes up a firm stand over "concessions" in which it detects "bad faith or irresponsibility." [10] It establishes its own lists of what is suspect—in the fashion of religious authority itself—and is ready to call that authority to order, if need be. Having made up its mind once and for all that there can be nothing reasonable in Christian beliefs, it brands as "liberalism" or "modernism" every effort made to disentangle Christianity in its real purity and its perpetual youth, as if this were an abandonment of doctrine. It can never see in the thought of men like Justin or Clement of Alexandria or their modern disciples anything but the concessions of an apologetic which sacrifices the "tough" element in dogma to the desire to please those whom it wishes to win over; Tatian and Hermas are the favorites, and their method alone is regarded as the only Christian one.[11] It maintains that "the Church can never cut loose from her past . . . religion is a whole which must not be touched . . . as soon as you reason about it, you are an atheist." [12] The principle is "All or nothing" —provided that the "all" is understood in the terms dictated—which are not those of the Church. Thus, for example, Renan, who would have forever involved the Catholic faith with the historicity of the Book of Daniel and other things of the same kind.[13] And it is a day of rejoicing in this quarter when voices are raised within the very heart of "the poor and aged Church" [14] which sound like approval. A false intransigence can certainly cause an enormous amount of harm in this way—quite in opposition to its own intentions.

The vistas opened up by all this should be yet one more motive for our distrusting ourselves. We should be wary of a certain kind of humility which borders on pride, cultivating a healthy fear of sacrilegious usurpation, and taking to heart the exhortation of St. Augustine to his fellow-fighters in the thick of the Donatist controversy: "Take your stand upon the truth without pride." [15]

We have to bear in mind, too, that our knowledge is always partial and that in this world we only glimpse the divine truth "through a glass in a dark manner." [16] Like

Newman, instead of settling ourselves into the Church as our private property and personal possession and more or less identifying her with ourselves, we should rather make it our business to identify ourselves with the Church, and without expecting any personal triumph from it.[17]

Criticism in the Church

There is another temptation from the opposite direction, which is certainly more frequent today, and sometimes more aggressive in the provocation which it offers— the critical temptation. This also very frequently advances itself cunningly under the camouflage of the good; it can easily put itself forward to the apostolic-minded as a necessary concern for clarity. And for this reason it cannot, in most cases, be avoided save by a preliminary "discernment of spirits."

The very word "criticism" means discernment, and there is, of course, a kind of criticism which is good—particularly self-criticism. That kind is a striving for realism in action—a determination to bar all that cannot justify its claim to genuineness. It is an examination carried out in humility, capable of recognizing the good achieved, but arising out of an essentially apostolic discontent and a perpetually restless spiritual dynamism. It is born and grows from attitudes such as the inability to be satisfied with work done and a burning desire for the best; integrity of judgment on matters of method; independence of will to break with customs that cannot be justified any more, to get out of ruts and put right abuses; above all, a lofty idea of the Christian vocation and faith in the mission of the Church. It stimulates an intensified activity, inventive ingenuity and a sudden outburst of exploration and encounter which must, doubtless, be brought under control on occasion—and which certainly often disturbs our habits a little too rudely. Criticism of this type is hard on the illusions which it tracks down, but can induce others which will soon be in turn the object of similar criticism. Yet how very much better it all is, still, than the naive self-complacency which admits of no reform and no healthy transformation—that certain comfortableness which gradually digs itself deeper and deeper into its dream-world, that obstinacy which thinks that it is preserving things, when all it is doing is piling up their ruins.[18]

We should be wrong if we wished to prevent on principle all public expression of this kind of criticism. When the Church is humble in the persons of her children she is more attractive than when they show themselves dominated by the all-too-human concern for respectability. Jacques Maritain once said, not entirely without his tongue in his cheek, that many Christians of today find any admission of our deficiencies "somehow indecent." "It will be said," he adds, "that they are afraid of putting difficulties in the way of apologetic. . . . The ancient Jews and even the Ninevites didn't stand on ceremony in that way." [19] No more did the saints in the past. Think of St. Jerome's famous address to Pope Damasus,[20] or St. Bernard's broadsides against bad pastors,[21] and the program of reform which he outlines in his *De Consideratione*,[22] or diatribes like that of St. Catherine of Siena against certain highly-placed ecclesiastical dignitaries: "O men who are no men but rather devils incarnate, how you are blinded by your disordered love for the rottenness of the body, and the delights and bedazzlements of this world!" [23] Or again, remember for a moment people like St. Brigid, and Gerson, and St. Bernardine of Siena, and St. Thomas More; or, to come nearer to our own day, St. Clement Hofbauer. Or think of the struggles of the "Gregorians" to tear the government of the Church free from the system which was enslaving it; or the audacity of a man like

Gerhoh of Reichersberg, addressing to Pope Eugenius III his work *On the Corrupt State of the Church*, like St. Bernard; or Roger Bacon, demanding of Clement IV that he should "purge the Canon Law" and cast out of the Church the pagan elements which had been brought into her with the ancient Civil Law; [24] or of William Durandus publishing his treatise *De Modo Celebrandi et Corruptelis in Ecclesia Reformandis;* of the Carthusian Peter of Leyden exhorting the Roman Pontiff at the opening of the edition which he issued in 1530 of the works of his fellow-Carthusian Denys.[25] This last example evokes the whole great movement of Catholic reform which is all too inadequately described under the name of the Counter-Reformation; an enterprise of that kind could not even have been outlined without an effective determination on self-criticism, of which history shows us more than one brilliant example.

Yet for every constructive complaint and each clear-headed and fruitful analysis there is still too much excess and recklessness. Each really courageous act is counter-poised by a mass of futile agitation. There is all too much purely negative criticism. Sanctity is not common, and the sincerest goodwill has neither the same rights nor the same privileges. And both competence and opportunity may be lacking.

Even if a given criticism is a fair one, we are nevertheless not always justified in making it. In addition, we have to bear in mind this important fact that today we do not have the same situation as existed in what we call the Christian centuries. Then, everything happened within the family circle, as it were; and irreligion was not perpetually on the lookout to turn this, that and everything to account in argument. Today, when the Church is in the dock, misunderstood, jeered at for her very existence and even her sanctity itself, Catholics should be wary lest what they want to say simply in order to serve her better be turned to account against her. We have to be on our guard against misunderstandings of a fatal kind; and this is a filial delicacy which has nothing to do with prudery or hypocritical calculatingness. It is not possible to give a hard-and-fast rule, but the Holy Spirit will not be miserly with the gift of counsel to the really "ecclesiastical" man, as I have tried to depict him above—that is, to the man who cannot but be truly spiritual.

Sterile Complaining

We must in any case make a distinction between healthy self-criticism, even when it is excessive or ill-directed, and all sterile complaining—everything that stems from a loss, or even a diminishing, of confidence in the Church. It would certainly be impious to use one or two unfortunate occurrences as an excuse to run down "contemporary Christianity's excellent and laborious attempt to diagnose its own deficiencies, and understand, love and preserve all that has grown up of value outside its own direct influence, and to venture out into the storm to collect the first materials for its new dwelling." [26] But if an attempt of this kind is to be carried out and bear fruit, we have to be careful that it is not contaminated by the breath of a spirit very different from that which is its own principle.

There are certain times when one sees springing up in every direction the symptoms of an evil which catches on like an epidemic—a collective neurasthentic crisis. To those who are afflicted by it, everything becomes matter for denigration, and this is not just a case of the irony, quarrelsomeness of bitterness which are at all times a perpetual threat to a certain kind of temperament. Everything gets a bad construction put upon it, and knowledge of all kinds, even when accurate, only serves to intensify the evil. Half-digested new discoveries and clumsily used new techniques are all so many occasions for believing that the traditional foundations of things have gone shaky. The spiritual life goes but limpingly—so much so that nothing is really seen in the light of it any more. People think themselves clear-headed when all the time it is precisely the essential that they have overlooked. We are no longer capable of discovering, sometimes on our very doorsteps, the fresh flowerings of the Holy Spirit's innumerable inventions—that Holy Spirit which is always in its own likeness and always new.

And thus, discouragement creeps in by a thousand and one different ways. Things that might have given us a healthy shock simply have the effect of paralyzing us. Faith may stay sincere, but it is undermined here, there and everywhere, and we begin to look at the Church as if from outside, in order to judge her. The groanings of prayer become an all-too-human recrimination.[27] And by this movement of Pharisaism—a sort of interior falling-away—which may be unadmitted but is none the less pernicious for all that, we set foot on the road which may end in open denial.

That this should be realized in time and that the appropriate reaction should take place is something devoutly to be hoped for. There is no question of blinding oneself to inadequacies. Those are always only too real. And there is no question of not feeling the painfulness of them; indifference can be much worse than excess of emotion.

The total and burning loyalty of our holding to the Church does not demand of us a puerile admiration for every possible thing that can be, or be thought, or done, within her. Christ wished his bride to be perfect, holy and without spot; but she is this only in principle. If she does indeed shine with a spotless radiance, it is "in the sacraments with which she begets and nurtures her children; in the faith which she preserves ever inviolate; in the holy laws which she imposes on all, and in the evangelical counsels by which she admonishes; and finally, in the heavenly gifts and miraculous powers by which out of her inexhaustible fecundity she begets countless hosts of martyrs, virgins and confessors." [28]

Her soul is the Spirit of Christ but her members are men, all the same. Well we know that men are never up to the level of the divine mission which is entrusted to them. They are never wholly amenable and submissive to the inspirations of the Spirit of Christ, and if they do not succeed in corrupting the Church (since the source of her sanctifying power does not lie in them), on the other hand she will never succeed in stopping completely the source of evil in them—at least, as long as the conditions of this world hold good. Their good will is no guarantee of their intelligence, and intelligence is not always accompanied by strength. The best among them will always be setting up innumerable obstacles to the good which God wants to bring about through them.[29] We may as well get it well into our heads, to start with, that nothing which they do should surprise us—a lesson which is most healthily rammed home by history.

Yet we are all men, and there is none of us entirely unaware of his own wretchedness and incapacity; for after all we keep on having our noses rubbed in our own limitations. We have all, at some time or other, caught ourselves red-handed in the very act of contradiction—trying to serve a holy cause by dubious means. And we must add that our most serious shortcomings are those very ones that escape our notice; from time to time, at least, we see that we are without understanding in the face of the mystery which we are called upon to live out. So that there are scanty grounds for making exceptional cases of ourselves—and none at all for the withdrawal implied in a grimly-judging eye. If we behave in that way we fall into an illusion like that of the misanthrope who takes a dislike to humankind, for all the world as if he himself were not a part of it. "In order to attain to a deep understanding with humanity, it is enough to be part of it, to cleave to the whole mass of it and all the intermingling of its members." Then, "we have no more grievances left, no more standing-back, no more judgments and no more comparisons." [30]

At this point, the staring contrast, between the human wretchedness of those who make up the Church and the greatness of her divine mission, will no longer be a scandal to us, for we shall first have become painfully aware of it in ourselves. Rather, it will become a stimulus. We shall understand how a certain sort of self-criticism which is always directed outwards may be nothing more than the search for an alibi designed to enable us to dodge the examination of our consciences.[31] And a humble acceptance of Catholic solidarity will perhaps be more profitable to us in the matter of shaking us out of some of our illusions. It will perhaps help us to fall in love once more, from a new standpoint, with those elements in the wisdom and the institutions and the traditions and the demands of our Church which we were coming near to understanding no longer.

The Problem of Adaptation

Today, however, disquiet often takes forms more precise than this, and the most lowly of active Catholics does not entirely escape it. He may ask himself with painful anxiety, Is the Church's action on our age properly adapted to it? Surely indisputable experience shows that it is tragically ineffective? For some time past at least that kind of question has been asked in many quarters, and we should not underestimate its seriousness, or dismiss it hastily as if we refused to look at it. If we do that we shall only add to the troubles of those who (perhaps because they are more wide awake than we) are at grips with it in a real "dark night." But here again we must make a sober effort at the discernment of spirits.[32]

In many quarters people are asking themselves questions as to the real value, not of course of Christianity itself, but of many of the parts that go to make up, as it were, the religious instrument, as the centuries have forged it. They find its efficiency at too low a level, and point grimly to the worn cogs and tired springs; many practices are put in the dock and there is talk of out-of-date methods and institutions. It will scarcely be a matter for surprise if there is in all this more than one illusion of the inside-out kind, and if certain errors creep into both the diagnosis of the evil and the choice of remedies for it; a genuine intuition of new needs may be accompanied by inadequate knowledge and a certain lack of grip on reality. It is not always possible to make an accurate distinction between what ought to be preserved and what ought to be changed, at the first shot. Sometimes we are overquick to despair of forms which, though apparently dead, are capable of reanimation. However, if our inspiration is sound we shall not find it difficult to make the necessary adjustments to a program rather hastily drawn up, and to round out a somewhat onesided effort by others more calculated to balance it.

But it is that inspiration, precisely, which stands in need of control. For here the worst may go cheek by jowl with the best. What is the real source of this concern for adaptation—or, which is very much the same thing, the felt need for what is often called a more effective "incarnation"—a concern in itself wholly justified [33] and frequently encouraged of set purpose by the supreme authority of the Church? [34]

Is it a pure overflowing of charity, as in the case of St. Paul who, following the example of Christ, wanted to make himself all things to all men? Or is there some ad-

mixture in it of the illusion that it is enough to make a
change of method, as all human undertakings may do, to
obtain results which primarily suppose a change of heart?
Realistic views, objective inquiry, statistics, the elucida-
tion of sociological laws, the drawing up of methodical
plans, breaks both big and small with the forms of apostolate belonging to the past, the perfecting of new techniques—all these things may be made use of by zeal that is
really pure and upright, and anyone who belittles them
puts himself in the right with a facility somewhat suspect
if he makes a mere opposition between them and the
methods of the Curé d'Ars. Yet all these things have to be
kept in their proper place, in the service of the Spirit of
God alone.

But—and this is something more serious—it may well
be that there is mingled with our disquiet in some more
or less subtle way a certain timidity, a certain deep-seated
lack of assurance and secret revulsion against the tradition
of the Church. We may, when we see ourselves as setting
ourselves free from what seems a spirit of senility, and as
struggling against ankylosis and sclerosis, be putting ourselves in the way of contracting "childish ailments"; [35]
what we take for an awakening of the personality may in
point of fact be the end-product of a blind aberration,
and we may set ourselves to judge all things in accordance
with criteria which are superficially "modern" and no
more. The secular values which the world spreads before
our eyes may begin to dazzle us, and in the presence of
those who stand for them we may, bit by bit, allow ourselves to be affected by an inferiority complex. Where
things that should be most sacred to us are concerned, we
may be on the way to accepting ideas about them held by
men whose blindness should in fact be matter for our sor-
row. We may be stupidly allowing ourselves to be imposed
upon by the manifestations of the "pride of life." To put

it in a nutshell, although our faith may not be flagging, we may be beginning to lose our faith in our faith, if one may so put it.[36]

This should be an occasion for recalling with greater explicitness certain constant truths. "I, when I have been lifted up from the earth, will draw all things unto me." [37] Those words of Christ are not, doubtless, an invitation to literal imitation, and we are not Wisdom personified that we should be able to be content to say, "Come over to me all that desire me: and be filled with my fruits." [38] St. Paul, conformed to Christ, travelled the world over, the precursor of a whole army of apostles. And the Church will always be a missionary. This is at least the symptom of a certain spirit. In other words, we are quite right not to want to be separated from men who are to be led to Christ—if by that we understand the necessity of breaking down the barriers which would be put between them and ourselves by forms of living or thinking which are superseded, and even more so by ways of behaving whose sole justification is an ideal of comfortableness or peace and quiet.

We are quite right not to allow ourselves to be shut up in any sort of ghetto, by ourselves any more than by anybody else.

But we have to be on our guard against misunderstanding both the truly central position which our faith guarantees us, to the degree of its own strength, and that essential condition of being *set apart from the world* which belongs to every Christian.[39] If we are really "turned to God," we have "abandoned idols" and cannot "bear the yoke" with those who are deceived by them.[40] And when we show real vitality in this sacred operation and the joyful practice of all that it imposes on us, others will certainly be drawn to this source of life and will not want to be separated from us. The miracle of the drawing power of Christ will continue in and through our lives.

We should, then, have no inhibitions about feeling a profound sympathy with the men who surround us. We should be fully human, for we are obliged to that by our duty of interior sincerity as well as of brotherly love; or rather, that disposition should be something so natural and congenital to us that there is no need to go looking for it. We ought not to get our loyalty to the eternal mixed up with an attachment to the past which is mischievous and even morbid. Yet at the same time we should beware of modern self-sufficiency. We should be wary of making our own the weaknesses and infatuations, the pretentious ignorance and the narrowness of the surrounding milieu, and of giving a welcome to worldliness, whether it be proletarian or middleclass, refined or vulgar. Or rather, we should be always extricating ourselves from it— for unfortunately we are always getting involved in it to a greater or a lesser degree. To sum up: we should always be adapted, and as spontaneously as possible. But we must adapt without ever allowing ourselves, either in behavior or thought, to adapt Christianity itself in the least—that is to say, to de-divinize it, or lower it, or make it insipid, or twist it out of shape. We should have a great love for our age, but make no concessions to the spirit of the age, so that in us the Christian mystery may never lose its sap.[41]

For some, this difficulty is made more acute at the intellectual level, and the pain more piercing at the depth of the soul, when it seems that in spite of every possible effort of adaptation the action of the Church remains far from effective, through causes which make all effort powerless. Far from making a perpetual advance, she goes back. Even where she is in apparent control and her influence is recognized and encouraged, she does not bring about the reign of the Gospel, and the social order is not transformed according to her principles.

Yet the tree is surely to be judged by its fruits . . . and *that,* surely, provides grounds for believing that the

Church has shot her bolt? It seems that we must fear that she can never realize other than symbolically what others feel confident of being able to realize eventually in truth. The conclusion would appear to be that we should transfer elsewhere the confidence which we once reposed in her.

There is much equivocation in this process of reasoning, apparently so simple. It is obvious that if each member of the Church were all that he ought to be, the kingdom of God would progress at a very different rate, though always through a perpetual piling-up of obstacles —as we saw earlier on—and always invisible to eyes which are not enlightened by God. And it is equally true that this or that historical happening and this or that social context can, independently of the will of the individual, create unfavorable conditions, deep-reaching misunderstandings and divergences, and thus set formidable problems. But if we are to have a chance of solving these—or at least of maintaining our confidence, even if we have to concede that some of them are, for the time being, insoluble—then a great many latent equivocations must be exposed. We will leave on one side all considerations of the sociological order, for it is with the preliminary "discernment" that we must concern ourselves to begin with.[42]

The Church Not a Visible Triumph

When the Church is in question we must not judge (success and frustration) of advance, and retreat, as we should do in the case of things which are of time. The supernatural good which the Church serves in the world is something that reaches its totality in the invisible order, and finds its consummation in the eternal. The communion of saints grows from generation to generation. And we should not regress into any dream of a Church exteriorly triumphant, for the Church's Head did not promise her dazzling and increasing success. If we say of the Church, as did Pascal, that she is destined to be in her agony until the end of the world, like Christ, this is not a relapse into mere rhetoric or the enjoyment of a romantic emotional luxury. We must not forget the demands of the "redeeming wisdom." [43] We should watch her at work in the life and action of Jesus; that will help us to pass through our disquiet and arrive on the other side, rather than drag us back to the hither side of it in a sort of resignation which may be a fall in itself. The apostolic-minded must know how to wait, and often have occasion to know how to accept the sense of being helpless; they *must* accept the fact of being nearly always misunderstood.

Above all, we must not get the wrong idea about the kingdom of God which is the end of the Church and which it is her mission to anticipate. Here the whole of the faith is involved; without in any way underestimating the urgency of the urban problem or the irreplaceable part wich the Church must play in the solution of it,[44] it is impossible to lose sight of the fact that her desire is to solve a problem no less urgent, but at a higher level and more far-reaching, more constant and more all-embracing. Like sicknesses that evolve in some germ-breeding environment, waging war on the remedies applied to them and cropping up again under a new form every time we think we have got them under control, the root evil which man carries in his depths flares up again, always the same in itself, under forms that change perpetually as society changes. Psychologies, customs, and social relationships change. Man remains, with his evil. This does not mean that we ought not to try everything in our search for betterment; the tenacity of evil can be nothing other than a challenge to a yet more determined and sustàined struggle. But assume for a moment a condition we are, unfortunately, far enough away from—a more or less perfect functioning of society: that is, not an economic or political machine more or less adequately powerful, but an exterior order which is as human as possible. With all that granted, the Church's work would not, in a sense, have been started. For her business is not to settle us comfortably in our earthly existence, but to raise us above it. Her bringing to us of the redemption of Christ means that she wants to tear us free from the evil that is in us and lay us open to another existence. The other side of the same fact is that if she were to give temporal effectiveness top priority, that very thing would not be granted to her. If she were to wait, in order to carry out in the world the work of salvation, for temporal conditions to undergo an eventual improvement (whatever the terms in which the ideal state of affairs were actually conceived), she would be playing false to her mission, which is to bring safely home not a future humanity at some time to come, but the whole of humanity throughout time—not a mythical humanity but the actual men of each generation.

If, then, we want to be realistic, it is none the less indispensable that our realism should not mistake its object. And if we are anxious to be effective, it is essential that we should not build our foundation on means which are too extrinsic and thus calculated to turn us aside from our end. If we rightly may (and sometimes should) be strict with those who call themselves Catholics—with ourselves—it is essential that we should understand what we do, and do it with reference to valid standards. We must not lose sight of the essential.

This essential, which cannot remain as even a distant objective on our horizon if we do not find a place for it in the heart of our present activity, is not something which can be judged from a quantitative point of view. God brings about the saving of us according to laws which are hidden from us as far as their concrete application is concerned, but which are imposed on our faith in principle —the mysterious laws of the community of salvation. Today the prayer of intercession and the sacrifice of charity have lost none of their secret power. Moreover, the existence of one saint alone would be sufficient witness to the divine value of the principle by which saints live. But the question is whether our sight is clear enough, and whether we have sufficient knowledge of where to look, to discern among ourselves, in this order of sanctity, the effectiveness of the Church? Let us at least try to catch a glimpse of it.

Massive appearance should not hide from us the central reality, nor should noisy ideological debate prevent us from hearing the silent breathing of the Spirit. At a time when he was the head of a community, and was without appreciable influence on the destinies of the Empire, the great St. Cyprian said, "As for us, we are philosophers not in word but in act; we do not say great things—but we do live them." [45] That saying remains true, in all its proud humility. The essential is very rarely something that can be much talked about. Christian vitality is in every age very much less dependent on all that is discussed and done and picked to pieces on the world's stage than we are often led to believe. There is here a life which is almost impossible to pass judgment on from the outside. And that life keeps itself going, passes itself on and renews itself under all the turmoil of politics, all the swirl of public opinion, the currents of ideas and the controversies, far removed from the scene of public debate, unsounded and untabulated. The blind see, the deaf hear, the dead are raised to life and the poor have the Gospel preached to them; [46] the kingdom of God shines in secret. Here and there there are sudden glimpses, patches of light break through, widen, join up with others. A point of light or two in the night suddenly shines more brightly, sometimes there will be patches of blood, to draw our attention. All are so many heralding signs.

Today, when there is so much discussion about Christianity and so much complaining about its "ill-adapted-ness" or "ineffectiveness," we should always be returning again and again to these very simple considerations. The best Christians and the most vital are by no means to be found either inevitably or even generally among the wise or the clever, the intelligentsia or the politically-minded, or those of social consequence. And consequently what they say does not make the headlines; what they do does not come to the public eye. Their lives are hidden from the eyes of the world, and if they do come to some degree of notoriety, that is usually late in the day, and exceptional, and always attended by the risk of distortion. Within the Church itself it is, as often as not, only after their deaths that some of them acquire an uncontested reputation. Yet these are responsible, more than anyone else, for insuring that our earth is not a hell on earth. Most of them never think to ask themselves whether their faith is "adapted" or "effective." It is enough for them to live it as reality itself, and reality at its most actual; and because the fruit of all this is often enough a hidden fruit it is none the less wonderful for that. Even if such people are themselves not engaged in external activity, they are the source of all initiative and action, all spadework which is not to be fruitless. It is these people who are our preservation and who give us hope, and it would be a bold man who said that they are less numerous and less active today than in the past.[47]

We should not become blind to the real fruitfulness of our Mother the Church for the sake of a dream of efficiency which may be no more than a mirage.

Notes

[1] A. Molien, "Simon (Richard)," *Dictionnaire de Théologie Catholique*, 14, col. 2112.

[2] Thus Tertullian, *Apologia*, ch. 32, no. 1; ch. 39, no. 2 (pp. 94 and 106 in Waltzing's edition): *Ad Scapulum*, ch. 2 (vol. 1, p. 541, in Oehler's edition): Melito of Sardis, quoted in Eusebius, *Hist. Eccl.* IV, ch. 36, no. 11.

Our Temptations Concerning the Church

3 One cannot read without profound sadness the reflections of non-believing authors on this subject, however exaggerated they may be; for example, those of Leon Brunschvicg in his *Le Progrès de la Conscience dans la Philosophie Occidentale,* 1927, I, pp. 221-222.

4 St. Hilary of Poitiers, *In Psalm.,* 67, no. 12 (pp. 287-288 in Zingerle's edition).

5 Bruno de Solages, *Pour Rebâtir une Chrétienté,* 1938, p. 174; cf. Leo XIII, *Letter to His Eminence Cardinal Rampolla,* Oct. 8, 1895: "Things human change, but the beneficent virtue of the supreme magisterium of the Church comes from on high and remains always the same. . . . Established to last as long as time, it follows with a loving vigilance the advance of humanity, and does not refuse (as its detractors falsely claim) to come to terms with the reasonable needs of the time as far as this is possible."

6 *Sermo* 105, no. 9 (*PL,* 38, 623).

7 Phil 2:5.

8 St. Augustine, *Sermo* 252, no. 3 (*PL,* 38, 1173-1174).

9 Renan, "Du Libéralisme Doctrinal," in *La Liberté de Penser,* May 15, 1848.

10 Renan, *Letter to the Abbé Cognat,* Sept. 5, 1846, quoted in J. Cognat, *M. Renan Hier et Aujourd'hui,* 1886, p. 203.

11 Renan, *Marc-Aurèle,* 3rd ed., 1882, p. 109; cf. pp. 403-404.

12 Renan, *Questions Contemporaines,* p. 423; *Drames Philosophiques,* pp. 279-280 (Act I of *Le Prêtre de Némi*).

13 *Letter to the Abbé Cognat,* in J. Cognat, *M. Renan,* p. 203; *Souvenirs d'Enfance et de Jeunesse; Questions Contemporaines,* p. 457.

14 Proudhon, *De la Justice dans la Révolution et dans l'Eglise,* new ed., IV, p. 332.

15 *Contra Litteras Petiliani,* I, ch. 29, no. 31 (*PL,* 43, 2509).

16 I Cor 13:12.

17 *Apologia pro Vita Sua,* ch. 5.

18 Cf. the panegyric on St. Rémi delivered at Rheims by Mgr. Chapoulie, Bishop of Angers; confronted with "the great upheaval which has been going on for more than a century in society," the duty of the Catholic is "to try to understand, and above all to desire to love." Certainly, "there are audacities we may not like, and certain 'discoveries' may seem to us to be naive," but "when all is said and done, is it really preferable . . . to shut oneself up within a disdainful and immovable refusal, to continue to seek a timid refuge in love of the past?" If we are to succeed in disengaging the eternal truth of the Gospel from a crumbling past, "as did St. Rémi," we must have "a powerful faith in Jesus Christ and the coming of his kingdom" ("Semaine Religieuse d'Angers," *Témoignage Chrétien,* Nov. 14, 1952).

19 *Du Régime Temporel et de la Liberté,* 1933, p. 139.

20 *Epist.* 15 (*PL,* 22, 355).

21 *In Cantica, Sermo* 77, nos. 1-2 (*PL,* 183, 1155-1156).

22 Particularly in Book IV (*PL,* 182, 771-788).

23 Letter 315.

24 *Compendium*, ch. 1 and 4.

25 Dedication to the *Opuscula* of Denis the Carthusian: "I address myself to Your Beatitude, not in my own name but in the name of many, not to say in the name of all. The act of solicitude we ask for, we call reform of the Church. . . . What is there in the Church which is not contaminated or corrupted? What is there left of integrity among the clergy, of honor among the nobility, or of sincerity among the people? All is put to confusion, wounded, ruined, mutilated. From the soles of the feet to the crown of the head, there is nothing healthy left."

26 Emmanuel Mounier, "Un Surnaturalisme Historique," *Georges Bernanos*, p. 113.

27 Cf. Paul Claudel, *Letter to André Gide*, Jan. 9, 1912.

28 Pius XII, *Mystici Corporis*.

29 This reflection appears several times in the correspondence of St. Francis Xavier, and he impresses it again upon his faithful disciple Gaspard Barzée in his final advice to him; cf. Catherine Ranquet's letter to Fr. de Bus of May 4, 1647: "Before God, I am nothing but an obstacle to his designs, and the destruction of his work . . ." (quoted in G. Gueudré, *Catherine Ranquet, Mystique et Educatrice*, 1952, p. 168).

30 Paul Claudel, *Interroge le Cantique des Cantiques*, p. 277.

31 Cf. Cardinal Wyszynski's letter of Nov., 1952, published in the Cracow Catholic weekly *Tygodnik Powszechny*: "The active presence of Catholics in the universal Church needs a deepening. . . . It ought to be the presence of *domestici fidei*, incorporated in Christ living in the Church . . . we must induce men to break with religious individualism; with the facile criticisms of far-off observers who impose on the Church (often conceived of in a highly abstract fashion) great demands, and forget that these demands should first be imposed upon oneself, since the Church . . . is ourselves" (*L'Actualité Religieuse dans le Monde*, April 1, 1953, p. 28). See also, de Montcheuil, *Aspects de l'Eglise*, pp. 77-79.

32 Here I am not envisaging any of the objective problems which may really present themselves. It is not that I wish to question the importance of such, but that to do so would be to go beyond the bounds of my subject. All I am attempting here is to define the attitude without which such problems would of necessity be misrepresented and would bear within their very formulation risks of misunderstanding or error.

33 There is a permanent value in what Fr. Alfred Soras wrote in 1938 in *Action Catholique et Action Temporelle* concerning the "law of incarnation," its depth, scope and problems.

34 One of the most recent examples of this was the allocution of Pius XII to the superiors of female religious gathered in congress in Rome in Sept., 1952: ". . . Where things which are not essential are concerned, adapt yourselves as reason and rightly-ordered charity counsel you."

35 Cf. Joseph Folliet, *Presence de l'Eglise*, 1949, ch. 3: "Maladies Séniles et Maladies Infantiles des Catholiques Français"; Louis Beirnaert's invita-

tion "not to entrench ourselves in resentment" in his "Fidelité à l'Eglise et Fidelité à l'Homme," *Etudes*, v. 151, p. 16.

36 This temptation will already be partly dissipated if we see how others before us have recognized and overcome it. Newman came close to giving way to it during his Anglican period—admittedly, within the framework of a situation very different from ours. It has been said of a certain type of politician. "He both believes in his truths and despairs of them" (Etienne Borne, in *Terre Humaine*, Oct., 1957, p. 7). It would be even more illogical for a Christian to harbor such an attitude of mind with regard to his faith.

37 Jo 12:32; cf. Bengt Sundkler's stimulating study, "Jésus et les Paiens," *Revue d'Histoire et de Philosophie Religieuses*, 1936, pp. 462-499.

38 Ecclus 24:26.

39 *Sanctus = segregatus;* cf. Acts 13:2; Rom 1:1: ". . . called to be an apostle, separated unto the gospel of God."

40 I Thess 1:9; 1 Cor 6:9-12; II Cor 6:14-17.

41 Rom 12:2: "And be not conformed to this world." I have treated of these questions at greater length in *Paradoxes*, pp. 41-45 and 73-85.

42 Cf. Jean Clémence, S.J., "Le Discernement des Esprits dans les Exercices Spirituels de Saint Ignace de Loyola," *Revue d'Ascétique et de Mystique*, 1951, p. 359: while the danger which threatens souls who are still mediocre is that of cowardliness, "that which threatens generous souls is illusion."

43 Cf. Alfred Soras, S.J., "Besoin Actuel d'une Sagesse Rédemptrice," in *Masses Ouvrières*, March, 1952.

44 The situation with regard to social Catholicism is rather like that with regard to Christian philosophy; it is not and can never be a completed system or a total success. In its most fundamental aspect the action of Catholicism on society is essentially indirect, as is its action on thought. However, during recent times, in which the conduct of societies and states has been so little under the influence of the Church, it is something to wonder at that "social catholicism" has been able to carry out work, in the sphere of influencing doctrine and leavening society, which is by no means negligible.

45 St. Cyprian, *De Bono Patientiae*, ch. 3: "Nos autem . . . qui philosophi non verbis sed factis sumus . . . qui non loquimur magna sed vivimus" (I, p. 398, in Hartel's edition); Minucius Felix, *Octavius*, ch. 38, no. 6 (*PL*, 3, 359a).

46 Lk 7:22.

47 Cf. *Paradoxes*, pp. 89-117 (on the subject of efficacity). The reader should also consult Henry Dumery's *Les Trois Tentations de l'Apostolat Moderne*, 1948 and Yves Congar's *Laypeople in the Church*, ch. 6, "In the World, and not of the World."

PART 4 *Understanding in the
Life of the Church*

CHAPTER **10** *The Church and Christian Understanding**

by Émile Mersch, S.J.

Author: Émile Mersch, who was killed during the German invasion of the Low Countries in 1940, was for a number of years professor of Dogmatic Theology at the Jesuit college in Namur, Belgium. He has the distinction of being the author of what many theologians rank as the greatest single volume of Catholic theology of the present century, *The Theology of the Mystical Body,* a tremendously vital and highly personal synthesis of dogmatic theology built around the notion of the Mystical Body of Christ. The present selection is taken from this book.

Article: There are in the Church "official" Catholic doctrines (called dogmas and, under certain conditions, infallible definitions). But there is also in each member of the Church a personal understanding of that Truth of Christ which he participates in through the light of faith and which is authentically presented to him in the 'official' doctrine of the Church and in the sources of that doctrine, the Bible and the Church's Tradition. In the present selection Father Mersch attempts to present and harmonize both the visible communication of Christ's Truth through the official Church hierarchy and the invisible communication of that same Truth by the Spirit working in the faithful. The whole article is an eloquent personal testimony to the importance and vitality of Christian

* "The Church and Christian Understanding" first appeared in English in Father Mersch's *The Theology of the Mystical Body* (B. Herder, 1951), pp. 520-533. It is reprinted here with permission.

[229]

understanding which official dogma guides but by no means stifles.

READINGS: For a fuller exposure to the thought of Father Mersch the reader should go both to his major work, *The Theology of the Mystical Body,* and to his earlier study of the notion of the Mystical Body in the Fathers and in Church Tradition, *The Whole Christ* (Bruce, 1938).

CHRIST'S TEACHING career was too important to come to an end with his mortal life. Can we conceive that the Word was made flesh with the purpose, as he himself declares, of giving testimony to the truth,[1] and that his voice should die away in silence after three years? Christ's humanity, subsisting as it did in the Word, was in itself a human teaching without limits, and was so great that it could not express itself fully except in the totality of the human race. Regarded as teaching, therefore, it had to spread over the whole world to be in all mankind a principle of knowledge, just as, regarded as life, it is spread over the whole world to be in mankind a source of grace. In the same way as Christ's humanity fashions for itself a living body out of mankind, a body vigorous with eternal life, it makes out of mankind an intelligent organism that has knowledge of eternal truth.

This living body, like Christ's humanity, is both visible and invisible. Consequently the life of knowledge perpetuated in it must be at once visible and invisible, and likewise the influx of knowledge by which the sacred humanity produces and maintains this life must be visible and invisible. But the knowledge communicated to the mystical body must be the same as that possessed by Christ the head, for in the unity of Christ the life of the whole Christ is one and the same.[2]

Invisible Communication

The invisible communication of this knowledge is accomplished in the souls of Christ's members. It is a donation of life and thought, a sharing in the mind of Christ in the life of Christ, enabling us to judge and evaluate in a way suitable for members of Christ. It is a participation in the consciousness Christ has of himself as head of mankind, a consciousness so human yet so penetrating that it can enlighten the consciousness of every man from within.[3] This interior illumination is not a simple elevation of the faculty of knowledge without any bearing on the new objects to be known. As a sharing in the consciousness of Christ it is related to every Christian dogma that imparts instruction about Christ. It is meant to express Christ; it conveys a kind of preliminary sketch of Christ that is not yet filled in. Since this knowledge is possessed by a member of Christ, it expresses Christ who has members in a body that is the Church, and who, being God the Son, is able to unite members to himself.

An illumination of this kind is not a passive reception of light-rays. To live is to act and, for a spirit, to know is to live; even material things do not shine in the rays of the sun without vibrating in turn. To receive light in any true sense, Christians have to cooperate with it by letting it penetrate into the deepest reaches which the soul can lay open to it. They have to think out their faith with living docility; they have to meditate on it with eagerness and continual adherence to Christ, so that, through the power of the head who is Christ, they may develop in themselves a mentality suitable for Christ's members.

The mention of a member implies an organism. Christians do not belong to Christ unless they are all joined together in him. They would not live their life of knowledge in Christ unless they all lived together, in a common reception and a universal collaboration; this is a phase of the communion of saints. Their collaboration must be both interior and exterior, because the nature of man has these two aspects.

This is the work of the immense collective life of the Church, so far as that life is intellectual. Every Christian has the ability and the duty to take part in it in his own way, either by expressing it in his life or by scientific investigation, according to his vocation, his talent, and his condition. His baptismal character, and particularly the character he receives in the sacrament of confirmation, invest him with the ability and the duty to render public and social testimony,[4] to teach, if not by authoritative instruction at least by his solidarity and fellowship in charity, and to engage in that communication of life, conviction, and thought that marks the adult.

Visible Communication

But the work would not be entirely human if it were purely invisible; such as influence on thought alone is too delicate and imperceptible to suffice for the sluggish minds of men and the rigorous precision required by supernatural truth. That is why Christ lives on in the Church not only by an invisible continuation in souls, but also by a visible continuation in social authority. In this authority Christ is prolonged as the exterior principle and visible, efficacious unity of the society that owes its existence to him. And by the visible teaching office he exercises in this authority, he is prolonged as the exterior principle and efficacious unity of the propagation of knowledge and light that come to us from him.

The interior teaching, the growth of each member in

truth for his own benefit and that of others, is not in full union with Christ and does not share in absolute certitude or infallibility unless it is in union with this authority. In this authority Christ still continues to teach externally and audibly; when we hear it, we can still hear him. His human word reflects the eternity he has as the Word; he does not cease to be uttered either in his divinity or in his humanity. His human word is the decisive word that judges every generation, and the act that announces it never ceases to function.

Such is the mystery of the teaching Church. "Peter has spoken through Leo, and Christ has spoken through Peter." This accounts for the superior character of this teaching authority; it is the superiority of Christ himself. The doctrines proclaimed by the Church are heard outside. Men may be struck by the firmness, the flexibility, and the time-resisting quality of this teaching. But no one can perceive from outside why it always remains the same.

Christ in His Vicars

We may approach an explanation by considering the divine Omnipotence that from heaven invisibly guards the deposit of revelation. But, in our opinion, we have not yet arrived at an understanding so long as we represent this assistance as a distant aid guaranteeing an invariable fidelity that is merely material. When Jesus Christ promised to remain always with his Church, he was not speaking of any such remote aid. He does not dwell in us, nor we in him, from the heights of heaven; he is within us and in our Church. The Church is his body; when the Church teaches, it lends him its lips, its voice, and its effort; but he is the one who speaks.

We hear the Church, but "he that is of God heareth the words of God." [5] We hear the words spoken by the

Church, but what we hear is not the Church. For the Church is the continuation of Christ. Just as the words uttered by the sacred humanity of Jesus did not have their first starting point in that humanity, so the doctrine of the Church is not its own doctrine. Jesus has given to the Church the words he himself received, and the Church speaks the works of God and the word of Christ.

The Father gave to Jesus the words he spoke, and the Father spoke them in him.[6] Our Lord's teaching existed in the flood of light that issued from the Light, "light from light," just as he himself subsists in him who sends him.[7] Such is also the Church and the teaching of the Church; this teaching comes from the Father and has its origin in the brightness of eternal light.

Accordingly this teaching is essentially Trinitarian in its content, in its origin and support, and in the mission of those who announce it. For this mission is connected with the eternal processions. "As the Father has sent me, I also send you." [8] When we stand in the presence of the teaching Church, we are in the presence of absolute mystery. Therefore, to grasp the message of the Church and to know what its teaching authority is, we need a revelation from the Father; only the Father can reveal the Son,[9] and he alone can tell us where the Son's voice is to be heard today.[10]

"The Church is the pillar and the ground of the truth;" [11] and "it is the Spirit which testifies that Christ is the truth." [12] The Church truly takes the place of Christ; yet we cannot say that the Church pilfers anything that belongs to him; he alone is the truth in the Church. Therefore we may say that the teaching of the Church is not less infallible than the teaching of Jesus, and yet that Jesus alone is infallible; he is infallible in the Church. The dignities are equal here, for they both are one dignity; on the one side it is personal, on the other it is mystically communicated; but on both sides it is the dignity of the uncreated light made flesh.

Human individuals do not count on these heights. The theological formation of the pope and the learning possessed by bishops gathered in a council are not important; in themselves they know nothing, they can do nothing, they serve no purpose. Even their deficiencies, however great we may suppose them to be, do not count. Jesus Christ is in them; can the insignificant clay that we are dam up God's omnipotence? We can say of their teaching office what we may say of their governing authority: in themselves and of themselves they have no power.

Yet they are Christ's vicars. They must tend flocks that are not their own with a care that is not their own in pastures that are not their own. But they alone have the duty of tending the flocks, and the sheep have but to hear, not the voice of these shepherds, but the voice of the one great Shepherd.[13]

Never, perhaps, did Christ so boldly place his reliance on men as when he said, "Feed my sheep." [14] When he said over the bread, "This is my body," he knew that the bread could not play him false, that it could never resist transubstantiation, that it could never give poison to souls instead of life. But when he told Peter, "Feed my flock," he knew well that man would always retain the power of going back on him. He was fully aware that man's mind is dull, often harried by blameworthy prejudices, and even by excessive eagerness to do well. Yet he dared to commit himself completely to one among us; he put his signature to this man's decisions and definitions before they were issued, so that, if this man were to fall into error, he himself would be in default.

A sort of "real presence" is found in the pope and the episcopate. The Son of man is sure enough of his mystical undertaking in our race to give us his pledge that he would reside in the pope and bishops until the end of the centuries, and that their shortcomings in knowledge would not keep him from being the truth in them, any more than the commonplace triviality of bread would keep him from being our life in the consecrated host. In the pope as well as in the episcopate, we repeat. Both make up the teaching Church, and both are infallible. Catholic doctrine is characteristic on this point, and for my part I do not see how it can be satisfactorily understood without appealing to the truth of the mystical body.

The power to teach is said to be twofold; it is truly found in the bishops and it is truly found in the pope. And the full teaching authority which is in the pope does not prevent the same power from being really in the bishops when they act as a body. Anywhere else such a régime would be impossible; what can a parliament do when the monarch is absolute? But the two are perfectly compatible in the Church. The pope's power is the power, not of his person, but of Christ who teaches through him. The same Christ also teaches in the assembled bishops, and has the same power in them. Yet there is only one power, because there is only one Christ; and although the two organisms are not identical as organisms, they will always be found to be in agreement, because they have but a single power.

A Christian is someone who refuses to see anything else than Jesus Christ. His docility to the bishops is the same as his docility to the pope, for it is the docility he has to Christ. The definitions of a council and the declarations of the incarnate Word are absolutely equivalent for him. They are, indeed, identical in the unity of the mystical body; the council continues Christ, as the voice that strikes the ear continues the voice issuing from the speaker's mouth.

Obviously the teachings of the magisterium do not all have the same doctrinal value. What we have said applies fully only to the cases in which the Church acts in the plenitude of its power, that is, in the totality of its incorporation in Christ, to define revealed truth. Other cases admit of correctives and explanations; theology treats of them, and we need not enumerate them here. We need only to point out that in these other cases human thought acts to some extent on its own responsibility, and that consequently the mystical Christ informs the teaching office less completely. However, the teaching office is always the organ by which Christ acts, and his action remains always a powerful preservative against error, even if it does not manifest itself in the infallibility that properly belongs to it. And therefore, whenever the Church speaks, an internal assent is to be given. But this assent can be based on the absolute competence or on the relative competence of the Church, as the voice through which truth speaks, according as the Church acts with the fullness of its authority or employs that authority only partly.

From this point of view, the teaching activity of the Church resembles the sanctifying action of the sacraments. The words pronounced at the consecration by the least worthy of priests in the most distracted of Masses are no less efficacious than the consecration pronounced by Jesus himself at the Last Supper. Similarly, the teaching of the Church is no less sure than that of Jesus.

This teaching of truth has its own proper efficacy. "The word of God is living and effectual." [15] Of its very nature it is incisive and penetrating; such it was in Jesus Christ, and such it remains in the Church. Christ spoke as one having authority. His teaching possessed the power of helping his hearers to understand and to believe. His miracles were no doubt numerous and impressive; but they were not indispensable; his bare assertion was enough to give a firm basis to faith.[16] On his testimony God has erected the whole economy of salvation; [17] and his testimony is valid for all those who are of the truth, for no other reason than that it is his.[18]

Christ's testimony has not ceased to be given; it is found in the teaching of the Church and constitutes the efficacy of that teaching. In former days his voice was heard across a few yards of space; now it is heard through the Church; such media cannot in any way cut down the power of the word. The people of Samaria once said to the woman who had announced Christ to them, "We now believe, not because of your saying, for we ourselves have heard him." [19] The situation is exactly the same for us Christians of the twentieth century; we believe, not because of what our priests, our parents, and our books have told us, but because we ourselves have heard him through the organs by which he himself speaks.

The Vatican Council declares that the Church is the custodian and teacher of revealed truth. The Church exercises this office with supernatural perfection, not only by transmitting and authentically interpreting the truth or by enjoying the constant assistance of him who is the author of the truth, but mainly by being, in a mystical sense, him who gives the truth and who sums up in himself all truth. Since he is there, his witness of the Church is not less cogent than was his witness of himself. Therefore this testimony, like the Savior's own affirmation in other days, can penetrate the soul and, if the soul's will cooperates, can rouse it to give the assent of faith.

Consequently we may say that the teaching of the Church is more than a rule and guaranty of the faith; it is also the ultimate foundation of the faith. This statement, of course, has to be rightly understood. We do not say that explicit submission to the external teaching authority is the only condition that makes an act of supernatural faith possible; if this were so, the souls of good will that are outside the Catholic Church could have no faith. Nor do we say that attachment to the bishops and the pope, regarded as persons who exercise an external office, is enough to establish us formally on the immovable rock of truth. What we are trying to bring out is that this point of view is not adequate. The Church is Christ, and Christ is God. When the Church as such speaks, we need not pursue our investigations farther. All we have to do is believe; and the one we believe is God.

Some may object that God is only the invisible protector who assists his ministers from without. That is true, if we are looking at the surface of things or at the body of the Church. But it is not true if we consider the true reality. Since the time of the Incarnation, God is not other than Christ; and since Pentecost, Christ is not other than the Church. On the one side, hypostatic unity; on the other side, mystic unity; but in both cases the unity is real. The Church is the word of God addressed to all the nations; the Church is the eternal Truth that has drawn close to us in order to become ours. When we believe in the Church, we believe in God.

The teaching of the Church begets faith; it is like the sacrament of the Eucharist, which is not only the sign of the life that is given, but is this very life in its source. And that is the case in the various ways of conveying this teaching as provided for in the structure of the Church, for example, in the teaching of simple priests or in the instruction Christian parents give to their children. Christ speaks everywhere, as he speaks always.

Christ in the Faithful

As the superiority of the teaching authority is that of Christ himself, its "interiority" is also that of Christ. The mystical body is a unique kind of entity; it is a single, living, supernatural being. Its life, which it receives from Christ, is expressed in a knowledge and love that also come unceasingly from Christ. As Christ is living, so this knowledge and love are living; as Christ lives more intensely than we do, this knowledge and love live more intensely than we do; and as Christ lives in us, they too live in us, and more ardently than we. The essential requisite of doctrinal progress is found in this fact. The formulas we succeed in expressing outwardly are vague and confused; but every living man knows what life is, and every Christian who lives in Christ by faith and love knows, by his faith and love, what this life in Christ is.

As the centuries pass, men in whom Christ dwells come to know him more and more perfectly. Through grace, the teaching of the Church, and their own reflections, men express and comprehend him better and better. The doctrine is not new; it is old; but it becomes better understood. The reality is now new; it is the same as it was in the beginning; but it is more explicitly possessed. The identity is complete; since the time Christ began to exist, no entirely new light has shone or will shine in his humanity. What we understand is the mutual gift; better still, the gift itself makes itself ever better comprehended by continually giving itself. Yet there is advance and growth. New jewels are brought out of the ancient treasury. But this development merely accentuates the living identity; the better we come to know Christ and Christianity, the better we perceive that we now possess more fully the gift that was unreservedly handed over to men at the beginning. The very acknowledgment of this fact shows how rich in definitive doctrine the origins were.

In this point, as in all others, the progress of doctrine surpasses any progress of which we have experience as much as the supernatural surpasses the natural. For the goal to which the progress of doctrine is to lead was realized from the start, since this goal is the beatific vision. Christ had this vision from the instant of his conception. Doctrinal progress wholly consists in communicating to the members what pre-exists in the head.

In this progress of dogma, the only thing that can account for its structure and internal coherence is union with grace. Here we are thinking of all our supernatural activities, particularly of faith. Faith is a union of the mind with Christ and his knowledge. Therefore it confers a special competence on our supernatural knowledge. This trait should be clearly brought out. Too often faith is represented, even by those who have the best of intentions, as an intellectual timidity, as a fear that keeps a man from thinking for himself and that induces him to accept the ready-made ideas of another. It is like that only when it is badly exercised. In itself, union with light tends to make vision more piercing and luminous. Submission to the teaching authority of the Church as such, that is as representing the incarnate Word, ought to impart to the mind a new boldness and a sort of rapture. We think, but not alone; we think in Christ, with Christ, through Christ. Truly we are the ones who think, and we think with all our heart and soul; but even for us our act of thinking is a rich and splendid mystery. And when Christ lends to our thinking his cooperation, his light, and his thought, our concepts are bathed in eternal light. Let us think, then, for when we reflect we let the rays of this brilliant light penetrate our souls. Let us think, out of love from him who is the Word and Thought and Truth; let us think, for our reflections are the only love our minds are capable of when they are in the presence of the truth that charms them.

But we should think with Christ, in him, and in dependence on him. He stands before us, very near, real, and attentive, in the magisterium of the Church. He is there to deliver to us the data of our undertaking, to sustain our effort, to correct our wanderings if need should arise, and to approve the result. What more could we desire? If we approach the work with a craven or irresolute spirit, the fault is none of his; for we ought to perform the task in him.

The part played by man in the vitality of Christian

teaching is very great, and we do well to assure ourselves on that point. To appreciate the fact better, have we noticed how important it was in the very founding of the Church? Jesus came to establish the Catholic Church on earth; but the ones who actually established it were men. Christ himself hardly preached to anyone except the lost sheep of the house of Israel; and during his mortal life he sent his disciples nowhere except to the villages of Palestine, directing them not to travel the roads of Samaria or to cross over to the pagan districts. He himself apparently wished to do no more than train the apostles and to make ready the seed that later, under his hidden action and his bidding, would be sown to spread the Gospel over all the earth. In point of fact, truly Catholic preaching, the diffusion of the true doctrine, is the work of the Church, not of Christ; or better, it is the work of Christ in the Church. The body of Christ has built itself up; as St. Paul says, it has achieved its own construction and growth; but it was able to do so because it was attached to the head and possessed the real though invisible power of the head.

Can we not say the same with regard to Christian teaching? Jesus has given us the whole doctrine; yes, indeed, but as a seed rather than as something fully formed. He spoke under the form of images, practical counsels, occasional lessons, parables, and especially examples. He never declared explicitly, in the precise formulas of defined dogmas, that he was one person with two natures; that he was one of the Trinity, consubstantial with the Father, and, along with the Father, the principle of the Holy Spirit; that he came to expiate, by vicarious satisfaction, an original fault and numberless actual sins; that his Second Coming, which was at hand, would be his return in the Church. In a word, he hardly gave any exposition of Christian doctrine, if by that we mean an orderly collection of propositions. What he taught was

[242]

rather the sketches or first drafts or, so to speak, the seeds of formulas. In general he was content to be himself, to be the summing-up of all truth in himself. He conducted himself as a man and as God, he acted toward God as a Son with his Father, and also as someone able to give God and to pour out the Spirit. He acted as a hostage coming to free all men, and as a founder coming to establish a society in which he himself would live mystically. But the formulation of the truth in words, the reduction of these realities to a body of doctrine, has in large part remained the task committed to the Church. The apostles had to piece Christian teaching together from what he said, displayed in his own person, and suggested; what has been accomplished is his work, but it has been performed by them. He would ever aid his Church, but from within; his Spirit would bring all truth to mind, and would also see to it that not so much as a superfluous comma would be added.[20] Yet the Church would draw up its Creed, its councils, and its theological summas in him; for the head and the body are inseparable.

A Christian is a member of the mystical body, not by his own effort, but through Christ. On the other hand, the act of knowing, which is a function of being, is construed as the being that knows. Consequently, although the Christian truly knows, he knows, not of himself, but through Christ. But Christ, who lives in souls by his "anointing" and his living truth, does not express himself outwardly and authentically except in the teaching authority of the Church. Therefore this "anointing," this living truth, in a word this Christian life, appeals to the teaching authority when it appeals to Christ, and its voice is lifted up in the councils. "Peter, teach us; you have the words of eternal life, and you have them for me."

Thus entreated by Christian life, Christ proceeds, not to restrain it or to supplant it or to suppress it, but to call it forth and to complete it. The theologians who keep silent for fear of attracting notice and are content merely to criticize or to treat of subjects that are safe and lacking in vital interest, are not those of the strongest faith; Christians who leave to ecclesiastical superiors the task of thinking out their religion for them, resigning themselves to a passive faith, are not the most fervent. As though the internal act of thinking were the exclusive prerogative of the external magisterium as such; or as though God had not fortified his Church with an unfailing authority for the express purpose of enabling men to think without fear!

Union of the Invisible and Visible Communication of Christ's Knowledge to the Church

The union between the authority of Christ in pastors and the life of Christ in souls is perfect. It springs up from the spontaneity of Christian life. What is outwardly submission, is inwardly supreme autonomy. Let this word frighten no one; it is necessary to bring out the glory of our faith. But such autonomy clearly implies that the faithful are united to Christ. As long as we dwell on their distinction from Christ, the case is different; but is the branch of the vine a branch merely because it is distinct from the vine?

The faithful are in Christ, and Christ is in them. Living faith brings Christ to dwell in his members. When the believer surrenders himself to Christ in faith, Christ is no longer a stranger: he is the believer's life and his all. And when Christ entrusts his truth to a believer, he entrusts himself along with it. From the instant of its coming, faith is no longer faith in someone extraneous and remote; it is faith in him who is more interior to us than we ourselves are; and from then on, we may say, it is faith in oneself, and is autonomous rather than heteronomous. However, it is autonomous, not with reference to the

Christian alone or to Christ alone, but with regard to the unity of the whole Christ; outside this union there is neither Christian nor Christ. A man believes in the mystery of unity only from within this unity.

In this mystery of unity, that is, in the true reality, the life of supernatural knowledge, or faith, is spontaneous and interior, like all life; but it is such in the same way as it is life, that is, in Christ. In his mystical body, Christ forms himself as the One who knows, "there will be one Christ knowing himself." On the empirical level, the magisterium appears to teach the faithful; in reality, Christ teaches himself, as St. Augustine says in a passage of his *Tractatus in Joannem* which expounds the ideas dealt with in this section, although the method of treatment is somewhat different. The saint there explains how Jesus can say, in St. John, that the Father will show him yet greater things, so that the disciples and not he will marvel, as though, in showing these things to him, the Father had really shown them to the disciples.

The magisterium of the Church is not the exaltation of a few individuals above masses kept in tutelage; it is the means God uses to elevate the whole populace. The office of the popes and bishops will pass away, and it is not because they have taught that they will see the Light in heaven, but because, like any of the faithful, they have believed. And everything else will pass away, *ex cathedra* definitions and infallibility in teaching. But infallibility in believing will remain, in the sense that the belief of the faithful will become, century after century, infallibility in seeing, the certitude of vision. Hence the greatness is shared by all, and all alike are illuminated; and this resembles a democracy. But the greatness comes through the ministry of some, especially of one; and only some, especially one, hold the torch; and here we have the monarchical principle. But this one and the others and all are illuminated because they are in the house; [21] and here we have the synthesis of both aspects. In reality, there are not, on the one side, those who teach, and on the other, quite separate, those who are taught; there is but one life, one mystical body, one complete Christ, head and members. When the head communicates light to the members, a single mystical man grows in knowledge. "There will be one Christ teaching himself."

Like all the others, and as much as the others, pope and bishops need to be taught by Jesus Christ. But Jesus Christ teaches them by means of the function they discharge. As private persons, they are subject to the power which, as public persons, they wield in the name of God. This is very revealing for the exact nature of the magisterium, for it shows that teaching is an action of Christ performed through men, and not an action of men. They can teach and they must teach; but the truth they teach comes from Christ, and is greater than they. As a priest effaces himself before the host he has just consecrated, they ought to efface themselves before the doctrine they proclaim. Their faith ought to be just as absolute as that of the priest at the consecration, and we may seemingly add that in all likelihood it is more meritorious. We of the general body of the faithful behold the arbiter of our faith in the majesty of liturgical functions; but they who hold this office know themselves in their workaday lives, and they appreciate better than anyone what imperfect and feeble instruments the Master has deigned to use. No matter. They have the strict duty of regarding their pronouncements as excluding all doubt, even to martyrdom if need be.

They have been but a channel of truth. And their pronouncements are not the product of their own reflections but come from the mind of him who, in the flesh hypostatically united to the Word, has brought us the doctrine of truth.[22]

Notes

1 Jo 18:37.

2 This visible influence and magisterium will be to the invisible influence and magisterium what the body of the Church is to the soul of the Church, and what the formulation of dogma in words and phrases is to the supernatural knowledge present in souls.

3 "The Word was . . . full of grace and truth" (Jo 1:14); "Every one that is of the truth, hears my voice" (Jo 18:37). "Christ is the master who teaches secretly in the school of the heart," says St. Augustine, *Confessions*, IX, 9.

4 Cf. *Decretum pro Armenis*, Denzinger 697.

5 Jo 8:47.

6 Jo 7:16 f.

7 Heb 1:1 ff.; Jo 10:37 f.; 14:10-13.

8 Jo 20:21; 17:18.

9 Mt 11:27; 16:17; Jo 6:45.

10 Cf. Jo 14:29.

11 Cf. I Tim 3:15.

12 See I Jo 5:6.

13 Jo 10:16, 27.

14 Jo 21:17.

15 Heb 4:12.

16 Jo 4:19; 20:29; Mk 13:22.

17 Jo 1:18; 8:14; 12:44; Apoc 1:5.

18 Jo 18:37.

19 Jo 4:42.

20 Jo 14:26; Mt 5:18.

21 Mt 5:15.

22 St. Augustine, *Epist.* 105, 16.

CHAPTER **11** *The Bible, Tradition, and the Church**

by GEORGES DEJAIFVE, S.J.

AUTHOR: Georges Dejaifve is professor of Fundamental Theology at the Jesuit theologate of St. Albert, Louvain, Belgium. He has written extensively on ecumenical questions, the nature of the Church, the role of the bishops in the Church, and the role of the Bible in the Church.

ARTICLE: One of the central topics in current ecumenical dialogue is the role of the Bible in the Church. Protestants hold that the Bible is the unique norm of Faith; Catholics hold that the Bible is the Church's book and the Church can (continually) interpret her own book. Some progress has been made of late, with Protestants admitting that the Bible must live within the Christian community and therefore necessarily involves some sort of tradition, and Catholics affirming more clearly than before the primacy of the Bible as God's Word to men to which the Church must be faithful—as she follows the guidance of the Spirit in interpreting that Word from age to age. But sharp differences still remain. Father Dejaifve discusses these differences and in the process shows why this is not some idle scholastic dispute but a central point which affects our whole notion of what it means to say that the Bible is God's book, or that the Church is the guardian and channel of divine Truth to the world.

* "The Bible, Tradition, and the Church," a selection taken from *Theology Digest* 6 (1958), pp. 67-72, is a digest of an article originally published in *Nouvelle Revue Théologique* 78 (1956), pp. 135-151. It is reprinted here with permission.

READINGS: A fascinating account of the dispute over the suffi-
ciency of Scripture in the history of the Church, with some
very knowledgeable applications to the current ecumenical
scene, is *Holy Writ or Holy Church* (Harper & Brothers, 1959),
by Georges Tavard, A.A.

Protestant and Catholic

WHEN CATHOLICS refer to the Church as the "Bark of
Peter," Protestants seize upon the figure and try to
turn it to their own advantage. For Protestants the Church
is an ancient hulk which survives only by some miracle as
it plows through the ocean of time. On board is heaped
the baggage of centuries snatched by her seamen from
every port of call: fragments of Greek temples, Alexan-
drine statuettes, relics from Rome's triumphal arches,
Gothic vaults, paintings from the Renaissance, baroque
adornments—all the curious bric-a-brac of history. This
strange Noah's ark follows a capricious course at the mercy
of wind and current. But it never strays far from land because commerce with this world is the secret of its survival.

The Reformation, on the other hand, boasts a flotilla
of light craft. This fleet steers its course for the high seas;
for it is the world beyond the horizon that lures men on.
Far from the false security of the land and guided only by
the written directions of the divine Shipbuilder, the fleet
sails before the unpredictable breathings of the Spirit, who
guides it by routes unknown.

As opposed to their own unswerving loyalty to the
written directions of the Bible, Protestants contrast the
fatal deviations of the Roman Church. At first the Roman
crews veered slightly off course, the better to hear the
Sirens' songs of flesh and blood. Little by little, they forgot

the goal of their journeying and ended up by acquiescing to the seductions of a sinful world.

A common Protestant view has it that at Trent the Church was faced with the task of justifying its doctrinal evolution. Confronted with the Reformers' cry of "Scripture alone," she replied by dogmatizing the role of Tradition. In this way the Church hoped to explain the many articles of faith and practice she had added to the Bible. But the only basis for such action was the arbitrary authority of the Church herself: the decrees of the Council have only a vague relation to "faith and morals." Their "apostolic" character is pure fiction; they are a clear indication of the rejection of the primacy of Scripture.

This Protestant view sees the dethronement of Scripture carried one step farther at the Council of the Vatican. Resolved to build a dike against the Modernist concept of evolutionary dogma and at the same time determined to reject the arguments of tradition against papal supremacy, the Catholic Church used an old trick. To obstinate conservatism she joined shocking innovation: Modernist evolution of dogma was replaced by the theory of the *development* of the Church, and with the new theory went the dogma of papal infallibility. Thus, Tradition canonized at Trent gave way to the supremacy of the teaching Church. What Scripture teaches, Tradition makes clear, said Trent. And it is the Church who decides what Tradition is, added Vatican. Thus the Church emancipated herself from all need of fidelity to the past by making herself the supreme norm for judging revelation.

Scripture becomes Useless?

This subordination of Scripture to the Church is, of course, anathema to the Protestant. If it is God who speaks to man in Scripture, Scripture must be given a complete and unqualified hearing. If the Church refuses this submission, she ends up only by engaging in a sterile monologue. Scripture becomes a useless entity for an infallible Church. Why bend over dusty parchments when one can listen to the Vatican oracle and learn what Christ reveals to the people of each age?

The force of these objections lies in their apparent simplicity. One would prefer countering with a simple denial. But since it is the teaching of the Church that is being misrepresented, the teaching of the Church is a good place to look for an answer.

First of all, is it true that the Church depends only on the charism of truth without regard to the sources of revelation outside herself? At the Vatican Council, in the very definition of papal infallibility, the Church is careful to indicate her dependence on such sources:

" . . . The Holy Spirit was promised to the successors of St. Peter not that they might make known new doctrine by his revelation, but rather, that with his assistance they might religiously guard and faithfully explain the revelation or deposit of faith that was handed down through the apostles" (Denzinger 1836). The historical dependence of papal pronouncements on objective evidence is next emphasized. " . . . The Roman Pontiffs . . . defined as to be held such matters as they had found consonant with the Holy Scripture and with the apostolic tradition" (Denzinger 1836).

Protestant critics will be quick to reply that all this is mere theory, devoid of meaning. But then how explain the practice of the Church—the long delays before the proclamation of a dogma whose meaning is not explicit in Scripture? Even some Protestants admit that the infallibility of the Roman Pontiff was being affirmed at the time of St. Thomas Aquinas. Recent mariological pronouncements, particularly the dogma of the Immaculate Conception, were common doctrine in the Church for centuries. What kept the Church from proceeding to a definition? Her sense of faith was there. If she is her own unique source of truth, why the hesitation?

The principal Protestant difficulty arises from dogmas which are not clearly taught either in Scripture or in the unbroken testimony of tradition from the beginning. The Assumption is cited as the chief example of such a dogma.

To get at the bottom of this difficulty one must first clarify the nature of tradition and its relation to the Church, on the one hand, and to Scripture and revelation on the other.

What Is Revelation?

The Catholic view of tradition depends on the Catholic view of revelation. Up to a certain point, this view agrees with recent theories of certain Protestant scholars: God intervened in human history by a series of events that culminated in the Incarnation. Far from minimizing the value of human history, the Incarnation consecrates it by linking the eternity of God with the brief duration of the God-Man on earth.

But then the Protestant and Catholic views part company. A prominent Protestant view holds that the Incarnation is only an intimation of the divine will calling man to an existential decision. No manifestation of the divine Nature, no communication of new truths is involved.

But is this view satisfactory? Does it explore all of the dimensions of revelation? Can God come to live with men without revealing something of his inner Self? Can man reach God, who is man's salvation, except through God's historical revelation of himself? If the Person of Christ reveals the perfect image of his Father, it is because his words and deeds—even his silences—are a part of history and necessarily reflect the mystery of God for souls prepared to receive him. Christ's life on earth was the supreme theophany.

How Is Revelation Transmitted?

Because this revelation of God in his only Son is the manifestation of a mystery surpassing flesh and blood, God must illumine from above the souls who welcome it. St. Matthew attests to this in the avowal of Peter at Caesarea Philippi (Mt 16:17). The Spirit of God adds his internal witness to external events and reveals the redemptive meaning of what is taking place. Just as the spoken word cannot reveal its sense unless it includes some reaction of a hearer, so revelation cannot be conceived adequately without taking account of the faith that gives it welcome.

If revelation is designed for all men, God can hardly be indifferent to its manner of transmission. God's Son came at a definite moment in time: God's message can reach men of later ages only through communication that is trustworthy. That is why Christ selected and trained a group of authorized witnesses. He gave his apostles the duty of announcing the good news to the whole world. To their witness Christ joined that of his Spirit, whose assistance he promised to his followers. In this way Christ established his Church as the unique depository of his Gospel.

Many Protestant thinkers today agree up to this point but differ from Catholics on the role proper to the Church. Does the Church's mission consist in repeating with literal fidelity a message to which Christ painstakingly fixed an authoritative and definitive expression? St. John's Gospel does not seem to support this view. The Fourth Gospel tells how Christ at the Last Supper attributes to the Holy Spirit the task of gradually leading his apostles to the full possession of the truth he had already revealed (Jo 16:13). A development in the understanding of divine truth is here affirmed as a normal thing. Christ has made a complete revelation. Nonetheless, his teaching has not been fully assimilated. An understanding of revelation by the Church is foretold, an understanding in progressive stages harmonized by the Spirit with the gospel message of Christ.

The Church as Witness

This role of the Church in assimilating and penetrating the gospel is indispensable when one considers the historical character of Christ's revelation. He gives his message to poor fishermen of Galilee. But he is also the Master of Time. He proclaims his message in such a way as to include successive adaptations and developments for men of all ages. If Christ is no longer present in person to guard the exact meaning of his words, where will the faithful transmitter of his gospel be found? Nowhere else than in the subject to which he originally entrusted it: his Church. The Son of God gave a living interpreter who would comprehend and explain his words to every age. The testimony of the Church succeeds the testimony of the apostles.

To deny the Church this power of authentic interpretation is to make the divine word literally a dead letter and a sealed book. If the Church did not have the power of authentic interpretation, the further removed a Christian would be from apostolic times, the less capable he would be of understanding the message of Christ. Some Protestant historians therefore speak of the corruption of the Church at the end of the first century and turn to the New Testament as the unique source of apostolic preaching. Some even contest the value of the New Testament and maintain that a critical reconstruction of Christ's original teaching is necessary. Thus the enigma of a scholar of the twentieth century trying his hand at discerning the real meaning of Christ's first message, a meaning misunderstood by the writers of the New Testament.

Much more in accord with divine wisdom to concede that Christ confided the charge of his mysteries to the Church. In her is kept alive for men of succeeding generations the message of Christ.

Subordination to the Holy Spirit

Since the role played by the teaching authority of the Church is so much misunderstood by Protestants, it is necessary to emphasize its subordinate nature. When the magisterium sets forth and interprets a revealed truth, it does not act in an absolutely autonomous fashion. Rather it uses a power given it by Christ, a power whose proper use is guaranteed by the presence of the Holy Spirit. A skilled physicist who lays bare the mysteries of the atom does not invent the results of his inquiry even though he alone, by reason of his special knowledge, can reveal the secrets hidden there. So with the teaching authority of the Church. She alone has the charism of authentically interpreting the "given" of revelation. But the truth is not her invention.

What is the given of revelation? Protestants maintain that it is Scripture and Scripture alone. Such a view was condemned by the Church even before she was faced with Luther's doctrine at Trent. The Church saw the revelation of the New Testament as the *comprehensive arrival of salvation,* not a list of rules and beliefs bound up in a book.

The living testimony of the life of Christ contains more than can be explicitly formulated in words. This testimony was communicated by the apostles not only through words but also through acts and rites and practices whose import in the work of salvation could not always be immediately grasped. This living testimony to a living mystery God communicated through his apostles to the Church. It is to the Church of Christ, formed from communities of the faithful, that God entrusted his message. The Church's teaching, working, preaching—all transmit the message according to the will of Christ present in her through his Spirit.

It is precisely this role of the Church as the historical intermediary of revelation that the theologians at Trent found wanting in Luther's doctrine. And it is this misunderstanding that they intended to correct by their insistence on tradition. More urgent tasks, however, prevented them from clarifying the relation of Scripture and Tradition to the Church.

Scripture and the Church

What is the relation of Scripture and Tradition to the Church? Historically, the revelation of Christ has come to men through the preaching of the Church made manifest in the various forms of the life of faith. The New Testament is within this life of faith as a part within a whole. To be sure, once the canon of Scripture had been formed in the second century, the New Testament enjoyed a certain normative role in the faith of the churches. One can even say that the farther removed in time the Church was from its origins, the more it referred to the New Testament as a privileged witness of the apostolic preaching. The belief in the divine inspiration of Scripture united the New Testament to the Old and gave to both a unique place in the teaching of the Church. But this is not to say that this unique place necessarily implied a devaluation of the Church's teaching. Scripture could not be separated from the Church which transmitted it and explains its meaning.

Right of Interpretation

If the New Testament did assume the place of honor, then the task is to explain how, at the very time this was supposed to be taking place, the bishops were making a point of asserting their right of authentic interpretation? Irenaeus, Clement of Alexandria, even Origen himself, clearly assert such a right and base their assertion on the existing faith of the churches. Much can be found in patristic exegesis to corroborate this view.

The tradition of the Church is the continuation of the original witness of the apostles but enriched by the insights of the centuries. It is this tradition on which the Church draws in her study of Scripture, and it is this tradition that guides the Church to an ever clearer understanding of the deposit of revelation. For the Church can proclaim the truths of revelation without realizing their full import; at times only the challenge of concrete problems stimulates her to look for answers in a deeper understanding of what God has entrusted to her care.

These influences from without, these challenges to progress in understanding faith are not alien to revelation. They are not something that finally ends up by corrupting revelation's first purity. This is revelation's proper history. Not a purely human history, of course, subject to the laws of decay, but the divine history of the people of God. It is a history directed toward the "last things," a history whose mover is not the spirit of man but the Spirit of God.

It is the Spirit of God who, animating the Church, draws it imperceptibly but surely toward its longed-for goal. Like the pillar of fire guiding the holy people through the desert, the Holy Spirit provides the means for discovering with full certitude the meaning foreseen and intended by Christ.

Such is the relation of the Church to revelation, such is the nature of Catholic Tradition with a two-fold movement of conservatism and progress. This two-fold movement appears contradictory to the outside observer, but in reality it is a sign of the Church's truth and of her fidelity to the Word of God.

The Church is attached to the past. If all the truths of salvation come to men through Christ incarnate, how can the Church be anything but anxious to preserve the continuity of apostolic testimony? If that testimony is inscribed in her concrete, historical life, how can she be anything but solicitous about conserving each fragment of it?

On the other hand, the attraction towards her final end quickens in the Church an insatiable thirst for the future. Faithful to the Lord, her only guide, she keeps coming back to scrutinize the intent of his revelation and to receive his teachings which he parcels out in wise progression. Her faith grasps and penetrates his meaning. What she finds is but an amplified echo of the unique Word coursing through time.

Initiative from the Faithful

In discerning truths implicit in revelation the teaching authority of the Church does not usually take the initiative. More often it is the faith of her members that anticipates dogma. This faith is examined by theologians and then sanctioned by the Church's teaching authority. In this way the teaching authority hears in the whole Church the voice of tradition. Confident in the power Christ gave her, the Church clarifies the intentions of his message.

The Church then does not draw revealed truth from herself. But the Church does impose the truth she possesses. How then can a man be certain that the Church has always been faithful to the message it originally received? The ordinary member of the Church cannot establish the continuity between the Bible and the teaching of the magisterium. Only an act of faith can give him assurance that the Church has been faithful to her Founder. This act of faith is based on evidence given in the New Testament, but in the final analysis its foundation is God himself.

No one comes to the Church unless God draws him.

Yet a theologian can present some corroboration of revelation as proposed by the Church. Rightly presented, this revelation would not fail to claim the assent of men who cling to God by supernatural faith.

If the Church is really loyal to Christ, it cannot but be loyal to the Bible. This loyalty can become visible to the believing soul if he submits himself to the Spirit which is the Church's guide. For the Spirit who speaks in the Church is the Spirit who spoke to the apostles, the Spirit of Christ who substitutes for him during the Church's journey here in the world of time.

CHAPTER 12 *The Development of Dogma**

by MATTHEW J. O'CONNELL, S.J.

AUTHOR: Matthew J. O'Connell is professor of Dogmatic Theology at the Jesuit theologate in Woodstock, Maryland, where
he teaches sacramental theology.

ARTICLE: The phenomenon of growth in the Church's authentic presentation of Christ's Truth to the world is called the
development of dogma. It is called a *development* because
the contemporary Church proclaims as part of Christ's Truth
a number of dogmas which, as propositional statements, simply are not found (explicitly) in the Bible or early sources of
the Church's Faith.

It should likewise be called a *problem* because the revelation accomplished in Christ is definitive. Revelation has been
'closed' since the apostolic age. No additions to revelation have
been possible in the intervening centuries. Father O'Connell
resolves the apparent conflict inherent in these two statements
by a deeper understanding of the nature of revelation itself
and consequently of the Church's role of authentically proclaiming revelation to the world throughout all ages. If revelation is conceived as a group of propositions about God and
Christ and man's salvation, the problem is insoluble. But if
revelation is recognized as the full communication to the apostolic Church of the person of Christ, a communication so rich
that the knowledge which results from it can never be ex-
haustively propositionalized, then the Church's progressive
proclamation of dogmas over the centuries becomes intelligible as her continuing reflection on (and propositionalization

* "The Development of Dogma" originally appeared in *Thought* 26
(1951), pp. 513-521. It is reprinted here with permission.

of) the Christ-event in all its depth and all its ramifications in human history.

READINGS: Another analysis of the phenomenon of development in terms of reflection on interpersonal knowledge is made by Karl Rahner in his essay on "The Development of Dogma," *Theological Investigations* I (Helicon, 1961), pp. 39-77. The two giant nineteenth-century forerunners of the contemporary renaissance in the theology of the Church, Johann Adam Möhler of Tübingen, and John Henry Cardinal Newman of Oxford and Birmingham, both were fascinated by this phenomenon of growth in the Church's understanding of Christ. Möhler's thought is best studied in his *Symbolism* (Gibbings & Co., 1906) and in the writings of Karl Adam, who was strongly influenced by him. Newman's thought is found in his *Essay on the Development of Christian Doctrine* (Image Paperback, $1.35) and in *A Newman Synthesis* (Sheed & Ward, 1945), edited by one of his outstanding German disciples, Erich Przywara, S.J. Another excellent introduction to Newman's prophetic anticipation of the contemporary accent in Catholic dogmatic theology is J. H. Walgrave, O.P., *Newman the Theologian* (Sheed & Ward, 1960).

THE PURPOSE of these pages is to attempt a schematic answer, along the lines of certain contemporary trends of thought, to two questions: first, "Where and how are truths which have been defined, or will yet be defined, implicit in the deposit of faith?" and second, "What in general is the actual process of development: its dynamism and its factors?"

The Nature of Christ's Revelation

To answer the first question we must return to the original revelation of Christ and examine its character. For the Christian religion was from its very outset specifically different from all others. The pagan cults sprang out of speculations and myths that sought somehow to grasp an incomprehensible and transcendent reality without point of insertion into history. As for the Jewish religion, the divine revelation which is at its origin gave it, of course, a quite different character, but the revelation was mediate. Neither Jew nor pagan, therefore, attained immediately in its concrete reality the object of his belief. But the Christian religion is based on the Incarnation; not on a teaching received from an invisible God but on God living with us. Christ is himself both object and revealer on the Christian's faith.

In Christ, revealer and revealed are one. He is the Word of God, the consubstantial image of the Father become incarnate, and therefore in the fullness of his temporal actuation he is the self-revelation of God. The object of the Christian revelation in its actual form, then, is primarily an acting person, a person who is Truth, but also a Life and a Way. This triple identification of Truth, Life, and Way is, perhaps, the key to an understanding of the communication of revelation, both initially and in succeeding generations; it is also the key to an understanding of the character of the deposit of faith, and to an understanding of the dynamism at work in dogmatic development and in the doctrinal life of the Church.

Since the Divine Word in its human manifestation as the man Jesus is the first truth that God would reveal to men, it is not merely the words of Christ that are revelation, but his person and his every action. All the divine truths which have been or can be enunciated, objectively gather in Christ. This centrality of Christ can be expressed in various ways. The central object of faith for St. John has been summed up thus: "Christ, the only Son of the Father, given to men by God as the source of eternal life." For St. Paul the primary object of his faith and preaching is the mystery hidden from eternity and revealed in Christ, namely, the mystery of Christ himself in his Mystical Body (Col 1:26-27). The Acts of the Apostles tell us simply that the apostles went forth and preached Jesus. And St. Augustine sums up this Christocentric tradition in these words, "There is no other mystery of God except Christ." All this makes it quite clear that the Person of Christ himself is the divine revelation and the first object of faith in its concrete form.

Communication of Revelation

But revelation had to be communicated to the apostles. It is evident that the full communication of such a revelation embodied in a person could not take the form of words alone. Nor was there any need that it should. St. Augustine again puts the matter briefly, "Christ is God's Word, and he speaks to men not by sounds alone but by deeds as well." There was, then, a communication by personal intercourse. Christ roused in his apostles a living faith in and love for himself which made them receptive of the lessons of his gestures, his actions, his attitudes. He transmitted to them a new personality. He gave them a vision of life and the world, orientated their minds and attention, evoked in them tendencies of thought and life which in turn developed in them his mind. In brief, he gave them a new supernatural consciousness, the "sense of Christ" of which St. Paul speaks (I Cor 2:16), which the Holy Spirit would guard in them and in the future generations to whom they would transmit this same Christian consciousness. The apostles *lived* Christ, the object of their faith. They grew in their possession of revelation not only through the truths which he taught them orally and by the judgments they formed, which were the immediate object of their assent, but also by growing in their interior living possession of Christ.

There is no need to enter into the detail of the lessons which Christ conveyed by example, lessons which we have no evidence for saying were formulated into explicit propositions by Christ or the apostles. Brief application to Marian dogma will suffice. To the question, "Why do the Gospels say so little of Mary?" Suarez answered, "When reality itself and the deeds with which Christ honored his mother cried out, words were unnecessary." Thus, for example, the role of Mary at Cana, a role which in all probability she played more than once, made it unnecessary for Christ to express in so many words her mediating power with God. It was a truth concretized in reality and lived by those who experienced it.

But this manner of communication raises an epistemological problem to which we must advert at least briefly: How can we possess a knowledge that is not explicitly formulated in our minds?

In our vital contact with being, and especially with persons, there are many things which we truly perceive, which are nonetheless not immediately elevated to the state of actual intelligibility in judgment, but remain latent in phantasms, in ways of acting and thinking impressed on us by being. These are intelligibles in potency, not merely an obediential potency but a state of virtual understanding that seeks actuality, a positive attitude, a drive toward actual intelligibility. In fact we have, in a certain fashion, an actual, though negative, understanding of these potential intelligibles, inasmuch as we grasp in our intellection the inadequacy of our concepts and formulations in relation to the fullness of the empirically known object. The greater our love for the person, the greater is our absorption or assimilation of him, and consequently the greater and more certain our realization that our explicit judgments do not do full justice to the object, and the greater our desire to penetrate it more deeply. For the transition from this lived implicit knowledge absorbed in communion with the object, to the level of explicit knowledge, no further actuation by the object is needed, but only the play of forces extrinsic to it.[1]

So in the relations of the apostles with Christ. He

[265]

spoke and they understood. They formed judgments which expressed the direct and primary content of their faith and which were the core of the deposit; but not the exhaustive and complete deposit. Christ also in his personal intercourse with the apostles formed in them an image of himself, an image whose lack of intelligible distinctness they could not immediately remove and which therefore contained many elements not actually conceptualized. As Father Lebreton has remarked, "This primitive adhesion to the divine reality, this completely concrete and living perception was the unique source from which all dogma would flow." But many of these dogmas remained latent, even for the apostles, in the richness of this living experience. These indistinct elements in the total image of Christ and his meaning were part of revelation because Christ intended to produce them in the apostles and would provide assistance both in his own lifetime and after his death for their infallible conception. Furthermore, Christ revealed himself to be assimilated by the apostles under various aspects: as announcing the Kingdom, as Redeemer, as forgiving sins, as uniting the disciples into a church, etc. Thus the potential intelligibles of revelation imposed on the Christian mind various orientations, existentially interconnected but not necessarily logically interconnected for us. Moreover, the impression made by Christ on various apostles was itself varied according to the individuality of temperaments and souls. For Paul, Christ was experienced primarily as Redeemer; for John, as Word, Light, and Truth. To use Newman's terminology, it was the totality of these "impressions" that formed the Christian "Idea"—which is the deposit of faith.

The Deposit of Faith

At the death of the last apostle, this deposit could be summed up thus: first, a well-marked Christian mentality, which included the great directive ideas delineated with full clarity in the doctrinal enunciations which had already been made explicit by the Church to meet the first needs and difficulties of the community and which were ready to be put to work in the symbols of faith. Secondly, there were formulas, fixed in the inspired writings or carried along in the stream of oral tradition. Thirdly, around these ideas, enunciations and formulas, were grouped other half-conscious, half-instinctive dispositions of mind, received from Christ and authorized therefore by him. Finally there were liturgical prayers and orientations of the souls of the faithful which obscurely, but no less importantly, implied truths; and habits of action and cult which concretized dogma.[2]

The detailed inventory of this deposit was not, of course, and could not then be made, nor shall it ever be, because of the infinite riches of the mystery of Christ and because also of the varied states in which the truths exist with relation to explicit enunciation.

In the great truths and formulas just referred to there was much that was logically implicit and could be educed therefrom. There were many lived-implicits, too, in all the other aspects of Christian life: in the sacramental life of the Church, in her liturgy, in the practices of devotion she encouraged, and—to the point at the moment—in the profound impression of the extraordinary character and singular position of our Lady. The germ, then, out of which—or better, the totality within which—development would occur was not merely a group of primitive texts but the whole of Christian life.

Tradition

The question arises at this point: How is the deposit of faith, this Christian "Idea" possessed by the apostles, to be transmitted to future generations, not only in its

explicit enunciations and its logically implicit propositions, but also in its lived-implicit content?

In transmitting the deposit the witness to Christ can
count on the secret preparation worked in souls by grace,
the connaturality placed in the soul by the habit of faith,
the Christian consciousness, the "eyes of faith." [3] Before
we ever hear tell of Christ, he has disposed our souls to
discover him; he has already prefigured himself in us by
baptism and its accompanying gifts. The Church has at its
disposal for the perpetuation of Christ the Scriptures and
the preaching of the word of God. Finally God sees to it
that the Church reproduces Christ in us, sufficiently in the
totality of his members, excellently in some of them.[4]
Action, too, plays an important part in the conservation
and transmission of the deposit; and thus the saints in a
special way have helped transmit to us the implicit revelation, the realization of the inadequacy between the Christ
we can formulate and the Christ who is lived in the
Church.

One brief remark at this point about the apostolic
plenitude of faith. Are we to regard the apostolic possession of the deposit of faith as somehow rudimentary and
unformed, and our own possession as more perfect? By no
means. We today have more dogmas to believe but not
more truth. The apostles' knowledge was less discursive,
less conceptualized, but far richer and more sure, a direct,
living, infused knowledge, rooted in their souls by Christ's
lessons and example, miraculously augmented and deepened by the Holy Spirit. We may adapt here St. Thomas'
doctrine that "the higher an intelligence is, the more able
it is to see things in wholes and in a single idea . . . and
the less need it has of its object being particularized and
detailed." Thus in the central intuition of faith in Christ
the Son of God, the apostles adhered to all revealed truth,
explicitly present to their minds, yet without distinct concepts and without perhaps ever imagining the form which

the development of the faith would take in future generations of Christians less graced than they.

Dynamism of Development

Our understanding of the actual process of development—which was our second problem—depends in large
measure upon a realization of the dynamisms at work in
the Church to make development possible and inevitable.
Christ's revelation is intended to lead the Christian to the
vision of God, and faith creates in us an orientation toward this vision. What has indeed been revealed to us is
the Truth itself, the perfect knowledge of which already
beatifies us in hope. While awaiting this perfect knowledge a double progress lies open to the individual Christian: first, growth in the explicit and detailed possession
of all the truths in the deposit of faith, a type of progress
possible even for a faith unformed by charity; secondly,
an interior and sapiential penetration of divine truth
under the influence of charity and the gifts of the Holy
Spirit.

This twofold progress is in itself distinct from dogmatic development, since it is individual and private
while dogma is official and social. Yet this private progress
will inevitably, within the ontological unity of the Mystical Body, intensify the inner life of the whole Church
and ultimately have social effect.

The same dynamism of faith may be seen from the
viewpoint of the Church as a social organism. The faith
is a common means of salvation for humanity, and therefore implicitly contained in the revealed deposit are all
the future propositions of faith which will be needed to
maintain the body of the faithful in their progress toward
the vision of God. The Christian revelation, being a
divine work, could not be *frustrated* in what is necessary
to accomplish its proper end, the salvation of humanity.[5]

St. John shows us clearly how faith implies dogmatic development. Christ, he tells us, is Truth, Life, and Way. Faith in him is the life of the spirit, a life of enlightened adhesion to the Truth. And the eternal life Christ brings, the good toward which faith is intrinsically orientated, is precisely the knowledge of Christ and through him of the Father. Our faith, then, is inspired from within by a love that urges us to understanding.

Finally, we have the promise of dogmatic development in Christ's promise to the Twelve, and through them to the whole Church, of the Paraclete, "the Spirit of truth who will lead you to the entire truth" (Jo 16:14). It would seem that in the apostles the Holy Spirit was to complete the work of revelation not by proposing new doctrines but by communicating a more profound understanding of the mystery of Jesus. He is the Spirit of truth and will enable the apostles and the faithful to understand the absolute Truth, Christ; he will enable the Twelve, and later the Church which will take up the apostolic mission, to interpret the message of Christ. He will remain with the Church until the end of time because the Church will never exhaust the intelligibility, the riches, of the revelation which is Christ. He will abide as a quasi substitute for Christ, to illumine the Gospel, to make it, in St. Paul's words, "the power of God unto the salvation of every man who believes" (Rom 1:16). The Gospel, the revelation, is such a power of salvation precisely because it is Christ, "known, tasted, possessed, transforming the minds and hearts of men." [6]

Factors in Development

In describing thus the faith seeking understanding, we have already seen the chief factor in dogmatic development. For the Holy Spirit of truth is present in the Church and in the individual faithful to lead them to an ever deeper understanding of their treasure, Christ. Among the secondary factors a most important one is Christian morality, because it is so intimately connected with the Person of Christ and develops the "sense of Christ" in the faithful; because the submission of the heart to God leads to a taste for and a judgment of the things of God. The assimilation of human nature to the divine leads men to a deeper perception of the divine truth contained in the law of God. The growth of charity in the souls of the faithful enables them to comprehend connaturally God's dispositions with regard, for example, to our Lady—dispositions which no amount of dialectical or analytic subtlety can deduce with certitude, because they are free dispensations of God, not intrinsic necessities. Analogous remarks apply to the role of liturgy as a factor in development.

But morality and liturgy will not of themselves necessarily lead to expression in proposition; for they are active mainly in the order of sapiential knowledge. There are, however, other forces leading to directly dogmatic expression: the intellectual needs of individual Christians, especially in the face of current philosophies and secular atmospheres; the impact of heresies; the work of theologians whose function is precisely to understand in ever more explicit form the content of revelation and to integrate it into a harmonious image of divine reality. The theologians are a most important factor in development, but it should be remembered that they too are, simultaneously, part of the 'learning Church,' and that their function is not a narrowly dialectical one but that of interpreting a living reality. Their contemplation is to bring to intellectual maturity the truth which is lived in the Church, the truth which they themselves live.

Standing over all, finally, is the magisterium which possesses Christ's Spirit in a special manner and which in the fulfillment of its social function of protecting and educating the Christian soul will seek an ever more explicit knowledge of the deposit of faith and will testify to the truths that become clearer in the piety and Christian life of any era.

Notes

1 Many of the ideas, and some of the expressions, in this and the following paragraph are borrowed from some of the current European thinking on our subject.

2 This summary of the deposit of faith is drawn from L. de Grandmaison, S.J., *Le dogme chrétien: sa nature, ses formules, son développement* (Paris: Beauchesne, 1928), p. 253, and H. Pinard, S.J., "Dogme," *Dictionnaire apologétique de la foi catholique.*

3 Here again acknowledgment must be made of the writer's debt to current European thinking.

4 In speaking of another problem (the substantial identity, from age to age, of the explicit belief of the ordinary faithful), Suarez states a principle which is basic in the solution of our present problem: "This Church [i.e., the Church of any given generation] is equally close to Christ." (*De Fide,* disp. 2, section 6, no. 12.)

5 For this discussion of the dynamism of faith, cf. H. D. Simonin, O.P., " 'Implicite' and 'Explicite' dans le développement du dogme," *Angelicum* 14 (1937), pp. 138-141.

6 J. Huby, S.J., *S. Paul: Epître aux Romains* (4th ed.; Paris: Beauchesne et fils, 1940).

PART 5 *The Mission of the Church*

CHAPTER **13** *The Holy Spirit and the*
Apostolic Body, Continuators
of the Work of the Church *

by YVES CONGAR, O.P.

AUTHOR: Yves Congar is probably Europe's most influential
writer on the theology of the Church. This outstanding French
Dominican has published and lectured widely on the nature
of the Church, the layman's role in the Church, Catholic ecu-
menism, and related subjects. The present theme of the importance of the Holy Spirit in the direction of the Church is
characteristic of much of Father Congar's work.

ARTICLE: Father Congar emphasizes the *twofold* continuation
of the directive work of Christ in the contemporary Church:
the hierarchy as the successors of the apostles *and* the Holy
Spirit as the continuing presence and dynamism of Christ in
the Church throughout the centuries. The apostolic mission of
the Church is one; the agents which direct the accomplishment of that mission are two, though these two harmonize and
complement one another perfectly and can never contradict
one another. But the work of the Spirit in the hearts of the
faithful does not simply parallel the work of the hierarchy in
the direction of the Church's apostolate: the Spirit retains a
certain autonomy and initiative which accounts for the "providential" adaptation of the Church to new situations and the

* "The Holy Spirit and the Apostolic Body, Continuators of the Work
of the Church" first appeared in English in Father Congar's *The Mystery
of the Church* (Helicon, 1960), pp. 147-180. It is reprinted here with permission.

dramatic mobilizations of all her forces at moments of crisis in the course of her history.

READINGS: A fine analysis of the missionary dynamism at the heart of the Church is presented by Jean Daniélou, S. J., in *The Salvation of the Nations* (Sheed & Ward, 1949). A highly personal account of the workings of the Spirit in the Church is found in *Aspects of the Church* (Fides, 1956), by Yves de Montcheuil, S.J. A testimony to the influence of the Spirit on the hierarchy as well as on the laity is *The Church Today* (Fides, 1953), by the great Cardinal of Paris, Emmanuel Suhard.

W E HAVE a threefold warrant in heaven, the Father, the Word, and the Holy Spirit, three who are yet one" (I Jo 5:7).

In one sense, Christ's work on earth came to an end with his "passage to his Father" (Jo 17:4); but in another sense, it still remains to be done and is to be continued by other persons than Christ himself. Thus, Christ speaks in the future tense, "I will come; I will see you again; I will speak; I will send you; the Father will give you another Paraclete" (Jo 14:18; 16:22, 25, 15:26 and 16:7; 14:16), "I will build" (Mt 16:18), etc. The messianic time is one of fulfillment, but it is also one of promise during the interval between the ascension of Christ and his second coming. This period, which is precisely the era of the Church, is characterized by a relative absence of its Head, who "must have his dwelling-place in heaven until the time when all is restored anew" (Acts 3:21), while his body is still being formed on earth. How is Christ, in his relative absence, to build up his body or his Church? How is he to complete in us the work he accomplished only in himself in the days of his flesh? The present study aims at showing (1) that Christ sent out to do his work two agents, his Spirit and his apostles; (2) that these two agents are conjoined so as to bring about together the Body of Christ; (3) that nevertheless the Spirit retains a sort of liberty or autonomy, which explains one of the features of the Church's life.

Two Missions: Two Agents

When the time came for him to leave the world and his disciples, Christ arranged for the continuation of his work, the sending of his Spirit and of his apostles. This disposition of his, a kind of final testament, he made known in the discourse after the Last Supper concerning the apostles (Jo 13:16, 20; 17:18; concerning the Spirit, 14:16, 26; 15:26). We will examine briefly both of these missions, their relations and economy.

The mission of the apostles is presented as already in being or, at any rate, as already inaugurated. In fact, the apostles had been called one by one and then collectively designated as such. Within the apostolic body, Peter had been set apart and nominated for the function of rock or foundation (Mt 16:13-19). The apostles had received special instructions from the Master, together with different powers to exercise over the future flock of believers in Christ (e.g., Lk 9:1 ff.; Mt 16:19-20; 18:18; 19:28; Lk 22:19; etc.). Their apostolic office, as would later become evident, was bound up with their having been not only chosen and instituted for it but also companions of Christ throughout his mission as Messias, that is from the baptism of John to his ascension (Acts 1:21-22; cf. 10:37 and 13:31, read in conjunction with Mt 3:13; 17:55; Lk 23:5). The apostolate is closely linked with Christ's life for us in the flesh—with his visible presence of those days, his powers and activities. It belongs to the sphere of the Incarnation, of the coming of the Son of Man, whose own mission it

[277]

continues. Christ, in the discourse after the Last Supper, emphasizes this important aspect, saying he now sends his apostles as the Father had sent him (Jo 17:16 and 18), and that men will treat them as they treated him (Jo 13:20; 15:18-21, 23; 16:2-3; 17:19; cf. Mt 10:40; Lk 10:16; I Jo 4:6 with Jo 8:47). In fact, from the Father to him and from him to them, it is one and the same mission that flows and, in consequence, also the powers belonging to the mission (cf. Jo 17:18, 22-23; 20:21)—the same mission which is, in the same degree, a mission of love.[1]

This is not the only case where we find two qualities, one of the purely spiritual or mystical sphere, the other a juridical one, conjoined in one and the same reality. The persistence of the mission which insures the movement of love on the part of God towards men is shown by the fact that the one sent and the person sending are equal in dignity, which is expressed in the Aramaic word for "sent," *saliah*. The one sent represents the person of his master and has the same authority; he is to be received in the same way as the master himself, from whom he has a power of attorney and whose functions he exercises in his absence. This is, undoubtedly, the whole idea of the apostolate instituted by Christ (cf. Jo 13:16, 20; 15:20; 17:9 ff., especially 18; also Lk 10:16; Mt 10:40).

The mission of the Holy Spirit is, in many ways, different from that of the apostles. It was not already inaugurated at the time of the Passion, but was then proclaimed as something in the future and made the subject of a promise (Jo 14:16, 26; 15:26; 16:7-15; cf. 7:39). It is not a consequence, like that of the apostles, of the Incarnation, the coming of the Word made flesh, which it was to continue, but is bound up with Christ's redemptive acts, with his passage to the Father and particularly with his glorification in heaven. It was necessary that Christ should go away, that he should be exalted, "glorified," for the Holy Spirit to be given (Jo 7:39; 16:7; etc.). As regards Christ,

[278]

the sending and the work of the Spirit are bound up with his condition of lordship, of domination over all things. The Holy Spirit indeed continues and accomplishes the work of Christ, but as linked with Christ's coming and his life in the flesh in a very different way from the apostles. The mission of the Holy Spirit is certainly presented as *a* continuation of Christ's, but not precisely as *its* continuation. It is a distinct mission; he himself is another Paraclete,[2] a Person distinct from Christ and one sent on a new mission which cannot be equated with that of the Incarnate Word, though in close connection with it.

The relations between the two missions, close though they are, remain profoundly mysterious in spite of the abundance of texts from which we may derive some idea of them.

The mission or work of the Holy Spirit and the mission or work of Christ are homogeneous, in the first place, by reason of their purpose and content. From this point of view, the work of the Spirit is, indeed, the work of Christ. His function is to "bring to mind" all that Christ said (Jo 14:26; cf. 16:12 ff.), to bear witness to Christ (I Jo 4:1 ff.; Jo 15:26; Apoc 19:10; cf. Acts 1:8). What he works in men has no other purpose or content than to bring to pass what Christ worked for the sake of men. This is one of the reasons why Scripture so often attributes spiritual activities indifferently to Christ (or the Lord) and to the Holy Spirit. It is unnecessary here to list all the places where the Christian is said to live, to sanctify himself, to feel peace and joy, to bear witness, etc., equally in and by the Holy Spirit and in and by Christ.[3] The identity of the work of each is such that it can be attributed indifferently to Christ and to the Spirit for, after all, the active presence of the latter is equivalent to that of Christ himself (Jo 14:18 ff.; 16:16, 22, 25). St Paul himself says: "The Spirit we have been speaking of is the Lord" (II Cor 3:17; and cf. 3:18). Our own conviction is, though we cannot argue it here, that this text can only be explained, that indeed the equivalence of action of Christ and the Spirit can only be explained ultimately by the profound Trinitarian concepts of the perfect consubstantiality of the divine Persons, their circuminsession and perichoresis.

Though the Holy Spirit performs the very work of Christ, he has, nonetheless, his own special function whose nature is clearly indicated in the New Testament. Christ established an objective reality of grace and truth, of salvation and revelation; the Holy Spirit applies it to the interior of each of us. Christ effected once and for all, in himself, the union of mankind with God; the Spirit brings within its scope a vast number of individuals. Christ proclaimed the Word of God; the Spirit brings it to the mind and inclines the heart to understand it. Christ built the house and the Spirit comes to dwell there (Eph 2:22). Christ gives us the quality of sons; the Spirit puts in our hearts the consciousness of this quality and makes us perform the corresponding acts and duties.[4] A more detailed study would reinforce and bring out fully these facts, which all lead up to the following conclusions—the mission of the Incarnate Word gives each individual soul, as it gave to the Church, existence in the new order of creation; it set up the structure of the Church and established an objective salvation with the various sources of grace and truth. The mission of the Holy Spirit makes these all produce their effects, gives the body of the Church its soul and brings the saving gifts to their fulfillment. Consequently, while acting always in accordance with the unique and decisive event of the Incarnation in time and "bringing to mind" what Christ said (Jo 14:26), the Holy Spirit continues to guide into all truth and to make plain what is still to come (Jo 16:13). He makes no innovations, he does not create anything that bears no relation to the work of Christ—this is a sufficient objection to the various movements based on an action of the Spirit independent of express relationship to the work already accomplished by Christ.[5] What the Spirit does is to bring all to fulfillment. He takes, as it were beforehand, what is Christ's and makes it known to future ages (Jo 16:15). He it is essentially who spoke by the prophets and brings into the Church a kind of prophetic dimension, a movement by which it is led to accomplish, right to the end, all that Christ placed in it in embryonic form. Between the two comings of Christ, between his departure and his return, the Pasch he accomplished for us and that which we shall celebrate with him, the Holy Spirit acts to bring all things to growth and fruitfulness.

The homogeneity of end and content between the work of Christ and that of the Spirit is due to a certain community of origin. This is not a community in every respect, a community of proximate principles, since the Holy Spirit is a Person distinct from the Word (Incarnate), and each is the object of a special mission. It is true that all the divine actions directed outside the divinity are accomplished by the three Persons to whom the divine essence, wisdom, and power are strictly common. There is, however, in whatever slight degree, something "proper," without which the words "mission" and "application" would have no real meaning. In the effects of grace, common indeed to all three Persons, there is something that corresponds mysteriously to what is proper to the Incarnate Word and the Holy Spirit, respectively.[6] Thus the distribution of properties between Christ's mission or work and the mission or work of the Spirit corresponds to something real; but by the very fact that the work or mission of each is distinct, those of the Spirit have a certain dependence on those of Christ. This is expressed in Scripture by the fact that the Spirit is sometimes said to be sent by the Father, but at the request and in the name of the Son (Jo 14:16, 26), and sometimes to be sent by Christ himself (Jo 15:26; 16:7; Lk 24:29; Acts

2:23). Thus, in the order of the economy of grace, the procession or mission of the Spirit is dependent on the Word. It is a Catholic doctrine that this dependence in the sphere of the temporal "economy" supposes a dependence in that of existence in eternity; and this allows us to take in their fullest sense, not merely "economic" but ontological, the expressions used by St. Paul in speaking of the Spirit of Christ in the same sense in which he speaks elsewhere of the Spirit of God (Phil 1:19; Gal 4:6; cf. Rom 8:9 and 15; cf. also I Pet 1:11; Acts 16:7).

It has often been observed that a theology which denies the eternal procession of the Holy Spirit from the Word tends to minimize the part played by definite forms or authority in actual life, and leaves the way more open to a kind of independent inspiration. The ecclesiology of the Orthodox Churches has a distinctly "pneumatic" tendency and declines to accept Catholic ideas of authority which seems to savor of legalism. This legalism, however, is closely bound up with values of profound mystical importance, as may be seen in the following passage from St. Thomas Aquinas which brings out strikingly the ecclesiological counterparts of the theology of the Holy Spirit.

"To say that the Vicar of Christ, the Roman Pontiff, does not hold the Primacy in the universal Church is an error analogous to that which denies that the Holy Spirit proceeds from the Son. For Christ, the Son of God, consecrates his Church and consecrates it by the Holy Spirit as by his seal or stamp. Likewise, the Vicar of Christ by his primacy and governance, like a good servant, preserves the universal Church that is subject to Christ. . . ." [7]

In fact, one cannot fail to notice the way in which Christ speaks of his Church (Mt 16:18), his sheep (Jo 10:1-16; 21:15-17), and how St. Paul speaks of Christ as "head of the Church, his body, of which he is the Savior, having given himself up on its behalf . . . to summon it into his own presence . . ." (Eph 5:23, 25, 26; cf. Acts 20:28). Now

Christ, as we know, builds up his Church by means of *his* apostles and *his* Spirit. These might almost be called his agents whom he has empowered to execute his work in the time of his absence, his "vicars" in fact; so, at any rate, his apostles are called in the liturgy "the vicars of your work" (*Preface of the Apostles*). Later, we will consider how the same expression may be used of the Holy Spirit. At the moment, we must examine more closely the relationship of these two agents to the Incarnation itself and its end.

This relationship may be expressed in two propositions: (1) what brings to pass the work of Christ proceeds from Christ himself in his Incarnation and (2) connects the seed with its fruit, the source to its fullness, the Alpha that is Christ acting alone for our sake to the Omega which we are to be with and in him, from him, and for him. Thus, the agents of Christ's work have a backward-looking relationship (if we may so express it) to his incarnation in time and a forward-looking one to its consummation at the end of the world. They function, in fact, throughout the whole of the interval between the two comings of Christ and this is, precisely, the time of the Church.

It has already been pointed out that the Church as an institution, which precedes and builds up the Church as a community of believers, consists of the deposit of faith, the deposit of the sacraments of faith and that of the apostolic powers bringing both faith and sacraments to men. It is from these that the Church derives its structure. Now it is essential to realize that they all come directly from what Christ was and did for us in the time of his earthly life. This is clear enough as regards the deposit of faith. Provided we do not exclude the revelation given by the prophets and the apostles, whose essential message is concerned with Christ, we may say that Christ himself is the revelation, the word of God, and he makes known to us the supreme mystery of the Father, the Son, and the Spirit.

As to the sacraments, they all derive from Christ's institution. This is brought out by St. John, both symbolically and literally, in regard to baptism and the Eucharist, the two greater sacraments and the most necessary to salvation, those Christ himself conferred and whose matter he directly determined and sanctified. St. John, in the epistle perhaps intended as an introduction to his gospel, tells us that Christ came by water and blood (I Jo 5:6), and shows us, in a passage of exceptional solemnity, this water and blood flowing from the side of Christ as he hung on the cross, dead but still warm (Jo 19:34 ff.). According to the commentators, he intended, in accord with the whole tone of his gospel and the content of his witness, to show thereby the intimate connection of Christ's mystical presence with his historical reality, the relation of the Christ of faith with the Christ who lives interiorly in his followers, with the Christ who came in the flesh.[8] This teaching is confined to St. John. According to St. Paul as well, the sacraments link the Church and the whole Christian life to the historical Christ who instituted them, and to his death. As with the apostolate (see above), all that exercises a kind of vicarious presence and action of Christ is expressly bound up with his deeds and sufferings in the flesh.

It is significant that, in neglecting to take proper account of these solid scriptural data, those who, for reasons of system, minimize the institutional aspect of the Church and see it only as the community of believers, see it too in connection with Pentecost, with the risen Christ, rather than with the "Christ of history" and with his deeds and sufferings in the flesh.

Yet the actual sending of the Holy Spirit is strongly and explicitly connected by St. John to the coming and passion of Christ, just as are the elements of the Church's institution. Like the sacraments, too, the fact is expressed in various places sometimes in symbolical form, sometimes literally. It is stated clearly in the celebrated passage of

John 7:39, whose interpretation, about which all are agreed, is basically independent of the punctuation or meaning of the two preceding verses, "The Spirit had not yet been given to men, because Jesus had not yet been raised to glory."

To this statement corresponds the symbol of Calvary, whether, on the basis of John 7:39, we see, in the water flowing from the side of Christ, the Holy Spirit, bound up with the blood of Christ's glorification, or else, seeing in the blood and water the sacraments, we consider the Spirit referred to in John 19:30, "Then he bowed his head and yielded up his spirit." [9]

In both cases, the sending of the Spirit is connected with the Passion, with the immolated body of the incarnate Word, the Lamb that the Apocalypse shows us sitting with God on a single throne whence flows the river of eternal life (Apoc 22:1 ff.).

Yet another passage of St. John shows clearly the connection of the Spirit of Pentecost with the acts and the mystery of Christ. On the very evening of the Pasch, the risen Christ came into the midst of his diciples, breathed on them and said "Receive ye the Holy Spirit. . ." The word used here, it has been pointed out, is expressive of the way in which a creation or a re-creation, a healing or destruction, is wrought.[10] The new creation of Pentecost is directly linked up by St. John to Christ.

Some writers are even of the opinion that John, to emphasize this connection, intended to place Pentecost, in a way, on the very day of the Pasch, not of course in a historical sense, as actually occurring then, but symbolically and doctrinally, as indicating the significance of the facts. As to the historical Pentecost, the word itself is sufficient indication of what it was, namely, the fiftieth day of the Paschal feast, the fullness and the fruit of the Pasch of the Lord. Liturgists are constantly pointing out that Pentecost is a part of the Christological cycle, that it completes the cycle of the Paschal economy, forming, as it does, with the Pasch one single feast. From then on, Christ's work is not carried out for us in his own Person exclusively, but is spread throughout his whole body, until the fullness of time comes which will bring in the Pasch of the Parousia.

Can we call the Holy Spirit the "vicar" of Christ, as we have seen the liturgy calls the apostles? Tertullian has no hesitation in so doing; but, despite his admitted genius in the use of language and the great influence he exercised on the development of the theological vocabulary of the western Church, he has not been followed in this. The traditional use prefers vaguer expressions, which convey the idea that the Holy Spirit does the work of Christ,[11] but without suggesting that he acts only through the power of Christ, as is the case of the apostles. Tertullian was basically concerned with expressing, in a somewhat rigid legal terminology, the great design of the Father sending the Son who, jointly with the Father, sends the Holy Spirit. The Fathers were fond of stressing this descending order, followed by a reverse order of ascent by which the Holy Spirit effects the work of Christ who, in turn, when all has been subjected to him, will give homage to him who has subjected all things to him (I Cor 15:28).

In this sense, there is indeed a kind of vicarious action of the Holy Spirit in relation to Christ and of Christ in relation to the Father, the one acting as if on account of the other. The Spirit, since he acts in conjunction with the Church in the interval between Christ's departure and return, desires, too, along with the Church, this return (Apoc 22:17). Swete observes that, after his return, Christ will himself exercise this function of guiding the faithful, for which, at the time of his departure, he had promised he would send the Spirit.[12] This might lead us to think that the action of the Spirit has a mediatory quality corresponding to a vicarious function, in some such way as Christ's action until the time when he shall have handed all things over to the Father so that God may be all in all.

Yet neither Christ in relation to the Father, nor the Spirit in relation to Christ, is in the same position as the apostles. These, indeed, were set up, in every respect, by the mandate given to them and, once they have discharged it, they will have nothing more to do as regards our access to God. The Holy Spirit and Christ, on the other hand, always retain their role in our regard. In heaven, Christ remains our high priest for ever. The Holy Spirit is always the living water (Apoc 7:16 ff.; 22:1 ff.; cf. Jo 4:14); he is not merely a vicar, he does not simply exercise a "ministry" of the Incarnate Word, he is not an "instrument." For all these reasons, even if we confine ourselves to our present subject, that of the agency of Christ's work, his position is very different from that of the apostles.

Nonetheless, he works along with them, in the period between the two comings of Christ; they, in fact, are sent as the specific realizers of his work in that interval. To this is due the fact that, in the function each discharges, there is one aspect turned, as it were, towards the past, to the historical facts of the incarnation and Pasch of Christ, from which all has its origin, and another aspect turned toward the future, to the fulfillment of the mystery of Christ throughout the range of his entire Mystical Body. In this connection, we may here, as we have done earlier, add to the apostles the other elements of the institutional Church, namely the deposit of faith and of the sacraments of faith. The entire ecclesiastical or apostolic institution it is, on the one hand, and the Holy Spirit, on the other, which, at the same time, bear reference to the Incarnation, whence they come, and to the final fulfillment.

The first aspect of their mission is that it assures homogeneity from Alpha to Omega; the homogeneity, that is, of all that is to develop in that period and of all that will be garnered at its term with what was laid down in the beginning. Each [i.e., the apostolic body and the Holy Spirit] assures this in its own province. The apostles and the institutional Church accomplish this in the realm of external means of grace and their objective identity with those which Christ set up in the exercise of his messianic power as king, prophet, and priest. The real meaning of the apostolate and the hierarchy is, as we have shown elsewhere, that they insure, in the visible order in which we live and where the Body of Christ is to be realized, that all comes from the one single event of the Incarnation and Pasch of Christ. But what the apostolic body and the institutional Church effect in the exterior and objective order, the Holy Spirit does within the institution itself and within individuals. He speaks and bears witness, but he does not speak of himself; he says what he has heard; he receives of Christ to declare it to us (Jo 16:13-15).[13] He brings each one into possession of the gift of Christ, and so brings about between all of them and Christ that identity we call mystical for want of any adequate analogy in the natural order. In this way, there comes into being that single reality which is both Church and Body of Christ, built up by what has its origin in him, Head and Principle, Alpha and First-born of all.

Thus the Holy Spirit and the Apostolate receive from what pertains to Christ only in order to produce for him the building-up of his body, the maturity of completed growth (Eph 4:12-13). Christ is, at once, the Alpha and the Omega (Apoc 1:8; 21:6; 22:13), and this well expresses the unity of the term with the beginning. But he is Alpha himself alone, although he is so for our sakes, whereas he is Omega together with us or we are so together with him, as forming a single body with him who is its origin. In absolute strictness, there is only one who goes up to heaven, he who came down from heaven (Jo 3:13); but we ascend in him. It is the same mystery, the same Pasch, but, between its first and its final moment, in that interval between the ascension and the Parousia, which is the time of the Church, there is communication and growth. The same passages which say that the Spirit will proclaim what he has heard point to him as leading the disciples into all truth, teaching them all things, making known what is to come (Jo 14:16; 14:13); the apostles are to do, in a sense, greater things than Christ (Jo 4:12); through them, through us, all things are to grow up into him who is the head, the Christ (Eph 4:15), so that he may be "fulfilled" in all (Eph 1:23).

It is this double law of identity and development—of reference to the unique fact of the historical incarnation, revelation, pasch and apostolate and, at the same time, a law of presence, of activity and growth throughout space and time—which is the law of the Church, placed as it is between the pasch and the Parousia to be the living link between them. Under the direction of the great principles of identity of which we have spoken, the activity of men is joined to the outpouring of God, in such wise that this latter is lived by all those to whom it has been predestined. The "passage" of Christ is celebrated, in baptism, the Eucharist and the other sacraments, after the manner which is characteristic of the liturgy, referring both to the past event, of which the sacrament is the memorial, and to the final fulfillment; in this way what Christ did flows into and fills the whole of time, which is made use of to prepare the plenitude of the Parousia. Here we have to do with the whole of the Christian meaning of time, the entire significance of the time of the Church. This significance is to be found in that realization of the outpouring through which, between the Alpha and the Omega, a function is enacted in no merely mechanical way, a function of such a sort that, at its term, there is found once again the same single reality set up at the beginning, like the talent shamefacedly buried of which the Gospel speaks.

This law is seen at work, not only in the case of the sacraments in their relation to the messianic acts and the passion accomplished once and for all, but also as regards Tradition in its relation to Scripture, development in relation to Revelation and the apostolate in relation to the mission of Christ. In each of these, in its own specific way, there is a single outpouring along with a realization of this outpouring in time and space, a kind of "recommence-ment," as Péguy calls it, a development and growth towards a fulfillment which yet will be found to contain nothing which is not derived from the initial stage.

The Holy Spirit and the Apostolic Institution Act Jointly

This joint action to bring about the Body of Christ is to be seen, both in the ministry in general, its constitution, authority and effects and, more particularly, in its two principal functions, those connected with the Word and the sacraments.

The apostles are such "by the Holy Spirit" (Acts 1:2; 13:4). The Holy Spirit and the apostles are manifested jointly at Pentecost; not that the apostolate had not been founded beforehand or that the Spirit had not already been given, but it was at Pentecost that the Church was definitely set up in the world and manifested as a new creation with its own specific energies, which consist precisely in the Holy Spirit and the apostolic ministry acting conjointly (cf. Jo 20:22-23).

From Pentecost onwards, the apostolate and the Spirit act in conjunction and the expansion of the Church is continuously brought about by their action; the witnesses to the Gospel are filled with the Holy Spirit (Acts 4:8; 13:9; 2:4; etc.), and are guided by him even in the details of their activities (10:19; 8:29, 39; etc.). As has often been remarked, the whole of the Acts could very well be summarized in the verse, "The Church . . . became firmly established, guided by the fear of God, and grew in numbers by the help of the Holy Spirit" (Acts 9:31); we might equally well translate, "by the invocation of the Holy Spirit."

The Spirit does not only join in with the ministry in its work, but intervenes to establish and consecreate it, or rather to bring about interiorly and in reality the consecration imparted in a visible manner by ministers already instituted; thus the prophets and doctors of Antioch lay hands on Saul and Barnabas, but the latter are also said to be sent by the Holy Spirit (Acts 13:3 and 4); likewise, St. Paul appoints the elders by imposition of hands (Acts 14:22), but, in addressing those of Ephesus, he says, "Keep watch, then, over yourselves, and over God's Church, in which the Holy Spirit has made you bishops" (Acts 20:28). The consecration of ministers is jointly the work of the Holy Spirit and the apostolic body. The authority of the apostles is, as it were, equated with that of God himself. Thus, Ananias, in attempting to deceive the apostles, in reality lied to the Holy Spirit and to God (Acts 5:3 and 4); and later, at the synod of Jerusalem, the apostles and elders made use in an official statement, legal in tone, of the celebrated formula: "It has seemed good to the Holy Spirit and to us" (Acts 15:28). It is a formula that recalls those of the councils of the Greek or Jewish world, in which is expressed a decision, not of an individual acting on his own judgment, but of a group of persons in communion with one another. Here there is a sort of sanhedrin of the Church, consisting of the apostles and elders, but their decision is taken in communion with the Holy Spirit himself, the chief personage, if we may dare to say so, of the council, whose authority is applied in conjunction with that of the apostles and elders.

The ultimate end and outcome of a ministry associated in this way with the Holy Spirit in its very constitution, in its authority and its acts, is the building up of the body of Christ. The apostolic ministry issues in the gift of the Holy Spirit (Acts 8:14-17; 10:44; 19:6). So it is not surprising to see St. Paul looking on the community of Corinth, formed by him, as a letter from Christ, written by him, not with ink, but with the Spirit of the living God (II Cor 3:2-3); he is speaking of a spiritual gift, but of a gift which is always bound up with the Person of the Holy Spirit. From the same point of view, it is very significant that, in the great texts where St. Paul speaks of the unity and life of the body, he brings into relation the unity of the spirit on the one hand, and the multiplicity of members on the other (I Cor 12:12 ff.; Eph 4:4 ff.).

There is, too, the same association and cooperation of the Spirit with the two great acts of the ministry, the preaching of the word and the celebration of the sacraments.

In the first place, since the apostles were made such by the Holy Spirit, they were also made by him men of the word. They receive him, and, immediately, they speak (Acts 2:4; 4:31, 33). It is by the Holy Spirit sent from heaven that the ministers of the Gospel proclaim and preach (I Pet 1:12). Once more, Christ's work is taken up after his departure by his two envoys, the Holy Spirit and the apostolic body. Christ taught (Mt 5:2; 7:29; Jo 6:59), but he arranged for the apostles to continue teaching after him (Mt 28:20; cf. 5:19), and for the Holy Spirit as well (Jo 14:26; cf. Lk 12:12). He even proclaimed expressly the law governing the joint action and agreement concerning the testimony given at one and the same time by the Holy Spirit and the apostles—"when the Spirit . . . whom I will send to you from the Father's side . . . has come, he will bear witness of what I was; and you too are to be my witnesses, you who from the first have been in my company" (Jo 15:26-27). Thus when Christ appoints the apostles his witnesses, he links up their testimony to the sending of the Spirit (Lk 24:48-49; Acts 1:8).

On the joint witness of the apostles and the Holy Spirit there exist many excellent studies, but no complete treatise. The apostles are not witnesses in a merely historical aspect, with a view to securing a purely objective recording and acknowledgment of the facts. They are witnesses solely as ministers of the Gospel, in their function of proclaiming the good news of salvation in Christ. Consequently their testimony is, in part, a narrative of the events in the life of Christ all the time they were with him, what they themselves had seen and heard and also, as was Christ's own preaching, an appeal to the prophecies and the fulfillment of all that was declared about Christ and of the preparation for his coming in the Old Testament. But it is, in addition, a proclamation of the future accomplishment of the messianic acts; for, as we have seen, the apostolate and the Church as constituted by Christ, along with the Holy Spirit, are constantly at work in the interval between Christ's pasch and Parousia to link up and urge on the Alpha of the former to the Omega of the latter. In the testimony of the apostles, the connection between the facts as already having occurred and their fulfillment in the body of Christ is brought out clearly in many places, particularly in I John 1:1-3 and Acts 5:30-32: "It was the God of our fathers that raised up Jesus, the man you hung on a gibbet to die. It is God who raised him up to his own right hand, as the prince and Savior who is to bring Israel repentance and remission of sins. Of this we are witnesses; we and the Holy Spirit God gives to all those who obey him."

How does the Holy Spirit give this testimony? First, he gave it, and continues to give it, in the prophets—cf. Heb 10:15; 3:7; 9:8; Acts 10:43; etc. He does so by the strength he imparts to the apostles in their witnessing—"They were all filled with the Holy Spirit, and began to preach the word of God with confidence. . . . Great was the power with which the apostles testified to the resurrection of our Lord Jesus Christ, and great was the grace that rested on them all "(Acts 4:31-33)." In the great judicial process going on after Christ's departure, a kind of revision or, at any rate, a continuation of what he endured, which will last as long as there is a "world," while the apostles bear witness "unto the ends of the earth," the Holy Spirit will "convince the world of sin" (Jo 16:8); whether it is that he brings the world to awareness of its sin, or that he strengthens in the apostles their conviction that the world is wrong and that Christ's cause is just, in short, that he refutes the world and brings out clearly its sin to the consciousness of the faithful, according to an interpretation not, indeed, widely accepted but well-founded. At all events, one essential aspect of the testimony of the Holy Spirit is to manifest the sin of the world and to strengthen the faithful interiorly. We know too that he does not leave the ministers of the Gospel to themselves, but acts as their guide (cf. above and Acts 20:22-23). God accompanies them too, "bearing them witness by signs and wonders and divers miracles and distributions of the Holy Spirit according to his will" (Heb 2:3-4: God himself "witnesses with"; cf. I Thess 1:5).

In addition to the testimony the Holy Spirit gives by eternal signs and within the apostles themselves, there is that which he gives within those who hear them. In a general way, he brings about within souls a work corresponding to that effected by the apostolate externally, the work of conversion and salvation by the preaching and reception of the Gospel. His work begins with a *call*. It has been justly emphasized that the act of calling or vocation is prominent among all the divine acts which result in the "convocation," that is, in the Church. Without unduly stressing the associated meanings of *klesis, kalein, ekka-*

lein, ekklesia, we must observe the relation between the call and the setting up of the Church; the people of God is gathered and constituted from the time of its being called, of its *klesis.* This is an act of God, proceeding from his free and eternal plan, an act most intimate and secret (Rom 8:28, 30; etc.); but this call of God is shown forth outwardly and concretely by the apostolic preaching of the Gospel (II Thess 2:13, with which cf. Rom 10:14 ff.), and this preaching is itself accompanied by an act of the Holy Spirit which is a kind of urgent call and prompting, the "paraclesis" by which, we are told in the Acts (9:31), the Church is built up and develops. Thus vocation, the divine act which in God follows upon election, is manifested to men by a twofold call to faith, one exterior, by the apostolic word, the other interior, by the prompting, the invitation and the drawing of which the Holy Spirit is the originator (cf. St. Thomas, *In Rom,* c. 8, lec. 6). To this corresponds the inclination of the heart, its readiness to answer the call and receive the word, of which the book of the Acts (16:14) speaks, and after it, the whole Christian tradition (cf. Acts 9:6; 10:5; *Summa Theologiae* II-II, q. 177, a. 1).

In this way, the Holy Spirit begins the movement of conversion which he continues by stirring up in us a conviction of sin, a rooted feeling of the need to change our life and to be truly converted. The Holy Spirit, too, makes us hear in the heart, as if directly and actually spoken to us, the calls of the scriptural witness: "If you hear his voice speaking to you this day, do not harden your hearts . . ." (Heb 3:7). If this witness, and that of the preacher of the Gospel, is received, the Holy Spirit gives us the grace of faith itself, for "it is only through the Holy Spirit that anyone can say 'Jesus is the Lord' " (I Cor 12:3). He pursues his work further in the whole 'life in Christ,' which is life on the basis of faith, by testifying to our spirit that, being forgiven, we are sons of God (Rom 8:16; I Jo 3:19-

24), by praying in us (Rom 8:26-27), instructing us in all things by his presence and the interior certainty he brings, by penetrating us deeply with his unction (Jo 16:13; I Jo 2:20-27).

The New Testament does not speak so expressly about the life and sacramental practice of the faithful as it does about the preaching of the apostles, but all the positive data it contains have been faithfully followed out and developed in liturgical and theological tradition.

The connection of the Spirit with Baptism and his working in it are quite evident, both from the proclamation of the baptism of the Spirit to be given by Christ (Mt 3:1; Mk 1:8; Lk 3:16) and from Christ's own baptism, in which, to signify the institution of the baptism of the Spirit, the dove rested upon Christ (Jo 1:32-33; cf. Mark 1:10), as well as from Christ's discourse to Nicodemus on the new birth from water and the Spirit (Jo 3:5) and the actual teaching and practice of the apostles (Acts 19:2-6; I Cor 12:13; etc.). We find, too, a similar connection of the Spirit with the sacrament of Penance (Jo 10:23), with the imposition of hands to impart the fullness of spiritual gifts (Acts 8:14-17, 18; 9:17; 19:6), with the imposition of hands for the exercise of the ministry (Acts 13:2-4; cf. I Tim 4:14 and II Tim 1:6)—even, in some respects, with the Eucharist, so closely bound up with the work of the Spirit,[14] and with the anointing of the sick, which is accompanied with prayer and invocation of the name of the Lord, that is to say, with an *"epiclesis"* (Ja 5:14).

Each of these topics calls for a special study, but here we are only concerned with the function of the Holy Spirit in the working of the sacraments and his connection with the visible actions performed by the Christian ministry. Theologically speaking, we have here one of the foundations of the necessity for an intervention of the Holy Spirit in the sacraments and, therefore, for an *epiclesis*. The question of the *epiclesis*, which has, anyhow, been somewhat artificially restricted to the eucharistic *epiclesis*, has been obscured by the secondary problem of the precise moment of the consecration; and has been even more fundamentally impaired through being treated in the theology of the sacraments, whereas it can be properly understood only as part of the theology of the Holy Spirit. We hope to return to this one day, as we cannot delay on it here; it is enough to point out its connection with our present subject, which derives from the fact that the Holy Spirit is, jointly with the apostolic ministry or the institutional Church, the active principle realizing the work of Christ. Their common function is that of applying throughout space and time the universal cause of salvation, of life reconciled in and through Christ. The specific function of the Holy Spirit is, on the one hand, to give the institution life and movement (and, in this sense of the word, effectiveness) and, on the other hand, to bring to individuals and to their innermost being the gifts of God.

If we look for the principle of this joint working of the Holy Spirit with the apostolic ministry or the institutional Church, we come to his function in the actual constitution of the universal cause of salvation, namely Christ himself. The very first coming of the Spirit, his first union with a human agency which was to cooperate with him, resulted in the conception of Christ "incarnated of the Holy Spirit and the Virgin Mary," in the words of the creed of Nicea and Constantinople. That was, indeed, the first and decisive coming of Christ among us, but his real "entry" as the Messias came with his baptism by John. Christ himself, as well as his disciples, called his baptism the beginning (Jo 15:27; Lk 1:2; 3:23; cf. Acts 10:37). John was, indeed, the precursor and even the consecrator of Christ; his function has been appropriately compared to that of Samuel in regard to David, the type of the Messias-King. Now, as the Spirit came down on Mary for the conception of Christ, he came down on Christ at his baptism to consecrate him for the messianic ministry. As he did formerly on David, the type of the Messias-King (I Kings 16:3), on the royal branch foretold as issuing from him (Isaias 11:1-2), on the Servant prophetically described by Isaias (13:1; 61:1-3; cf. Lk 4:17-21), the Spirit came down on Jesus and rested on him. That here we have the origin and the reason of the joint action of the Spirit and the water of Baptism is obvious enough, but it means something more. The consecration by the Spirit at Christ's baptism was his consecration to the messianic ministry. He had been sanctified in himself from his conception (Lk 1:35), and now he was sanctified in view of the ministry, and so as source of grace for us, at his baptism as Messias. For this reason, he is, a second time, called Son—and would be, a third time, in the mystery of his "passage," his death-resurrection-ascension (Acts 13:33)—as if sent into the world a second time, as source of grace, in whom the Father was well pleased (Lk 3:22). At his incarnation, the Word of God espoused our human nature as to its being and life, so as to share our human manner of life; at his baptism, he espoused the Church—and this espousal was to be consummated in the mystery of his Pasch, by which the sacraments and the whole work of the ministry would become efficacious. He espoused, not human nature as such, but the Church: the organism of the messianic work, the visible body containing the means of grace and constituted such from the moment of his baptism. Christ was constituted Son of God at his conception, but was declared Son and became such *for us* at his baptism, in which was instituted the baptism of the Spirit, that of our own sonship. This was the beginning of the sacramental order, of the order of the ministry and of that association of the Spirit with each which has been the theme of the preceding pages. The foundation of the union between the Holy Spirit and the institutional

Church is the union of operation present, from the beginning, between the Holy Spirit and Christ. This union, deriving from the mystery of the divine being, of the eternal relations in God, of the consubstantiality and circuminsession of the divine Persons, was proclaimed, as regards Christ, at his baptism and, as regards the Church and the apostolate, at Pentecost, their baptism by the Holy Spirit.

We are now in a position to state more precisely the nature of the union of the Holy Spirit with the institutional Church founded by Christ in his life on earth. The union is not incarnational, despite the analogies various distinguished writers have pointed out; [15] consequently, however mysterious and difficult to formulate are the relations between the Spirit and Christ, the Spirit and the Mystical Body, the latter is not the body of the Holy Spirit but of Christ. Not only is the action of the Holy Spirit wholly relative to Christ and is to effect within the disciples, after Christ's departure, the same as he did while still with them, [16] but the Spirit came to give life, motion, and effectiveness to a body, to sacraments, to an apostolic ministry already constituted, and constituted by Christ in the time of his deeds and sufferings in the flesh. It has been repeatedly shown by Catholic writers that Christ instituted a ministry, a body of doctrine, sacraments, a Church, before his Pasch, though the sacraments received their efficacity from his Passion, and the hierarchical mission of the apostles was definitely given only after the resurrection. Many non-Catholic writers express themselves on this subject in just the same way as we would. [17] In this connection, it would doubtless be appropriate to make use of the categories of *structure* and *life* we have already suggested earlier. No doubt, too, there could be found, in the various parts of the Bible which speak of a creation, significant analogies suggesting a kind of law of God's working—the creation of Adam (Gen 2:7), the vision of Ezechiel (38)—

a function of the Spirit of completing a work already laid out in its structure or skeleton. First comes the organization, and afterwards life and movement; first the letter, afterwards the understanding.[18] Accordingly, the Holy Spirit comes essentially for the purpose of animating and giving movement to a body constituted by Christ and which is his body; he is, for the threefold deposit of the faith, the sacraments, and the apostolic powers, what the vital principle is for an organism.

We can understand that Tradition gives the Holy Spirit the title of soul of the Church. It is not, however, to be taken in the sense of a soul entering into composition with the body of the Church and being united to it in a physical and substantial union, like our souls and bodies. There is no question of an incarnation, of union in actual being, such that all the actions of the Church would be physically and personally the actions of the Holy Spirit and have no other subject of attribution than him. They certainly come from him, but also from that body instituted by Christ as a subject in its own right, a collective person, which he himself called "my church," the Church we know too to be his spouse. This is not the place to try and work out what is the inmost reality of this body or quasi-person which is the Church. For our present purpose, it is sufficient to point out that the Holy Spirit does not enter into composition with it as a form with matter, but unites himself with it as with a subject already constituted in being. So it is that Scripture makes use of expressions which suggest the idea, not of a soul as a part of a composite being, but of one indwelling and acting: *to be with* always (Jo 16:16), *to be given (ibid.), to be present, to inhabit,* as if in a sanctuary, to be given by God as something one has (I Cor 3:16; 6:19), and of which one can be filled. In addition, there are all the texts, of which we have already cited a fair number and which may be found in a concordance, where all kinds of operations are attributed to the Holy Spirit—bearing witness, causing a rebirth, praying, guiding, teaching, etc. It is clear that, if these operations imply what we may call an ontic ontology or physical production, the texts which express the relation of the Holy Spirit to the Church in terms of *habitation, being with,* imply in an intersubjective ontology. The Holy Spirit does not inform the Church by entering into a physical composition with it to constitute a single substantial being which is both divine and human; he is with it to guide and assist it, to enable it to perform actions which, while outwardly human, are bearers of a divine virtue, the 'power of the Holy Spirit.'

What sort of a union, then, is it, if it is not one of actual being? It is a union of alliance, grounded on God's decree for man's salvation and on his promises, that is to say on the design of grace God is to realize in the time fixed by him. Since the good envisaged rests on a decree and promise of God, it has the strongest and most certain warrant conceivable, infinitely more solid and assured than any bond created by an undertaking and a promise on the part of man. Now, if God pledged himself, under the old disposition of his alliance, to succor his people, guide and strengthen them, he has pledged himself, under the regime of the new and final disposition made in the blood of Jesus, to give his Spirit in such a way that it really dwells in the new Israel. The Spirit is the specific gift of the messianic era. He rested on Christ in all his fullness; but this fullness Christ raised up to heaven, communicated to his own (Jo 1:16; Acts 2:33). The Spirit, after having come at Pentecost in fulfillment of the promise of the Father and of Christ (Lk 24:49; Jo 14:16; etc.), remains with the Church; and the "acts of the apostles" that St. Luke relates were to such a degree guided and accomplished by the Spirit that the Acts have been called the Gospel of the Holy Spirit. The regime of the new and final disposition is a regime of an abiding gift, of a permanent presence and assistance, closely bound up with a *being with* which is an indwelling. The post-pentecostal ministry is a "ministry of the Spirit" (II Cor 2:4-18).

If the Holy Spirit is the soul of Christ's Mystical Body, and if he is, as we have shown, conjoined with the institutional Church and the apostolic body—these latter doing externally and visibly what he himself does interiorly—it might be said that the elements of the institutional Church and the apostolic body are, externally, the soul of the Church as the Holy Spirit is its soul internally. This, indeed, is held by some of the Fathers, and the same idea is developed by Journet in *The Church of the Word Incarnate*. However, in view both of tradition and of speculative theology, we prefer to reserve the title of soul of the Church to the Holy Spirit exclusively and to speak of formal cause or formal principles in connection with the exterior elements of the institution or of the apostolic powers.

Whatever be the terms employed, it remains that the certainty of God's promise and the union of alliance existing between the Church and the Holy Spirit are the ground of the infallibility of the hierarchical actions, of those, that is, by which the visible Church receives visibly its structure and is linked, by the visible bond of apostolicity, to Christ's institution. The relevant passages of the New Testament are well known and, in any case, fully developed in Catholic works on the subject of the Church. The Acts, too, and the Epistles obviously suppose that the apostolic ministry performs the actual work of God and by the power of God. But from these texts to those of the apostolic Fathers, Clement and Ignatius, from the latter to St. Irenaeus, St. Cyprian and the Fathers of the classical era, from these to the affirmations of the Councils claiming their own decisions to be those of the Holy Spirit himself, as the synod of Jerusalem had done before, finally, from all this to the statements of classical theology, of the magisterium, even to those of the most exact scholastic theory speaking of immediacy of power in the mediation of the subject, where can be found any breach in the consciousness and the vindication of the fact that, thanks to the bond of alliance between the Holy Spirit and the institutional Church, the latter, in those major actions concerning its very structure, enjoys the guarantee of God's promises and, for that reason, of some kind of infallibility?

Why, indeed, should it not? In the natural order, for example, we see God intervening, so to speak, to give an immortal soul to what the union of man and woman has placed in an existence which was, in the first instance, an animal one. God, as St. Thomas shows, must give directly, and alone can give, the first and the final spiritual perfection, the immortal soul and deifying grace. He gives the soul by his unfailing cooperation with the human work of the flesh, faithfully observing the laws of his own creation; why then should he not give his grace in cooperation with the visible work of the apostolic ministry, faithful in this to the institution of the alliance sealed in the blood of Christ? On these lines we come, not merely to a reconciliation—which is absolutely demanded by Catholic tradition—but to a perfect equation of the "Church of the community of bishops" and the "Church of the Spirit" which Tertullian, as a Montanist, tried to separate and oppose.

None the less, in the spiritual sphere and, particularly, in that of grace, a kind of physical sequence of cause and effect is not the whole of what theology has to say. All that we have said so far is true enough: there is a union of alliance, grounded in the will of God, between the Holy Spirit and the institutional Church which implies some sort of infallibility in the acts of the ministry, so that the consecration of the sacred species is effected by the prayer of the Church and absolution from sin by the pronouncement of the priest, the sacramental bond of marriage, before God, follows on the contract blessed by the Church as infallibly as the gift of an immortal soul on the physical generation of a human offspring. Yet, though the Church's ministry is so sublimely fruitful, it is neither an entirely sufficient nor an absolutely necessary condition for the gift of grace. It is not entirely sufficient, because it is not a question of a purely automatic effect of a physical kind. The sacraments always have, as it were, an element of uncertainty, which derives from the necessity for man to elicit an act of faith and commit himself to God for them to produce their effect. Nor is the intervention of the regular ministry an absolutely necessary condition for the imparting of grace. This point is so important and requires such close exposition that we will devote to it a special section.

A Certain Freedom or Autonomy as Features in the Life of the Church

What Scripture tells us is not confined to the propositions just stated concerning the bond of alliance between the Holy Spirit and the institutional Church. Though the activity of the Spirit is ever directed to the building up of the Church as the community of believers or of the saved, it is not presented as invariably bound up with the established means, but rather as preserving a kind of autonomy which shows itself in two series of facts—the charisms and the sudden visitations or unpredictable leadings of the Spirit.

The charisms appear in the New Testament as spiritual gifts of a manifest nature, which are ordered to the building up of the body of Christ and given directly by the Holy Spirit or the glorified Christ (Rom 12; I Cor 12:4-11—the Spirit; I Cor 14; Eph 4:11-12—the glorified Christ). Of course, there is no opposition between the charisms and the hierarchical ministry. In the first place, the ministers were themselves chosen from among these who had been given the gifts of the Spirit, and the Spirit too had intervened in their appointment (Acts 13:2-4; I Tim 4:14; cf. I Tim 1:18). Later we shall see to what extent the apostles and their fellow-workers were, so to speak, formed by the Holy Spirit. Likewise, it is clear that many of the charisms enumerated by St. Paul represent actual ministries and strictly hierarchical functions. The ministers appointed in the early Church are seen to be essentially charismatic persons, filled with the Holy Spirit.[19] In this respect, the theology of the pseudo-Areopagite only systematized what was the ideal and, often enough, the actual case. In reality the charisms and the hierarchical functions overlap.

At the same time, long before the pastoral epistles and the so-called "catholicizing" of Christianity which supposedly followed the death of the apostles, the charismatic inspiration was assimilated to the unity of the Church by being made subject to an objective rule of faith (I Cor 12:13) and to the apostolic authority (I Cor 14:37-38). Just as the Holy Spirit has no radical autonomy, but is sent to do the work of Christ, to bring to mind what he said, the gifts imparted by the Spirit have no other end than to build up the body of Christ. Consequently, they have to be assimilated to the rule of apostolicity, which is that of continuity with the work done by the Incarnate Word, under the double form of apostolicity of doctrine and apostolicity of ministry. These are, indeed, the two criteria of unity, and so of authenticity and validity, that we have just met with in St. Paul. We find them too in St. John (I Jo 4:2, connected with 4:6 and 2:19). In both we find references to apostolicity of ministry and apostolicity of doctrine, the latter being, as it were, the internal content of the former, and in addition an insistence on submission by the faithful, however gifted spiritually they may seem to be, to the apostolicity of the ministry and, thereby, to the true apostolicity of doctrine. The spiritual gifts are assimilated to the unity of the Church through their regulation by the hierarchical ministry and the apostolic institution.

All the same, the charisms, a large number at any rate, do not arise from the hierarchical acts. But they are not unrelated to the hierarchical ministry and they have to be subject to it in order to be accepted in the Church for the building up of the body of Christ; still, they do not come from the apostolic ministry, but from the Spirit. We have here a whole body of facts of which the life of the Church has always been aware, which nothing in her theology gainsays, but which are practically ignored in present-day theology and ecclesiology. The facts, however, and the Scriptural texts are plain enough.

Invariably, the spiritual gifts present in the hierarchical organism of the ministry appear, at the same time, as having been freely given. This is especially the case with "prophecy," which occupies a very considerable place in the apostolic writings, from the Acts to the Apocalypse itself, notably in St. Paul. The early Church looked on itself as a Church in which the Spirit was continually raising up prophets, and held this to be one of its most convincing features over against the Synagogue as well as the pagan world. The very same Church that claimed so close a bond between the acts of the hierarchy and the Holy Spirit (cf. Clement, Ignatius, Irenaeus, Cyprian) was conscious that it was built up, in addition, by additional supports given unexpectedly; its structure may be compared with that of a fabric made on a woof in conjunction with a warp. The apostles had previously shown hostility to a messianic work that did not proceed from their number (Mk 4:37; Lk 9:49-50); but, after Pentecost, they learned that, though the Spirit is the soul of the Church, he also breathes where he will. They realized that, if the imposition of their hands gave the Holy Spirit, he could come, too, before the apostolic sacrament (Acts 10:44-47) or through the imposition of other hands than theirs (Acts 9:17).

Finally, they found themselves confronted with a thirteenth apostle, an apostle through the direct intervention of the glorified Lord, one who credited himself with never having known Christ according to the flesh, an apostle by effraction, so to speak, yet one the Church does not hesitate to call, even to this day, purely and simply "the Apostle." It is true St. Paul made use of his authoritative status (I Cor 4:21; 5:3; etc.), but he preferred to appeal to the spiritual gifts he had received and to the visible fruits of his apostolate (e.g., I Cor 7:40; II Cor 3:1-3; Gal 4:12, 20; II Cor 7:2). As an apostle added to the others over and above the normal rules of institution as such, he seems to have preferred the criteria of life and effectiveness to those of structure and legitimacy. Nonetheless, he was aware of the decisive importance of these. As the possessor of charisms would be unworthy of credit if he remained outside the institution and the apostolate set up by the will of God, Paul knew that he would be running in vain if he were not approved, both as to his teaching and his mission, by the apostolic center at Jerusalem. It has been ably shown how solicitude for preserving unity and communion dominated St. Paul's conduct and is the real reason for his collection for the "saints." We will go no further into these matters which are well known and, in any case, require treatment on their own account. What concerns us here is the obvious duality of the ways in which the Spirit works, and so of those whereby he builds up the Church. They have been called, respectively, "institution" and "event," though they can hardly be fitted into a precise system. This duality is, admittedly, relative but it is real, nonetheless; what follows will make clearer the scope of each.

The Holy Spirit is continually at work to effect in-

teriorly what the hierarchical ministry does exteriorly, according to the bond of alliance between them that we
have already explained. But he intervenes also directly
and, in the first place, in the conduct of the apostles themselves, to direct, as it were, personally the growth of the
Church and the building-up of the Mystical Body. Thus,
there is not only the regular exercise of the powers or
offices entrusted by Christ to his disciples, but together
with, over and above this—we might even say *within* it—
a kind of sovereign liberty of action on the part of the
Spirit who is truly the "Lord of the apostolate." He effects
all the increases in the Church (Acts 9:31). He designates
Paul and Barnabas for a mission to Cyprus (Acts 13:2 and
4). He prevents Paul from going over to Asia (Acts 16:6-7),
but later, at any rate according to Codex D, he impels him
to take the road to Macedonia. As regards St. Paul, his
docility to the indications of the Spirit is conveyed by his
repeated expression of a feeling that a door is opened to
him in this or that place, or in the idea that, in the midst
of dangers, the way remains open to him, which is a sign
that he is still to bear fruit (Phil 1:22). We find, too, in
the other apostles—Peter in regard to Cornelius, Philip on
the road to Gaza—the same docility to the sudden visitations and leadings of the Spirit. The particular personality of each of the apostles appears, in this way, as if
moulded at every moment by the Holy Spirit who, the
indwelling soul animating the Church, is also the ultimate
ruler of the movements of the body. He inhabits and animates the institution, but the activity he unfolds within it
is not reducible to the fact that he is given and bound
closely to it. This activity of his makes it evident that,
though given to the Church and faithful to the promises
of the new alliance, he remains transcendent to the Church
he dwells in. He is not just a divine force giving supernatural efficacy both to the ministry and to the sacraments,

but a Person sovereignly active and free. He is not made use of by others, but himself directs events.

The episode of Philip and the eunuch of Candace is a striking example of how the Spirit acts by himself for the building up of the body of Christ. An interior inspiration urges Philip to take the road to Gaza and the statement of the Acts, that it was desert, seems to imply emphasis and, perhaps, motive. A strange inspiration, then; yet it is there that he meets the eunuch in his chariot, a meeting like so many that chance puts in our way as time goes on. But the inspiration becomes more detailed; on seeing this man unknown to him, met by chance, Philip feels impelled to speak to him. The rest is familiar enough: how the meeting gives occasion to Philip to tell the man about Christ, and concludes with the celebration, by baptism, of the mystery of water and the Spirit.

This kind of thing, which seems so extraordinary to some, has always occurred and still does. The body of Christ is built up by the regular mediation, functional and hierarchical, of the appointed ministers, the sacraments and the other rites of the Church, but also by the unpredictable, occasional and fraternal mediation of the various conjunctures and unexpected happenings brought about by the Spirit and signs of his working, which he offers to souls ready to accept them. A whole volume could be filled with examples drawn from the lives of saints and men of God, from one's own experience and that of many others who have confided in us. The *Confessions* of St. Augustine, for instance, contain many examples of what may be called the law of occasions or conjunctures: Alypius attending, by chance, a lecture given by Augustine when still a Manichean and, by what he heard, delivered from his passion for the theater and the circus; Augustine himself hearing Pontianus tell about the life of St. Anthony and being fired with spiritual ambition in company with Alypius and, shortly after, in the garden, hearing, as if sung over and over again by some child, the *tolle, lege,* "take and read," and then chancing on the epistles of St. Paul. How often, too, in the history of the Church, important decisions about vocations, foundations, even canons of Councils, have been taken as a result of a dream, a word, a consultation of Scripture, in short of an intervention of the type of "event." And this, not only in the first and second centuries, which abound in such cases, but during the whole of the Middle Ages and, doubtless, later as well. This subject, which has never been studied as a whole, certainly deserves investigation. We ourselves are convinced, as a result of a few haphazard soundings, that there could be disclosed here one of the most constant and decisive elements in the Church's life.

Thus we are led by various ways to admit that, if the Church is always the work of the Holy Spirit who dwells in it, it is not that of the Spirit exclusively as bound to the institution and working in and through it. The Holy Spirit retains a kind of freedom of action which is immediate, autonomous and personal. In this way, there exists a kind of free sector which constitutes one of the most salient features of the life of the Church.

Notes

1 "As my Father sent me, so . . ." corresponds exactly to "as the Father has loved me, I also have loved you"—Jo 15:9; 17:23, 28.

2 Jo 14:16. Christ had been a Paraclete to his followers, and he still is, in heaven (I Jo 2:1).

3 We find this even in the Gospels. Thus, the bearing of the disciples when brought to judgment is attributed to the Holy Spirit in Mt 10:18-20 and Mk 13:10-12, and to Christ in Lk 21:12-15.

4 Cf. Gal 4:4-6; Rom 8:15, and H. B. Swete, *The Holy Spirit in the New Testament* (London, 1909), pp. 204-206.

5 We refer in particular, as regards the past, to the ideas of Joachim de Flora on a Church of the Spirit following a Church of the Son, ideas which only escaped the censure they deserved because of Joachim's supporters in the Papal Curia. In our own time, certain interpretations of the

spiritual technique of moral rearmament are open to the same kind of criticism.

6 Even in the Latin and Thomist view (minimalist, in this context), it can be held that something is attributed to a divine Person, not as caused by him to the exclusion of the others, but as representing what is proper to that Person. Further, there is something impossible to specify exactly, yet real, a relation of each Person respectively to the essential attribute which represents them, namely, power, wisdom, and love (or, as St. Paul says, love, grace, and communion—II Cor 13:13).

7 *Contra errores Graecorum, lib.* 2, *prolog.*: "In our own day, too, there are those who dissolve Christ and do their utmost to lessen his dignity. They do so when they say that the Holy Spirit does not proceed from the Son, whereas the latter is his Spirator together with the Father. Along with this, when they deny that there is a head of the Church, the holy Roman Church, they clearly dissolve the unity of the Mystical Body, for they cannot be a single body if there is not a single head, any more than a community without a ruler."

8 For the sacramental interpretation of the blood and water, see E. C. Hoskyns, *The Fourth Gospel* (2nd ed., 1947), p. 552 ff.

9 Thus Hoskyns, *op. cit.*, pp. 530, 532; L. S. Thornton in *The Apostolic Ministry* (London, 1946), p. 98 ff., and an allusion in *The Common Life in the Body of Christ* (2nd ed., 1944), p. 416. The same idea is taken up by Mascall, *Christ, the Christian and the Church* (London, 1946), p. 133.

10 Hoskyns, "Genesis 1-3 and St. John's Gospel," *Journal of Theological Studies* 21 (1920), pp. 210-218; cf. 215; *The Fourth Gospel*, p. 547.

11 The encyclical *Mystici Corporis*, 1943, says: "The divine Redeemer sent the Spirit of truth, who, performing his own function. . . ."

12 Apoc 7:17; Jo 16:13—the same word in each case. Cf. Swete, *op. cit.*, p. 357.

13 This is shown in the letters to the seven Churches of the Apocalypse. They are called upon to hear "what the Spirit says to the Churches" (Apoc 2:7, 11, 17, 29; 3:6, 13, 22), yet, at the beginning of each message, it is Christ who is said to be speaking (Apoc 2:1, 8, 12, 18; 3:1, 7, 14).

14 Cf. Jo 6:62-63 (everything to do with "spirit" involves the action of the "Spirit"); according to St. Paul, the Eucharist and the Spirit both produce the same effect, namely, the unity of a single body (I Cor 5:17 and 12:13; Eph 4:4).

15 Analogies between the Spirit's coming at baptism and his coming at the Annunciation (cf. Swete, *op. cit.*, p. 46), between the bond that John (3:4) points to between the Spirit and the water and that existing between the Word and the flesh. Manning proposed, at the Vatican Council, that the bond between the Holy Spirit and the Church should be conceived "according to the analogy of the Incarnation, without however any *hypostatic* union."

16 Christ was with his own (Jo 15:5), who were to remain in him, with him, and keep his word; they would do this by the Holy Spirit (Jo 14:25 ff.; 16:22 ff.).

17 This is quite usual in Anglican writers, whose ecclesiology is closely linked with the Incarnation. See, in particular, Wotherspoon, *The Ministry in the Church in Relation to Prophecy and Spiritual Gifts* (London, 1916), p. 103 ff.

18 Christ taught. His disciples were to understand later. There is a whole theology of the apostolic witness and of the relation between Scripture and Tradition to be developed in this connection.

19 This is clear enough in the New Testament. Polycarp, bishop of Smyrna, is qualified as an "apostolic and prophetic teacher" (*Mart. Polyc.* 16, 2); the *Didache* (15, 1) requires the election of bishops and deacons worthy of the Lord, men who are mild, disinterested, truthful, and proven, "for they too fulfill, in your regard, the ministry of prophets and teachers."

If we read the epistle of Polycarp, bearing in mind the charismatic title given to him, we will be little likely to fall into the temptation of forming a romantic idea of the charisms and their possessors. The whole work has a classical and balanced quality.

CHAPTER **14** *The Layman's Position in the Church**

by F. X. ARNOLD

AUTHOR: F. X. Arnold is professor of pastoral theology at the University of Tübingen and the author of a four-volume history of pastoral theology. He is a recognized authority on the theology of the layman and has published extensively on this topic.

ARTICLE: Father Arnold outlines the historical developments that in the past have somewhat obscured the importance of the layman in the life of the Church and endeavors to give a balanced account of the essential role of the laity within the Body of Christ, the complementary contributions of clerical and lay Christians to the well-being of the Church, and in particular the unique opportunity laymen have to serve the Church precisely as Christians working *in the world* and dedicated to the gradual transformation of the world into a Christocentric cosmos glorifying the victorious Lord of history.

READINGS: An excellent group of essays on the position of the layman in the Church in America is collected in *The Layman in the Church* (edited by James O'Gara; Herder and Herder, 1963).

---

* "The Layman's Position in the Church" was originally published in *Worship* 37 (1963), pp. 388-398. It is reprinted with permission.

A LMOST TOO much has been spoken and written on the subject of the layman since Pope Pius XI, open to contemporary problems to a degree few theologians have equalled, began his pontificate in 1922 with a call to the laity to "participation in the apostolate." The matter has been discussed so much that a person might well fear being led into sterile theological verbosity when producing another article on it. No affirmation about the rights of the layman, sincere and emphatic as it may be, seems able at times to allay the suspicion that "they preach a mature laity but really want a docile laity."

It is hard to remove this latent crisis of mutual confidence between ecclesiastical leadership and enterprising laity. The mistrust feeds on the suspicion that ecclesiastical authorities and their theologians are not really serious about the maturity of laymen that they talk about so much. What they assign to the layman in practice is usually an extremely subordinate role, one that does justice neither to his abilities nor to his claim to status.

If we want to advance this problem, we cannot remain with questions on which agreement has been reached, at least in theory. Nevertheless, we must at least cursorily examine those great truths without which the dignity and vocation of the layman would not be evident. Hence a glance at the *Church in its entirety* is called for first of all. For it is false to consider the laity in isolation, as if they were a group of persons who exist alongside the Church or in contradistinction to her.

The Lay State Isolated

The lay state must be understood as a genuine, essential, and integrating component of the Church herself. The layman doesn't just "belong" to the Church. The laity themselves *are the Church*, Pius XII declared. In fact, the Church is unthinkable without the layman. This state of affairs can best be corroborated by the fact that the biblical word *laos,* from which the term 'lay' derives etymologically, originally did not mean the 'people' in contrast to the 'leader,' but rather *all* the baptized—clergy *and* laity. It included both together as the chosen 'people of God' by way of contrast to heathens.

Even when, somewhat later, colloquial speech referred to the 'laity,' the people gathered for worship, as to a group distinct from the official leaders of worship, 'lay' still did not mean a civil or secular status. Rather it signified a sacral-ecclesial status; it was a concept associated with cult and liturgy. The layman was aware that together with the clergy he constituted the people of God.

The opposite of the laity was originally not the clergy or even the Church, but the world hostile to God. It was only after Constantine the Great that the laity began to view its pole of opposition no longer in the 'world' but in the clergy. The conflict between Church and world, between Church and state, had been eliminated. As a result of the reconciliation the clergy became a rank in its own right, and not only in a religious, theological sense, as it had been until then; now it also became a distinct social class, privileged by civil law. The subsequent centuries-long dispute between 'spiritual' and 'secular,' between *imperium* and *sacerdotium,* gave rise to the popular opinion that the Church was an affair of the clergy, and that the laity belonged to the 'secular' class.

More and more the position of the layman shifted, as a matter of principle, into the area of the 'profane.' Nor was the 'profane' regarded any longer as an 'ante-room' to the sanctuary, as the term originally indicated. Rather it stood for the opposite of holy. The modern label 'laicism' shows how much the relationship between Church and laity has evolved in contemporary terminology in the direction of diametrically opposed poles. It would appear that the layman no longer had anything to do with the Church and that the Church had no concern about the layman's world.

Stemming from a long and tragic development, this distinction between the world of the Church and the world of the layman destroyed the unity and wholeness of the Church in the consciousness of many generations. We have to restore these concepts by patient labor. For the originally existing order of relationships is valid *for all times.* That is precisely what Cardinal Newman, that bold spokesman for the laity in the nineteenth century, meant by the expression: "The Church without the laity is meaningless." We have to stop regarding the lay state as something isolated and separate. A *total view* of the Church is needed.

This total view, however, requires overcoming to some extent Counter-Reformation positions and the consequent hardening of Catholic thought about the Church. In its defense against anti-hierarchical tendencies, the Counter-Reformation had exaggerated, as might have been expected, the hierarchical factor at the expense of the lay state. Thus the impression could arise that the Catholic Church regarded herself quite simply as "the Church of the clergy, consisting of pope, bishop, and priest." Only they have full rights of fellowship and citizenship in the Church; the laymen are the 'clients,' the people to be instructed and guided, the 'object' of the hierarchy's activity.

An Integrating Approach

The truth, of course, is that the pope is not the Church; he is rather the rock on which the Church is built and the manifestation of her unity. Pope, bishop, and priest are not the Church; they are teachers, shepherds, and servants of the Church. Cyprian calls them the *pleroma,* fullness, of the Church, just as the people in their turn are the *pleroma,* fullness, of the hierarchy.

Christ's Church could not exist as a hierarchy without a people; but neither could it exist as a people without priests.

Where Peter is, where the bishop is, there is the Church. But the obverse is also true: where the Church is, there is Peter, there is the bishop. One is not possible without the other. *Both* principles are necessary: the hierarchical principle of command and subordination, as well as the community principle binding together clergy and laity. That is what the nature of the Church requires, because she is a unified organism. There is a unity in the multiplicity of her members, union in freedom and freedom in union. "Hierarchy without brotherliness would be paternalism; brotherliness without hierarchy would be false democracy," says Congar.

Unquestionably, hierarchy implies command, subordination, and obedience. But anyone who regards the Church solely or primarily from this viewpoint runs the risk of reducing the hierarchy (as Rudolph Sohm did) to a system for putting consciousness under tutelage and enslaving them. Such a system would leave no place for freedom, initiative, and personal responsibility on the part of the layman.

The Church, on the contrary, though conscious of her hierarchical structure, also and indeed primarily sees herself as Paul did, from the viewpoint of the common membership in and responsibility of *all* the baptized to the one body and priesthood of the glorified Lord. Anyone who takes that grand and total pneumatic view seriously knows that dignity and freedom and apostolic mission in the Church are not the privilege of a leading caste. They are the inherited right and the inalienable duty of every single Christian person. That was how Peter saw the Church when he extolled the totality of the faithful as the one holy people and the royal priesthood of the new covenant.

[317]

The thought of Leo the Great and Augustine points in the same direction: that the one sacrament of high priesthood is operative in the whole body of the Church and makes all members of one priest, Christ. That too is what Thomas Aquinas meant with his too little noticed teaching about the entire *societas sanctorum* cooperating, through faith and charity, through petition and reparation, in the forgiving of sins and the conferring of grace. And the Roman Cathechism, the most official of all catechisms, as well as Peter Canisius, similarly speaks of the Church in terms of the spiritual communion and the commonwealth of grace of all her members.

But then the struggle with the Reformers, who viewed the Church as a 'people without a priest' and without a hierarchy, clouded the vision of Catholics in regard to the general priesthood, dignity, and mission of the layman, and obscured the unifying pneumatic image of the Church. Only in recent times has the narrowed concept of the Church which these polemics occasioned been overcome on the part of Catholics by a truly Johannine pneumatic theology.

This theology began with Sailer and Möhler during the transition from the Enlightenment to Romanticism, continued in the liturgical and kerygmatic movements of the twentieth century, and climaxed in the great encyclicals of the recent popes. Möhler's message of the Church as a people quickened by the Spirit; the awakening of the whole Christian people and their becoming a worshiping community through the liturgical renewal; the call of the latest popes to participation in the apostolate by the laity; and especially the encyclicals of Pius XII on the liturgy and on the Church as the Body of Christ—these have, to use Congar's words, taken up in a positive way "the Protestant side of the Church" without detriment to Catholic dogma and hierarchy. They have paved the way for a reawakening of the laity and for a renewal of the total view of the Church in the spirit of Christian antiquity and the best theological tradition.

The general priesthood has been seen anew. The liturgical activity of the layman has taken shape more and more. His share in the theological dialogue and writing of the period has increased. All this unquestionably must be counted among the most hopeful phenomena of the Church's life in this century. This is the image of the Church in the light of which the laity must be viewed both religiously and theologically.

It follows that the Church and her activities can only be rightly seen and shaped if, as in ancient times, *two aspects* are simultaneously observed and maintained. On the one hand, the view of the Church as the institution established from above by God through Christ and existing *before* the faithful, with hierarchical ranks and fullness of powers, must be safeguarded. But on the other hand, we must also retain the view of the Church as the fellowship and holiness-conferring community of the faithful, ever renewing herself *from below* through the faith and charity of her members. The first aspect emphasizes the structure and formation of the Church through the hierarchical principle. The second gives due prominence to the sacral status and active function of all the baptized.

Complementaries in Action

What this means in detail will be clear if we apply both aspects to the *modes of activity of the Church*. First of all, as regards the service of the word and of the faith, i.e., the prophetic element or the teaching office of the Church, it is without question exclusively a matter for the hierarchy and its authority to make doctrinal decisions, to formulate and proclaim dogma. The Church's people are bound by these decisions and have to listen to and obey them. But the Church's service to the word

[319]

and to faith is not exhausted in a simple formulation and proclamation of dogma. *All* members of the Church have to bear witness. The faith has been entrusted to all of them. That is why in ancient times the Apostles' Creed was entrusted to the candidates for baptism, who then gave witness by reciting it publicly. Every baptized person is both bearer and subject of the testimony to God's word and command.

But baptism finds completion in confirmation, the sacrament of Christian majority, of the maturity and fullness of Christian personality. The Christian may not barricade himself against the public. Confirmation consecrates him to an ecclesial ministry to the world, to independent responsibility and initiative in the world, to the apostolate. He is called to a confession of faith, a confession corresponding to his situation. The task of the layman is thus determined by his position *in* the world: not by renunciation *of* the world, but by entry into this world and its milieus. To this the layman is not only called, but also empowered by the graces of baptism, confirmation, and marriage. Congar, therefore, is not exaggerating when he calls the laity a garden of faith within the Church and in the very midst of the world.

The ways in which the layman can and often has proved himself as the garden of faith are many. *Parents* pass the faith on to their children. It is not enough to have the children baptized and then depend upon the catechist to instruct them. Far more significant is education in the faith by the father and mother through the unconscious assimilation of the believing atmosphere of the parental home. Augustine, who as few others experienced what a mother can mean for the faith of her son, does not hesitate to address parents, especially the father, as "my fellow bishops."

Besides the parents, there is the *community,* the *general public.* These too can advance faith or destroy faith.

One need only think of the press, its direct and immediate influence upon millions. It can bear witness to God's word and command to countless people whom the priest's word doesn't reach. For that reason, among others, a press is needed which does not live in a ghetto, but preaches from the housetops.

The teaching authority of the hierarchy *and* the witnessing of the laity in the world—only if *both* collaborate closely does the prophetic ministry of the Church achieve its role. Viewed historically the witnessing, the confession, preceded and precedes the formulated dogma. First of all there was the message, the confession, and only after that the dogma. On this point Martin Dibelius was right. There were periods in the Church's history in which the witness of the believing *people* in the battle against Arius or against the rationalism of the eighteenth century sometimes proved more powerful than the word of their spiritual leaders.

And aren't there still situations in our own times in which the witness of a layman carries more weight than the statement of an ecclesiastical official? Aren't there quite a few people who pay attention when a layman testifies, but who shut their minds to the words of a priest? "The priest has to talk like that," they say. But if a layman speaks of God and confesses the faith, a famous physicist, for example, or a courageous laborer, this suspicion disappears. What would dogma be today without the witness of the faithful?

As in the case of the service of the word, so too the *service of the altar* requires not only the official priestly action but also the liturgical activity of the layman. Doubtless it is exclusively the privilege of the ordained priest to make present by means of the consecration the sacrificial offering of Christ on the altar. But the celebration of Mass is more than consecration alone. It is the sacrifice of the *whole* Church, the common sacrificial offering of Christians; it is the thanksgiving, the *eucharistia*, of the plenary assembly of Christ's members for the Gift that he has become for us. All are called to spiritual collaboration in the liturgical action and then to its moral completion in *agape*, benevolent love. Only if *both*, priest and people, collaborate actively does the priestly liturgical ministry of the Church find its full expression. That is the leading idea of Pius XII's liturgical encyclical *Mediator Dei* of 1947.

Union with the hierarchical structure of the Church does not mean the exclusion and destruction of the layman's own spiritual life and freedom. It does not mean that the freedom of a Christian person is reserved for a clerical leader caste, as Rudolph Sohm maintained. Hierarchy in its deepest sense does not mean dominion but service, ministry; not *dominium* but *ministerium*. It is only its humanly deficient excerise, not the office as such, that endangers the freedom and initiative of the laity.

Correctly understood, hierarchy does not mean the inhibition but the releasing of lay initiative, its guarantee, a guidance that innures attainment of the goal. Because it is anchored in the mystery of Christ, says Karl Adam, the ecclesiastical ministry saves the laity from domination of the part of Führer personalities. The believer recognizes in the priestly office Christ's ministering love and feels himself thereby united with Christ, the Head of the Church. On his part, the bearer of the priestly office is stimulated to the fullest and most selfless service of his brothers by the knowledge that he is Christ's servant.

The priest's task is not so much to rule the laity as to inspire them; to enrich even more than to preside. Not only does the layman have to listen to the priest, the priest must also listen to the layman. Cyprian, a bishop of Christian antiquity, wrote to this effect in a letter to his priests and deacons. "From the beginning of my episcopate I resolved to do nothing without your advice and the concurrence of the people" (*Ep.* 15: 4). In this way Christianity and the Church fulfill the ideal of becoming a mutually helpful community.

These theological considerations have an eminently practical bearing; for without a recognition of these truths and without the admittance of the layman to the service of the word and the altar, he will lack motivation and his actions will have no impact on the world.

Approaches to Reality

But it is precisely *in the world* that the Christian layman has his specific work to do. To the layman is assigned "the consecration of the world," to use the expression of Pius XII. Of course, the layman's vocation also has, like that of the priest, an orientation to the things of heaven. Both vocations share the heavenly inheritance; both are called to eternal salvation. But not in precisely the same manner. There must be people in the Church who are directly and exclusively concerned about the kingdom of God. That is the task of priests and monks. They are, as was the tribe of Levi, freed from planned engagement in the work of the world.

The case of the laity is different. Their business is a planned and direct engagement in this world. Unlike the monk, the layman does not have to live exclusively for heavenly realities. He has God's work to do *in this world,* as this is to be done in the world according to the Creator's will. Consequently, the relationship and the way of the layman to the final goal is less direct and exclusive. It leads of necessity *through* and *by means of* the things of this world.

Hence the attitude of the layman to the things of this world differs from that of the priest. The layman must be concerned about the substance of earthly things themselves, in and for themselves. For the priest, on the contrary, the things of this world are not so much significant in themselves, but only insofar as they have a relationship to God and to souls. This involvement with the transcendent brings with it the danger of minimizing the immanent intrinsic value of the things of this world: respect for the inner truth and essential dignity of wordly things can easily be lost sight of.

The 'purely Christian' viewpoint can easily lead to one that is Christian in name only, to the neglect of the spirit of dedicated scientific research and labor in the various fields of knowledge. History teaches us that the undue involvement of theologians in the worldly domain, without the necessary expert competence in the respective area of specialization, has not infrequently led to an attempted tutelage of a world and of a scientific research that had long since come of age. We need only recall the classic example of Galileo. Is the embittered this-worldliness of modern times perhaps a reaction to such exaggerated other-worldliness?

Even in post-Tridentine Catholicism, Friedrich von Hügel believed it necessary to lament an attitude of stubborn resistance and fearful mistrust towards the contemporary world and, as a consequence, a lack of "incarnational power." He considered this lack of essential cause of the estrangement from God in the contemporary world. For him there was a causal connection between a 'godless world' and a 'worldless religion.' Hence the estrangement from religion and the Church on the part of specialists, scientists, and politicians that did occur was not founded in the nature of things themselves.

The order of salvation does not abrogate the order of nature, but rather presupposes it. There is an intrinsic, even if not absolute, autonomy of the branches of civilized learning within this world. In these the expert, the specialist, alone is competent, not the theologian. Scientists, physicists, chemists, technicians have the task of investigating and of making useful the laws and potentialities of the universe from the nature of things themselves.

Biology does this for the laws of organic life. The economics scholar has to draw the principles of economic laws from established data and from experience, not from the Bible. Similarly the politician is limited in his decisions to act or not to act by the possibilities and necessities inherent in any given situation. In all fields the most exact special competence possible in the respective area of reality is needed to act rightly and objectively.

But because every isolated field of learning always furnishes only partial aspects of the total reality, it needs completion and perfection through other sciences which deal with the same material from different aspects. But even this synthesis of the various partial aspects can lead to the full truth only if the acquired specialized knowledge is viewed in its relation to the entire cosmos and to the whole of human existence. Every single branch of civilized learning has to be assigned its place, rank, and meaning in a universal system, in a proper hierarchy of values.

We all recognize how the very existence of humanity today depends upon whether the demands of technology, economics, and politics can be successfully fitted into the broader context of human values and of human community life. These sciences have gradually become extremely powerful and are clamoring for total autonomy. As never before, the recent developments of technology have imposed upon us the pressing duty of a concern for the right use of matter and for a proper ordering of human social life.

The Layman's Incarnational Service

In all of this we have been discussing the role of the layman in the world today. It has become more vitally important than ever before. His service to the world and in the world dare not consist in a retreat to a Christian ghetto. Nor can it be restricted to moral trumpeting from the heights of a safe bastion. What is required is the genuine incarnational entry of the layman into the world and its milieus, a genuine and serious acceptance of the world and work in it, new forms of Christian incarnationalism.

What the worker, the technologist, the economist demand today is not condescension and pity, but recognition and esteem for their rank. They seek the recognition that their sciences and their services to the world are included in God's plan of salvation. A new heaven *and a new earth* have been promised us for the day of Christ at the end of time. According to divine revelation, therefore, not only the Church and its activity in the care of souls is ordered to this 'kingdom of God,' but also all the rest of creation, of which the Logos is the Head: that is to say, the entire universe and the service of the layman to it.

The world in which we live is something and the work that we do for and in this world is something. The eternal Logos did not become man for nothing. He entered the world in order to bring it home with him on that day when "God will be all things in all and everything will be subject to him" (I Cor 15:28). In this hope we—priests and laymen—do our work in the Church and in the world. Whatever the work may be, it always carries with it the possibility of service to God and fellow man with a view to the fulfillment at the end of time.

CHAPTER **15** *The Mystery of*
*Religious Life**

by HENRI HOLSTEIN, S.J.

AUTHOR: Henri Holstein is on the staff of *Études,* the monthly
journal of opinion published by the Jesuits of France. He has
published and lectured extensively on a variety of subjects in
the areas of fundamental theology and the contemporary life
of the Church.

ARTICLE: As a complement to Father Arnold's discussion of the
layman's role in the Church, the present selection presents the
mission of religious life in the service of the Church. It attempts to make religious life meaningful not to religious themselves but rather to lay Christians, who can learn from it the
importance of the apostolic activity and public witness which
make religious life so valuable for the Church as a whole and
such a source of pride for all Christians. Religious are not
Christians who somehow extricate themselves from the business of Christianity's basic mission to the world. Rather they
partake of this mission by striving to realize the fullness of
Christian life in themselves and, even apart from directly apostolic activities, to manifest to the world by this fullness of life
the reality of Christ and his Church. Father Holstein is concerned that lay Christians appreciate the *primary,* and not
merely the surface, values of religious life and understand its
cooperative mission in the common apostolate of all Christians
to witness to Christ in a world that does not know him.

* "The Mystery of Religious Life" first appeared in English in *Review
for Religious* 20 (1961), pp. 317-329. It is reprinted here with permission.

[327]

READINGS: A stimulating analysis of religious life in comparison with the life of a lay Christian is found in *Toward a Theology of the Layman* (Herder & Herder, 1963), by John Gerken, S.J.

R ELIGIOUS LIFE [1] interests contemporary man; this interest, in fact, constitutes one of the curious paradoxes of our times. However surprising and unexpected this may seem to be, our contemporaries' interest in religious life is shown by the success of the novelized memoirs of ex-religious, especially when they are transposed to the film. Books about religious are a financial success; this is true even in the case of expensive publications like the recent volume of Messrs. Serrou and Vals on the Poor Clares; [2] this volume, illustrated by remarkable photographs that give the reader a realization of the life of the religious, is a continuation of a series on various contemplative orders of men and women.

Mlle. Cita-Malard, who lived with the permission of the Holy See within the cloister of most of the important orders of women and who is able to make them known in an intelligent and respectful fashion, has published a brief, well-written volume to introduce French readers to "a million religious women." [3] And on the stage in Paris, Claudel's *Diégo Fabri* presents the Jesuits [4] to an audience which from all appearances is deeply attentive and thoughtful—and despite a somewhat flamboyant plot. (The playwright has imagined the action on the frontiers of that part of the world cut off by the Iron Curtain, and here the problem of the contemporary apostolate is placed.)

What is the source of this interest and curiosity which in general is sympathetic even if it is aroused by anecdotal or vestimentary details rather than by what is essential to religious life? I believe the reason is that religious life poses a problem for modern man; in its own way religious life is a sign of contradiction which angers, shocks, impresses, and at time arouses inescapable questions. If one reflects and considers the matter, religious life by its demands and by its numbers is a social fact to which modern man can not remain indifferent, desacralized as he is and living in a paganized atmosphere. This has been stated by Cita-Malard when she writes of religious women, the number of whom she estimates to be a million:

> Isn't it a paradox that out of two and a half billion human beings and out of about five hundred million Catholics, one million women have renounced forever— and in most cases even before personal experience in the matter—the pleasures and the servitudes of the flesh, and that they have stripped themselves of everything, even their own will, either to follow publicly the strict and minute obligations which impose a common life on them or to free themselves for a more or less hidden apostolate in their milieu and profession, an apostolate which makes of their life an oblation without reserve? What they have pledged themselves to is directly opposed to the liberties claimed by our independent, self-centered, sensual age.[5]

To this situation, so loudly underscored by the indiscreet means of communication of our era, only we Catholics can bring the answer by our life and our witness. Doubtless, this witness will come from religious themselves, for even if people do not admit it to us they nevertheless watch us, since the religious dress and way of life attract public attention; but this witness will come especially from Catholics who should be able to explain to any man of good will what "religious life" in the Catholic Church means. Accordingly, our task is to present here

the principles we must know in a kind of theological synthesis, and give in a simple way the constitutive essentials
of the religious life.

Of the two parts of this discussion, the first will examine religious life as the fullness of baptism; the second
will emphasize the nature of the witness given in and for
the Church by the religious who is a witness of heaven as
well as a witness of the love of Jesus Christ for all men,
our brothers.

Religious Life: The Fullness of Baptism

"Religious life," canon law tells us, "is a stable and
community way of life in which the faithful besides the
precepts common to all propose to observe as well the
evangelical counsels through the vows of obedience,[6] chastity, and poverty" (c. 487).

In analyzing the obligations of religious life, this legal
text first mentions the precepts common to all Christians
to which, it is evident, religious are also bound. It then
adds that besides these religious take on the observance of
the evangelical counsels, obligating themselves to these
by the observance of the required vows lived out not in
isolation but—as far as there is question of religious life
in the proper sense of the term—in a stable and community life.

This description might seem to say that religious life
claims of those who profess it something more than the
Church demands of "ordinary Christians." This, however,
would not be completely exact. Our Lord's command to
be perfect as the heavenly Father holds for all: the exi-
gencies of baptism are the same for all the faithful. But
the religious, in responding to a call that comes from our
Lord and is acknowledged as such by the Church when she
admits to the vows of religion, intends to live this baptismal perfection in a radical way that by a definitive and

irrevocable intention suppresses the obstacles that might hinder or retard his fervor.

"Every Christian," Pius XII said, "is invited to strive with all his powers for the ideal of Christian perfection; but it is realized in a more complete and sure way in the states of perfection." [7]

In religious life there is no question of a Christian ideal of life other than that imposed on every baptized person; it is rather a matter of a complete and total effort to live out in an authentic way the life begun by baptism. The same program of perfection is proposed to all; the Gospel is directed to all Christians; religious know no other code of perfection. The originality of religious consists in the adoption of radical means which permit them to give full realization to their baptism; this is done in a prescribed and organic way within an institute or religious family approved by the Church.

In response to a call of our Lord, there takes place at the beginning and origin of religious life a consecration which is complete and irrevocable for the heart which makes it even before the person's lips are authorized to formulate it publicly before the Church. The consecration, which has all the fervor and generosity of those espousals with our Lord of which St. Paul speaks, is a clear-sighted and exacting renewal of baptismal consecration.

The life of every Christian is a consecrated one, since an ineradicable character marks it with the baptismal participation in the death and resurrection of Christ. Every baptized person is conformed to Christ; that is, he is regenerated in his likeness, is a member of his Body, and in him is an adopted son of the Father. Religious profession is not a second baptism: there can be no such thing, but only renewals, more or less fervent, of the baptismal promises. Religious profession—and this is its grandeur and its seriousness—is a decisive act which binds the one who makes it to the obligation of a strict living out of his baptism by forbidding to him everything which could be opposed to the life of the new man.

The negative aspects of religious life—separation, renouncement, despoiling—which are the first things to capture the attention of the general public as well as of relatives who are present at an investiture or a profession, are nothing else than the execution of this program of radical renouncement which baptism implies. "We are dead with Christ . . ." says St. Paul. "Regard yourselves as dead to sin and living for God in Christ Jesus. Let sin rule no longer in your mortal body . . ." (Rom 6:8-12).

The demands of baptism are understood by the religious with a total fullness. If it is necessary to renounce sin, then it is necessary to separate oneself from all the occasions of sin, from everything which would be capable of attaching us to a master other than Christ, from that world for which Christ refused to pray. To renounce sin, says St. Paul, is to refuse to submit to lust. Accordingly, the religious renounces those earthly lusts which are represented by money, by the body, and by self-will; he separates himself from these by his vows of poverty, chastity, and obedience which in their very austerity represent for him a welcome liberation.

In this there is no unconscious self-pity or masochism. There is only the liberating conclusion of a logic which dares to take literally and without gloss or casuistry the abrupt words of the Gospel. Ever since an Anthony left his town and his family to bury himself in the desert when he heard read in church the gospel message, "Go, sell what you own," and ever since a Francis of Assisi despoiled himself of all he possessed and returned it all—even his clothing—to his father, religious life has known the joyous liberty of understanding our Lord literally and of leaving all to follow him.

This would be a childishly imprudent act were it not

dictated by a total confidence in the promise of our Lord. "The folly of youth," say the wise, when they hear of young men and young women who joyfully put themselves within the cloister or who bring themselves to enclose their whole lives within the barriers of obedience and chastity. But it is not the folly of youth; it is the folly of God who is wiser than the wisdom of the prudent. For it is not self-confidence which brings a person to religious life; and if one should enter in a burst of enthusiasm, the long months of the novitiate would suffice to extinguish it. What leads one to religion is a humble confidence in our Lord who calls, a confidence that is capable of checking an understandable apprehension and even at times a fear bordering on panic. Like St. Peter, the religious makes up his mind to let down the net only at the word of Jesus.

And when the inevitable illusions of the first fervor have yielded place to that maturity of religious life which has been described so profoundly and accurately by Father Voillaume in his recent *Lettres aux fraternités* of the Little Brothers of Jesus, then there appears in all its naked grace the power of hope to sustain the religious. More than in his early days, he realizes that what he proposes is humanly senseless; but he also realizes that the power of our Lord sustains him day after day and that it allows him to advance up the steep road which he has chosen. Those who come to us, Ignatius of Loyola used to say to his first companions, must pray over it for a long time so that "the Spirit who urges them may also give them the grace of hoping to be able to carry the weight of their vocation with his aid." [8]

But religious life must not be defined by its negative characteristics, as though a religious placed his happiness in the restrictions of strict cloister and of stifling prohibitions. The truth about religious life—and unfortunately this was left in the shadows in the memoirs of Sister Luke —is that it is the road on which one accompanies Christ as closely as possible; it is the means of imitating and following him as loyally as human weakness permits. If he avoids the sources of earthly desires, the religious knows very well that this is done only to remove the obstacles which spring up between him and Christ. "Whoever wishes to be my disciple," said Christ, "must renounce himself, take up his cross, and follow me." It is not a case of the cross for the sake of the cross nor suffering for the sake of suffering; it is for the sake of being with Jesus. As Charles de Foucauld wrote in his notes:

> I cannot conceive of a love [of Christ] without an overwhelming craving for likeness, for resemblance, and above all for a share in the pains, difficulties, and hardships of life. . . . To be rich, comfortable, living contentedly with my possessions when *you* were poor, uncomfortable, living a painful life of hard labor for me. . . . I cannot love *you* in such a way.

The separation and the renouncements of religious life which each day accomplish in the religious the "death with Christ" of his baptism are considered by him as so many means of resurrecting with Christ. Better still, his vows appear to him as the attitudes of a person already resurrected.

For religious life is not a life of dying, it is a resurrected life. The Lord who is followed is not only the poor workman of Nazareth and the crucified one of Golgotha. He is also the Lord of glory, who appeared on the radiant morning of Easter. And the One to whom virgins give themselves on the morning of their profession and whom they choose as their Spouse is not only the agonizing Christ of Gethsemane but is as well the Lamb in the paschal splendor of his triumph. Already they belong to the procession of virgins who follow the Lamb wherever he goes; their virginal promise is the beginning of the eternal espousals which the Lamb intends to anticipate with them here on earth.

By virginity, Christ becomes the only Spouse of their

heart. At first view, the vow of chastity is a refusal. Its effect seems to be that of a total renouncement—renouncement of the senses, renouncement of affection, renouncement of a family. It demands that one leave his family; and it forbids all hope of ever founding a family. In reality, however, the vow of chastity is an assuming of a total and exclusive belonging to the Lord. The religious who assumes it refuses all idea of a partial belonging; thereby he expresses his desire for that total consecration which religious life realizes as the fullness of baptism. This is the behavior of the new man for whom nothing of the old man, nothing of the partial, nothing of the worldly can make sense.

Furthermore, chastity gives its meaning to the vows of poverty and obedience which in turn give to it their own dimension not of repression, but of a complete spiritual expansion in total love. For poverty is not the sad acceptance of small privations and of petty dependence; it is the gesture of confidence by one who is no longer anxious about those things which the heavenly Father knows we have need of. Moreover, poverty is a refusal to be weighed down by the things of earth and by the cares which afflict those who possess things, making them always fearful of losing or decreasing their precious little treasures. The religious knows of another treasure: the love of our Lord which leaves him no time to be occupied in the acquiring of riches, the manipulation of capital, and the preserving of property. Poverty is the testimony of the love given to the divine Spouse by one who has chosen him in an undivided way. Not only does the religious place his confidence in him with regard to his temporal life, he also detaches himself from every self-anxiety and from the monopolizing desire for possessions, doing this in order that he might give himself wholly to the Spouse of his soul. Chastity, which is the choosing of our Lord alone, and poverty, which refuses to allow a person to be monopolized by any selfish interest, mutually complement each other.

And by the conjunction of these two, obedience receives all its meaning. Obedience can easily appear to be an infantile submission; actually in the eyes of faith it is a preferring of the will of God. Defined in the negative terms of renouncement of initiative and independence, obedience is a caricature that is ridiculous and hateful. It has value only so far as it is an ardent search for the good pleasure of the One who is loved. Christ himself said that his food was to do the will of his Father. Accordingly, the religious has only one nourishment: the will of our Lord which is the will of the Father who is the only guide of the activity of the only begotten Son. "I always do whatever is pleasing to him."

The superior, this brother or this sister who commands me, is important for me only because he represents Christ. "The abbot," says St. Benedict, "takes the place of Christ." It is Christ whom through faith I hear and see in my superior. The man does not interest me, even though he be a saint, a genius, or a dear friend. It is Christ who is the object of my obedience; it is to him that I render my homage in performing what is commanded me in his name. There is good reason for saying that "obedience is an attitude of faith and love only if it is chaste; that is, if it is inspired by the exclusive love of our Lord." Otherwise it becomes degraded and turns into an interested conformism or into an unacceptable infantilism.

In religious life, all the elements are consistent with each other; chastity, which is an espousal and a consecration to Christ, gives its own characteristic mark to a life that is poor and dependent through obedience; for these two vows, if they are to be genuine in both great and little things, imply an exclusive choice of Christ as the only Spouse of one's soul.

This is why there must be a question here of vows, of statutory promise which oblige one's whole life, thereby surpassing the unstable impulse of a moment of fervor.

Love demands definitive commitments, it engages the whole life, it gives assurance for the future.

All this which among men is often only an illusion which the future may soon contradict unless the love is rooted in prayer and nourished by recollection is made possible for the religious by his original and constantly renewed confidence in the grace of him who has called.

The religious vow is the instrument of that consecration which realizes the baptismal consecration in all the plenitude of its demands. If at first view it appears as an all-out effort to exclude and eradicate the obstacles which are opposed to the perfection of baptismal life, nevertheless the religious vow signifies the total consecration of one's whole life to our Lord. It is included in the initial "consecration" which Christ made when he came into the world: "I have come, O Father, to do your will!" The Servant has no other intention than that of accomplishing the work for which he was sent into the world; for that reason his sole occupation will be to do the will of the Father. In line with this consecration of our Lord and in participation of this "intention" of the Incarnate Word, the religious places himself in the hands of God. As Father Bergh has said:

> The vow is the expression of a positive consecration to divine love. God loved above everything; there in short is the meaning of religious life. . . . Its program should not be enunciated precisely in the abstract terms of poverty, chastity, and obedience, but rather under the concrete form of a loving imitation of Christ poor, chaste, and obedient, of Christ the Servant of the Father and of men.[9]

Religious Life a Witness in the Church

Up to this point we have looked at religious life only from the viewpoint of a personal relation that unites it to our Lord. Now, however, it is necessary to consider it in the Church. To do this, we shall consider two points: first, the significance of religious life in relation to the Church; and second, the testimony to the Church which religious life gives to the world.

What then does religious life signify in relation to the Church? In other words, why does the Church, without whose consent there could not be a community or an institute professing the life of the counsels, recognize among her baptized children the existence of groups which in order to live out their baptismal life in a more radical way oblige themselves publicly to the observance of poverty, chastity, and obedience? It seems to me that by the religious life the Church expresses her own proper mystery. The purpose of religious life is to concretize and to give realization to the mystery of the bride who is without spot.

In the admirable fifth chapter of the letter to the Ephesians, St. Paul presents the Church as the bride whom Christ has chosen for himself. In order to make her holy and to "present to himself the Church in all her glory, not having spot or wrinkle," he delivered himself for her. Being submitted to Christ, the Church has for him the deference and respect, the discreet and fervent love which the Bible constantly presents as the expression of the response of the creature to his Creator. This is a virginal union which is consummated in those "nuptials of the Lamb" to which the angel invited the seer of the Apocalypse. "Come, I will show you the spouse of the Lamb . . . And I saw the holy city, the new Jerusalem, coming down from out of heaven from God, made ready as a young bride adorned for her husband" (Apoc 21:9, 2). The holy bride has no gifts other than those given her by her Spouse—the glorious heritage which he acquired by his blood; could she, then, have any other desire than to follow her Spouse and to accomplish his entire will? "The Church," says St. Paul, "submits to Christ" (Eph 5:24).

If all Christian living manifests in its own way the mystery of the Church, isn't it fitting that certain ones should have the particular duty of manifesting the mystery of the virginal bride in its complete authenticity? These are those who among all the redeemed have the singular privilege of following the Lamb wherever he goes. For, "they are virgins." Theirs is an absolute and undivided love which blossoms in holy poverty and loving obedience; it is the mystery of the Church and her consecrated ones.

Through religious life the Church manifests her own proper mystery to herself and to the world. This is why religious life is so dear to her. It is the reason why through the voices of her leaders, especially the recent popes, she never ceases to increase her efforts to maintain the correctness of religious life in its striving for sanctity.

> Holy Mother Church has always striven with solicitous care and maternal affection for the children of her predilection who have given their whole lives to Christ in order to follow him freely on the arduous path of the counsels that she might constantly render them worthy of their heavenly resolve and angelic vision.[10]

Religious, by reason of the vocation which surpasses them and which they know themselves unworthy of, are an intimate witness to the Church herself; at the same time they are a witness of the Church to all those who see them live. Nourished in the Church and directed by her, they bear witness to her and show forth that the Church in its innermost reality is truly the bride whom Christ has chosen for himself.

First of all, religious give testimony to the sense of God. Our modern world has lost this to the extent that even many Christians do not understand the contemplative life; their attitude is a questioning one, "What use is it?" To this I would answer that to judge religious life by its relation to human utility is to condemn oneself to misunderstand it. I readily maintain the paradox that religious life is *not* justified by its usefulness for men—but by its value in the sight of God. In its primary meaning it appears useless to the city of man, for the precise reason that it exists in its entirety for God.

Speaking of contemplation, Cita-Malard quotes the phrase of Joan of Arc, "God, the first to be served." I would be tempted to emphasize this even more by saying, "God—the only one to be served." This is why there are in the Church contemplative orders, monasteries of prayer—Carmelites, Poor Clares, Carthusians, Trappists. Their proper witness is to recall to men the importance of prayer, the urgency of penance, the necessity for adoration.

But this same witness is also given by every genuine religious life. Under pain of an anemia that would quickly become fatal, religious life must always include prayer. It can exist and is able to flourish only by reason of a spirit of prayer which animates every hour of the day, no matter how filled it may be with the care of the sick, the education of children, the help of the aged or the underdeveloped. In order to create a suitable climate, there is added to prayer religious observance, the rule of silence, cloister. One may be tempted to smile at these or to be scandalized by them. Every tradition can manifest a certain rigidity; at times inevitable minutiae may make religious life out-of-date or unadapted to the times. But these are simple human weaknesses which the Church herself will remedy. But to judge religious tradition by such details is to give proof of pettiness of spirit. What is at stake here and what justifies the observances of religious life is the need and the desire to set up a favorable climate for prayer.

For religious life is a present heralding and anticipation of the eternal life to which we are destined by our baptism. It shows forth that this present world is not the only one, but that there exists a true city in comparison with which the city of this world with its bustle and its narrow cares is vanity. This is the often emphasized eschatological meaning of the vow of chastity: it is an anticipation of the life of heaven; on this earth where the body and sensuality count for so much, it represents "the life of angels" as lived by beings of flesh and blood. Turned toward the heavenly Jerusalem, religious already attempt to live that which will be their condition in heaven. "That which we will all be," said St. Ambrose to the virgins of his time, "you have already begun to be. Already in this world, you possess the glory of the resurrection; you live in time, but without the defilements of time. In persevering in chastity, you are the equals of the angels of God."

This eschatological witness must be extended to the entirety of religious life. As Father Giuliani writes:

> Being a complete break with the world, religious life is a witness given to the kingdom of God. Through his life of poverty, chastity, and obedience, the religious makes apparent a reality that is begun here below for all, but which will be revealed in its fullness only in the world of the resurrection. He is poor in order to affirm that God constitutes the riches of the elect in the city of the blessed; he is chaste in order to affirm that there will be no other nuptials other than that of God and his people; he is obedient in order to affirm that the liberty of the creature consists in submission to the full accomplishment of the will of God. Thus it is that in the Church on earth the religious is a witness to the Church of glory.[11]

But at the same time and by a sort of paradox, religious life also manifests in the Church the charity of Christ who willed to share our condition. To present religious life only as an anticipation of heaven risks considering it as a comfortable evasion, a charge often enough directed against it. Are religious dispensed from one of the two facets of the great commandment, the one that commands love of neighbor? God forbid, for then they would no longer be Christians. Besides, one has only to recall the multiplication in the Church of charitable orders, institutes, and congregations to reduce to nothing the objection of laziness and flight made against religious life.

Contrary to this objection, it can be shown that religious life in its essence is a life of devotion to the neighbor. Pius XII in the constitution *Sponsa Christi* stated this unambiguously:

> Since the perfection of Christian life consists especially in charity, and since it is really one and the same charity with which we must love God alone above all and all men in him, Holy Mother Church demands of all nuns who canonically profess a life of contemplation, together with a perfect love of God, also a perfect love of the neighbor; and for the sake of this charity and their state of life, religious men and women must devote themselves wholly to the needs of the Church and of all those who are in want.

If out of love for Christ a religious consecrates himself to only one thing, the following of Christ as closely as possible, then it becomes unthinkable that he should be disinterested in the work of redemption, the salvation of the world. The love of God, which is sovereignly jealous, is also sovereignly generous; this love desires the good, even the temporal good, of all men. The commandment of mutual love is primary for all religious, and religious life gives testimony in the Church to the charity of God.

The witness of religious, then, will be a witness of fraternal charity, of a charity that is patient, inventive, characterized by the unfetterable impulses of missionary zeal, of pedagogical discoveries, of paternal solicitude. Is there a single kind of suffering, of sickness, or of infirmity which religious life has not sought to care for in the course of history? The almost infinite variety of hospital and teaching congregations represent a sort of diffraction of charity towards the neighbor; it is touching to discover at the origin of a given institute the desire to take charge of a particular type of misfortune which seemed to the founder not to have received sufficient care. Although admittedly it is often dispersed, such an attitude is a magnificent and multiform witness given by religious life of a tireless and tirelessly inventive charity, renewed each day by prayer and union with Christ.

This last characteristic must be emphasized. The apostolate and the devotion of religious draw their strength and their constancy from the consecration of their life to the Lord. It is this consecration that enables religious to be kind and sympathetic to the unfortunate and the afflicted. Likewise it is this consecration that makes it possible for a religious to interest himself in *everything that is human,* in science, in literature, in the arts. Did not the Lord who took on himself every infirmity, also assume by his incarnation every authentic human value?

Conclusion

This is the witness to the Church which is constantly given in silence and modesty by religious life. It does not give witness for itself but for the Church, which has inspired, accepted, encouraged, and has ever shown tremendous interest in it. Moreover the religious does not give testimony for his own limited congregation, but for the entire Church of Christ.

Religious life manifests the magnificent fecundity of the Church; Vatican Council I speaks of this. In the fraternal diversity of vocations and spiritualities, religious life is a permanent sign of both the catholicity and the unity of the Church. For on the magnificent path which our Lord calls all of them to follow, there is the same love of Christ, the same faithful adherence to the Gospel as the unique rule of their attitudes, the same charity welcoming every appeal of suffering, of education, of the apostolate. And all this takes place in the calm and serene joy of those who, having given up all for the Lord, know that even here below they have received the hundredfold.

Who are better witnesses than religious of the joy of the children of God and of the children of the Church? True, they have no monopoly on this, for they lay claim to nothing, not even the peace which radiates from their faces. But the joy of their Lord which they always bear about with them—they know well that no one can take this from them.

The joy of religious life is perhaps the most constant and the most efficacious trait of its witness. This is so precisely because it manifests itself spontaneously without being conscious of itself and without imposing itself upon those it meets. Julien Green relates that on a walk in the United States during the war he visited the scholasticate of a religious order. Of the young man who was showing him through the large establishment, he wanted to ask a single question, a question more important to him than all the details of architecture and theological programs that the young man was giving him.

The question he wished to ask would have been addressed to the young man personally, since he was a person whom some would think had enclosed his ardent vitality within the sad walls of a seminary and the complicated prescriptions of a rule. The question was this, "Young man, are you happy here?" But, continues the diary of the novelist, "I did not have the courage to ask the question. For my guide had about him the radiant air of those who feel themselves loved by heaven." [12]

Notes

[1] This article was originally a conference given at the University of Louvain as the conclusion of a series of lectures on religious life.

2 *Les Clarisses: les pauvres dames de sainte Claire d'Assise* (Paris: Horay, 1960).

8 *Un million de religieuses* (Paris: Fayard, 1960).

4 A critical review of this drama was given by P. L. Barjon, S.J., in *Etudes* (February, 1961), pp. 251-257.

5 *Un million de religieuses*, pp. 6-7.

6 In constitutions and new formulas the order is usually reversed: "poverty, chastity, and obedience." Was not the purpose of the legislator, however, to show here the preeminence of the vow of obedience as mentioned in the well-known text of John XXIII on this matter?

7 *Discourse*, December 9, 1957. *Acta Apostolicae Sedis* 50 (1958), p. 36.

8 In *Christus* 7 (1960), p. 250.

9 In *Revue Diocesaine de Tournai* 15 (1960), p. 18.

10 *Acta Apostolicae Sedis* 39 (1947), p. 114.

11 In *Etudes* (June, 1957), p. 397.

12 Julien Green, *Journal*, v. 4, p. 106.

CHAPTER **16** *The Liturgy: 'Action' of the Church**

by I. H. DALMAIS, O.P.

AUTHOR: I. H. Dalmais is on the staff of *Maison-Dieu*, the publication of the influential Parisian Center for Pastoral Studies, and has published a number of articles on various aspects of the liturgy and pastoral life.

ARTICLE: "The Liturgy: 'Action' of the Church" is a selection from Father Dalmais' well-known *Introduction to the Liturgy*, one of the most balanced presentations of the essential nature of the liturgy. The present selection locates the liturgy within the more comprehensive mission of the Church in our day. The liturgy's basic task of uniting Christ's members to the Father in the divinizing worship of the official, visible, communal Church is analyzed as an "action" which both constitutes and symbolizes the Church, the Body of Christ working out its salvation in the course of history in union with its Head.

READINGS: A fine presentation of the liturgy's role in the Church is chapter six of Charles Davis' *Liturgy and Doctrine* (Sheed & Ward, 1960). Joseph Jungmann, S.J., studies the Mass as the sacrifice of the Mystical Body in *The Sacrifice of the Church: The Meaning of the Mass* (Challoner, 1956), chapter 1. A penetrating analysis of the role of private prayer in the Church is offered in chapter three of *Prayer,* by the ex-

* "The Liturgy: 'Action' of the Church" first appeared in English in Father Dalmais' *Introduction to the Liturgy* (Helicon, 1961), pp. 38-48. It is reprinted here with permission.

tremely perceptive Hans Urs von Balthasar (Sheed & Ward, 1962).

―――――――――――――

Liturgy as 'Action' of the Church

W(HAT IS most commonly lacking in our view of the Church is *faith*, which discerns the presence of God at the heart of the most exterior aspects of the Christian mystery. We lack, too, the living experience of the unity of man with himself and with others, through which the union of body and soul and of individual and community are sharply perceived, if not explained. This lack both of living faith and of human wholeness accounts for such unsatisfactory definitions of the liturgy as, "The liturgy is the official, public expression of the Church's worship."

What interest can a Christian who longs for God for his own sake and for his brethren in God's love have in a display or spectacle, even if it is a sacred one? Rather is he seeking unity with God, with himself and with all men. The liturgy might be defined as the giving of unity to the Church through the act of worship. Nothing is less exterior, and yet all the external elements in man's being are in the liturgy taken up into their places.

It is this wealth of the liturgical reality which the idea of *action*, as used here, is intended to convey.

Action, that is, realization, making actual or real, the reality and life of the Church. *Realization*, the Church is constituted by the liturgy, for it is the Word of God which is at work in it, the Word of which Isaias said: "My word shall not return to me void, but it shall do whatsoever I please, and shall prosper in the things for which I sent it."

Reality, the very being of the Church is liturgical. The outpouring of the Spirit is sacramental and there

[348]

could be no Christianity without an objective and very real link with this liturgical datum. Consider, for example, that if the celebration of the Mass were to stop absolutely in the world the Church would disappear.

Life, the whole wealth of activity and expression which flows from the fullness of a being still appertains to that being.

So it is with the praise of the Church, with the charity of the Church, with the unending sacrifice of all Christians "in a living victim, holy, acceptable to God." All this is intrinsically liturgical, for it is the living and communal expression of the Bride's love for Christ, for God. It is the ultimate realization of the hidden mystery of which St. Paul speaks. So far must we go to understand the liturgy in all its reality and effectiveness.

How may we best define the liturgy's function in relation to the Church? One category suggests itself at once: activity. From the beginning we have seen that this is a constituent of all liturgy: communal, sacred activity. But this does not go far enough to express the real nature of Christian liturgy. We have already seen the insufficiency of all analogies taken from the life of man and especially the image of the nation to express that unique kind of community which is the Church. A new creation, the Church regenerates man in his inmost being, making him a citizen of the divine world. Liturgical celebrations cannot therefore be put on the same plane as profane activities; they spring from the inmost being and involve man in his fullness. It seems preferable therefore to define the liturgy as a *'sacred action.'*

Action means more than activity. Since Aristotle, philosophy has chosen *action* as a word to express reality, as opposed to mere possibility. One speaks of immanent actions which differ from other actions precisely because in them the subject realizes itself fully without modification of relationship to the outside world. It is obvious that the liturgy is not an action of this kind, but it too expresses and makes real the fullness of being. In this sense the liturgy can be defined as the action of the Church, for it is there that the Church makes real the fullness of her being. And for everyone who takes part in it, although the liturgy is not at every moment an (exteriorized) activity, it is the 'action' of the servants of God, and for the baptized it is the action of the sons of God living in the Spirit of the life of Christ.

If it is abnormal that in the Church one group of the members of the community should have no more than the passive role of presence (there are no mere onlookers in the liturgy), it is normal that the members of a particular order—especially laymen—should not take part in certain liturgical activities (for example, many sacramental activities). But all, from the very moment a liturgical function begins, are *enacting* the official service of God; a potentiality fundamental to every man is realized or, as the scholastics would have expressed it, becomes actual.

The liturgy is that action by which the Church as a social body becomes aware of herself as she is established in this world: as the dispenser of the mystery of salvation to mankind.

But this 'action' is effected only in activity, and it is this which gives the liturgy its special place in the dispensation of the mystery of salvation. The liturgy is not primarily a form of teaching, although, as Pope XI said, it is the *didascalia*, the official instruction, of the Church and the chief organ of her ordinary magisterium; [1] it must be approached from the practical rather than the speculative standpoint. The documents of the liturgy, especially liturgical texts, however great their importance, are not the liturgy; they become the liturgy only when they are set in action, like a musical score. Less still are ceremonies, and the rubrics explaining them, the liturgy. They are only the medium for its performance, and become liturgy only when they are seasonably performed at the right time for the purpose for which they were instituted, that is, for the communication of the mystery of salvation.

The Action Constituting the Church

Seen from this point of view, the liturgy has a twofold function in the Church. It *constitutes* the Church, and it *expresses* the Church. The first is the work chiefly of the sacramental liturgy, the second that of the liturgy of praise.[2] And the Eucharistic liturgy lies at the very heart of the life of the Church; it is preeminently *the* sacrament, the sign and bond of the unity of the Body of Christ.

Quite obviously the sacraments of Christian initiation occur first to the mind when speaking of the liturgical action constituting the Church. The Fathers pictured them as the fruitful womb from which Mother Church brings forth new children to Christ. But this image renders the reality only imperfectly, for the Church is herself established in this very act of generation.

It is in faith and in the sacrament of faith that there is effected the integration of the sons of God, hitherto scattered abroad, into the Body of Christ, the Church. The whole of the baptismal liturgy, with its diversity of rites bearing witness, through allusions to its multiform aspects, to the richness of the mystery—recruitment to the militia (the profession of faith), the struggle against the powers of evil and liberation from their ascendancy (the exorcisms and pre-baptismal anointings), the bath of regeneration and burial with Christ in the mystery of death and resurrection, admission to the nuptial feast with its eschatological implications (post-baptismal ceremonies, anointing, the baptismal robe and candle): the whole of this liturgy, abounding in images and, in the Roman tradition, full of allusions to the most varied scriptural archetypes, forms the setting and means of admission to the

[351]

Church. The essential, of course, is Christ's efficacious act operating in the properly sacramental formula and rite. But to reduce the rest to secondary ceremonies which can be postponed even when there is no grave reason—indeed it may be wondered if there is any other save immediate danger of death—is to ignore the living nature of the liturgical acts and, to use a somewhat crude image, to resort too lightly to caesarian-section. The birth of a Christian, and the general health of the Church, deserve closer attention than a juridical theology would generally afford the liturgy.

This is even truer of confirmation, the solemn administration of which requires the direct intervention of the head of the local Church—either in person or through his delegate—for the complete integration into it of the new faithful. This sacrament is too often disfigured by a deficient liturgy which is poorly expressive of its properly 'ecclesial' character.

The Eucharist, as we said above, is worthy of special attention. It is through the Eucharist that the life begun in baptism is, as a rule, sustained. It is the Eucharist which gathers the community of the Church together for the Lord's meal. "For we being many are one bread, one body; all that partake of one bread" (I Cor 10:17). There can be no question of putting in the first place, as though it were a separate value, the personal union of each individual with Christ, when all the teaching since the New Testament, the liturgy, and the most strongly guaranteed doctrine of the Church, show it as the fruit of the unity of the Body which is the Church. Why then do we so often fail to show how there is found in the Eucharist not only the sign but also the immediate principle of this unity, and how in it is rooted the mystical bond between the Christian and Christ?

The eucharistic celebration brings the community together for its most fundamental action. The Body of Christ is 're-actuated' daily in this sacrament which is the effective sign of the divine and human reality which forms a single being, a multiform but coherent organism, soundly articulated, pervaded by a single sap and by an influx from him who is both its head and its fullness—or fulfillment—animated by a single Spirit which operates differently in its various members, but through the ministry of all prepares the harmonious growth of the Body to the full stature of the perfect man, until that day when there shall be but the one Christ presenting himself to the Father in the finally perfected sacrifice (cf. Eph 4:11-16).

Understanding the Mass thus, as the act which at the same time constitutes and expresses the reality of the Body of the Church, should render indefensible the individualism still too common among Christians and priests. To be "present" at Mass, to celebrate "my" Mass—these are meaningless phrases which are the result of a mistaken piety. And what deep significance real community Masses, conventual and chapter Masses, assume once more—even when, under present discipline in a community of priests they seem to duplicate the eucharistic ministry of each individual member! Even in a privately celebrated Mass, the priest bears with him, invisibly, the community of all those whom he names in his intentions, and whose reality is expressed by the sacrament; and in the community Mass it is his own membership of the body that he expresses and makes real in the most vital way imaginable. How one wishes that a slight change of discipline would make it possible to give this 'realization' its own sign: communion in the very Bread that is consecrated at that Mass in which all are taking part.

We could follow out through the whole sacramental structure those signs which, directly or indirectly, are agents in constituting the Body of the Church: the reincorporation of its members in Penance; the handing down of hierarchical powers and the perpetuation of apostolic tradition in the sacrament of Orders, whose very name evokes the organizing function in the life of the Church; and finally Matrimony, which raises to the level of the special interests of the kingdom God's command to the species, increase and multiply. Even when we come to the Sacrament of the Sick, we must say that its purpose is the building up of the Church. By adapting a Christian in a spiritual manner to meet his special role as an invalid, it gives expression to the new function that has been entrusted to that member—a privileged function, immediately expressive of one aspect of the mystery of our redemption.

But there is no reason why this mission, this 'making actual' the mystery of the Church, should be confined to the sacraments. Of course, they do this in a very special way since the essential grace of Christ uses them as instruments which carry on the redemptive work of his humanity. The whole body of mysteries which, universally or even locally, the Church has thought should be added to them, would not merit the name of liturgy if they did not have a part in that great and ultimate mystery which is the realization of God's eternal plan to gather all things together in Christ. The most important among them— the consecration of places and persons—have a special part in this since they delegate their subjects—virgin, religious, church or altar—to a more direct cooperation in the priestly ministry of Christ and to the expression of some particular aspect of his mystery. In the same way, the funeral liturgy is not just a magnificent expression of the consummation, by one particular member of the Church, of his way of the Cross; it would have no meaning if it did not express the oneness of the Church here below with the congregation of saints and angels and with those who still await their final deliverance.

The Action Expressing the Church

However, in the case of the great sacramental rites and even more with the multitude of secondary liturgical rites, it is the *expressive* aspect of liturgical action which is most prominent. What is more, the philosophical concept of 'action,' to which we have already referred, insists on the indivisibility of these two aspects. It conceives of the action as both the dynamism which brings into existence what is merely possible and as the fullness which expresses the existing reality. The liturgy acts thus; and this is why it can be termed, in the strict meaning of the word, the *action* of the Church. At the same time that it constitutes her it expresses her, and these two aspects can be separated only by a process of mental abstraction.

It is this second aspect of the liturgical action that most appropriately brings into play its character as 'mystery.' A mystery expresses and makes present (both functions are essential) by means of sensible signs and symbols, a divine reality which, in itself, is inaccessible to us in our present state.

It is not inconceivable that the Church should have been constituted and her life maintained without the use of signs; but God did not choose this for the economy of the Incarnation. So then, since the Church is herself a parable and a sacrament of the kingdom, her liturgy is necessarily expressive, in mystery, of the ultimate realities of this kingdom. And this expression is in no way accidental or an afterthought. It forms the resplendent brightness of that human and divine reality which is the Church. By the very fact of her existence, by the modality of that existence, she expresses what she is and what she brings into being. Nonetheless, it remains true that this expression will always be endowed with all those human values that the Church integrates within herself; she will always bear the mark, and the burden, of the cultures in which she has her roots. Because of this she never expresses distinctly more than one aspect of the mysterious fullness to which she bears witness and there can never be too great a variety of rites, varying with the diversity of human cultures and historical periods, effectively to emphasize the many aspects of a mystery surpassing our understanding. Too much insistence cannot be laid on the necessity of referring to all the liturgical creations, of both East and West, if we are to gain a precise idea of what the Church, in the self-awareness that she has so far achieved, intends to express in her liturgy. A characteristic emphasized in one place will appear only in outline in another. Would we discern it in one place if it has not been encountered more clearly delineated elsewhere? On the contrary, this comparison, rather, this synoptic view, alone enables us to recognize the fundamental constant and the secondary developments, the fruits of the local needs or tastes of a given community.

There can be no question here of going into details; they are of interest only insofar as they are based on all the sources of information we have just mentioned. But it was necessary to draw attention to one aspect of the liturgy, whose theological value has not always been perceived, either because the diversity of rites was considered in their purely human aspect, such as the manifestation of folklore, or because they were arbitrarily laid under contribution in favor of a preconceived theological position. On the contrary it is important to see these rites for what they are, that is, expressions, albeit deficient or clumsy, of a reality of which we must bear in mind both its divine aspect—perfect and unchangeable—and the human, ever changing and dependent on the conditions of the milieu in which the Church must live. Moreover, a sign like this, insufficient, clumsy, forced though it be, very often draws attention to some aspect which the classic lines of the great liturgies in their massive equilibrium have obscured.

Thus, by reason of its sobriety, the Roman liturgy is often in danger of concealing from too perfunctory an examination some nuance which it has contrived to indicate discreetly.

Despite its shortcomings and false notes, the Christian liturgy taken as a whole forms a wonderful mirror of the mystery of the Church. More faithfully than in her Fathers and Doctors, who were especially alert to the needs of their hearers and the concerns of the moment, more fully than in the acts of her magisterium, which always bear the marks of controversy and of the errors requiring correction, the Church expresses in her liturgy her *action* par excellence, the exercise of her ministry of salvation, which she effects throughout the whole of time and to the profit of every human nation.

The Communal Nature of Christian Liturgy

Being the action par excellence of the Church, the liturgy is necessarily a social action. An individual liturgy, in the strict sense of the term, is inconceivable. Liturgy is performed by the community of the faithful; it is God's people who come to meet their Lord and stand before him. If rubrics and legal prescriptions are indispensable to liturgy, that is because they are so to every action of a human community. The meticulous ordinances of the Mosaic law and the multitudinous prescriptions of Leviticus are not unworthy of the word of God, because on grounds greatly superior to those of legislative prescriptions properly so called, these ceremonial laws organize God's people in a much more essential matter, its sacred actions. The 'convocation' at Sinai wrought a more or less turbulent association of nomadic tribes into an *ecclesia*, a holy people, worthy to come into contact with the awesome divine holiness, whose lightning flashes annihilated whosoever dared approach it without being in a state of holiness. It was the people itself that was sanctified by sprinkling with the blood of sacrifices, that was made a nation of priests. Because this holiness was social of its nature, it had to be regulated by exact laws. But these prescriptions had a religious significance only because the 'law of holiness,' the apex of the code of Leviticus (chapters 17-26), is preceded by the law of offerings (chapters 1-7). And in the definitive form of the Sinaitic legislation (Exodus, chapters 19-40), the whole of the considerable body of laws concerning the sanctuary (chapters 25-31 and 35-40), like the second form of the code of the Covenant (34:12-28), came to stress the capital role played in the life of Israel by the mysterious presence of Yahweh over the 'propitiatory' of the ark within the tabernacle.

When, after Pentecost, the first Christian community realized that it was the *ecclesia,* the 'convocation' of the people of God, the new Israel of which the Sinaitic community had been only the figurative anticipation, it organized itself at once, 'persevering in the doctrines of the apostles and in the communication of the breaking of bread and in prayers' (Acts 2:42). A new ritual quickly took shape and the Apocalypse clearly seems to bear witness to an already developed form of worship. The prominence given to ritual prescriptions in the oldest collections of Christian legislation which have come down to us (the *Didache,* the *Apostolic Tradition* of Hippolytus, the Syrian *Teaching of the Apostles,* and the great collections of the fourth century: the *Apostolic Constitutions* and Clement's *Octoteuch*) are not evidence of a Judaizing tendency, but of a deep-seated need in the life of the people of God, culminating in the direct service of the Lord. The life-giving law of the Gospel, written in their hearts, the law of charity, animates the multitudinous prescriptions to which it gives rise for the safeguarding of the holiness, not only interior, but also social, of the divine service.

Because the Church lives in time, the Church is subject to the conditions of the age. In each era, its liturgy is inspired by the norms of social life proper to each community. It borrows from social life ceremonies and forms of expression, so that it can infuse into them the efficacy of the mystery of salvation. From this point of view, nothing is more revealing than a comparative study of liturgies, which show with what flexibility and how sure a touch the things universal to Christian worship—Eucharist, the Office, the sacramental rites, consecrations and blessings— are adapted to the spirit of every culture.

Provided always that the liturgy preserves its social character! [3] As soon as it becomes the business of the clergy alone, it grows rigid and fossilized and the Christian people are reduced to finding substitutes for it: devotions, which for a Christian community are the normal overflowing of its life, become the sole refuge of its piety. And, because of their very nature, devotions, even when they are collective, as with confraternities, are not in themselves social. Religion becomes, thus, an individual affair. Liturgy itself suffers the aftereffects; even when it is not stripped of all its community characteristics (as is all too often the case today with the administration of the sacraments), and even when it is not completely abandoned by Christian people (like the Divine Office or the blessings of the Ritual), it is performed in the presence of a handful of individuals, by the ministry of the clergy alone. How can we recognize in this sort of thing the image and anticipation of the heavenly city? Can we still speak of the liturgy, of 'social worship,' when the people of God are reduced to the role of passive spectators? Can they truly be 'enacting' the divine service when they can no longer reply *Amen* to the sacerdotal Eucharist? There can be no city worthy of the name if the citizens do not exercise their civic rights. The Church—the anticipation in time of the heavenly city—calls on all her members to take part in the liturgy that the saints celebrate together on the heavenly mountain. For "you are come to Mount Sion and to the city of the living God, the heavenly Jerusalem, and to the company of many thousands of angels, and to the church of the first-born" (Heb 2:22-23).

Notes

1 Cf. Dome Capelle: *Revue Grégorienne* (1937), p. 79.

2 In saying this, we do not forget that the sacramental liturgy is also—and more fully than the liturgy of praise—expressive of the mystery of the Church, for in it the word, endowed with the power of Christ, effects exactly what it says.

3 Cf. J. Travers: *Valeur social de la liturgie d'après saint Thomas d'Aquin,* 'Lex Orandi,' 5 (Cerf, Paris, 1946).

CHAPTER 17 *The Era of the Church**

by ANDRÉ FEUILLET, P.S.S.

AUTHOR: André Feuillet is a distinguished French New Testament scholar and a professor at the Institut Catholique de Paris. He specializes in New Testament eschatology.

ARTICLE: This selection is an analysis of the *present* position of salvation history, as this is depicted in the Gospel of John and the Apocalypse. (These two books of the New Testament should certainly be read in conjunction with Father Feuillet's article.) By identifying the present age of the world as the Era of the Church, the selection concludes this book of readings with another portrayal of the Church as the living presence of the victorious Christ effecting the salvation of mankind and the universe throughout this, the final age of the world. Here is a Christian theology of history, presented in the great symbols and often in the very words of the most profound of the Apostles.

READINGS: For a study of the thought of St. John, cf. Louis Bouyer, *The Fourth Gospel* (Newman, 1964). For a fuller development of the Christian theology of history, cf. Hans Urs von Balthasar, *A Theology of History* (Sheed & Ward, 1963).

---

* "The Era of the Church," a selection taken from *Theology Digest* 11 (1963), pp. 3-9, is a digest of an article originally published in *La Maison-Dieu* 65 (1961), pp. 60-79. It is reprinted here with permission.

The Gospel of John

THE HISTORY of the Judeo-Christian religion is a history of salvation, a history that progresses through three phases or "ages." There is the Old Testament age of preparation, the age of Christ's sojourn on earth, and the age of the Church—the time from Christ's ascension till the parousia.

Each of these eras is distinguished by its own particular characteristics. A man who is Christian finds himself in religious surroundings very different from those of a Jew living under the Old Covenant or from those of a disciple hurrying after Jesus on the roads of Galilee or Judea. The age of the Christian is the age of the Church, which was born in the redemptive drama of Good Friday and the victory of Easter morning. The following pages attempt to define the characteristics of this third age in salvation history.

The synoptic Gospels show us a Church, a messianic community, inseparable from the conviction of Jesus that he was the promised Messias. The Gospel of John is richer even than Matthew in ecclesiology in proportion as it is Christological, showing the Incarnate Son of God revealing to men the mysterious treasures of divine life. John is the only one of the evangelists to emphasize the connection between Jesus and the Church. John's whole theme is the 'Hour of Jesus,' which is also the hour of the Church and of the sacraments. Christ's ministry, his preaching, his miracles are seen as more than a mere anticipation of a distant future. "The hour is coming and now is here" (4:23; 5:25).

Apocalypse a Complement

Difficult though it is, the Apocalypse is an almost indispensable complement to the Fourth Gospel—not because it offers any entirely new insights but because more clearly than the Gospel it expresses certain concrete aspects of the Age of the Church. More than that, the Apocalypse locates the Christian community within the context of the history of the world. It can be seen as a kind of continuation of the prophets, of I and II Isaias especially; it is a kind of Christian Book of Daniel. That is why we plan to give the Apocalypse a supporting role in our presentation, which we will conclude by a consideration of the magnificent figure of the Woman—the people of God—a symbol which recapitulates what John teaches us about the Age of the Church.

We proceed then directly to the heart of the Fourth Gospel where we find—in the Last Supper discourse— Christ's teaching about what his disciples are to be after he has left them. This teaching is completed and illustrated by chapters nineteen to twenty-one, where details of the death and resurrection awaken us to a realization of what it is Jesus has promised his followers.

Man's greatness is focused by the Bible on the fact that he can enter into dialogue with God, as contrasted with the Greek stress upon his abstract reflection on what God is in himself. The dialogue of the Christian with the divine persons is typified in three points of the fourteenth and sixteenth chapters of John's Gospel: (1) Jesus will go away but will return, to be more closely than ever united with his disciples; (2) the Father will care for them with special solicitude from the time of Christ's departure to the time of the parousia; (3) the Father and Son will send the Holy Spirit to enlighten and fortify the disciples.

We will first examine what the Gospel says about the Hour of the Church in reference to man's relationship with each of these three Persons. Later we will discuss briefly the era of the Church from the viewpoint of the disciples' interrelationships.

Christ with Men

The efficacious presence of the risen Christ is the outstanding characteristic of the Age of the Church according to John, chapters 14-16. Disturbed by the prospect of Christ's departure, the apostles are reassured that they will not be left orphans (14:18). It is true that the unbelieving world will think Jesus has disappeared forever, that he has faded away into history. But the disciples will know that his saddening departure is to be followed immediately by his return—and by a joy at his return like the joy of a mother who has brought a new human being into existence (14:18 f.; 16:19 f.). Though he will be yet invisible to the world, the Savior will make himself visible to his own. "Yet a little while and the world no longer sees me; but you see me, for I live and you shall live" (14:19).

These promises are made not only to the Twelve but to all believers of all times, according to the measure of their faith in him. Their assurance of the presence beside them of the glorious Christ will fill them with a joy which "no one shall take away" (16:22) because it will be in his divine victory that they will be made joyful (17:13). He will come as a friend and, together with his Father, will dwell with them (14:23), that they may be led to the many heavenly abodes prepared for them (14:2-3). The only condition for these remarkable benefactions is total fidelity to the word of Jesus, the Word spoken by the Father.

Two episodes from John 20 and 21 illustrate what we have been saying. Mary Magdalen is forbidden to touch the Savior for, as he says, "I have not yet ascended to my Father" (20:17). The most profound contact we can have with Christ is not the physical contact that the crowds experienced along the roads he walked during his public ministry; paradoxically it is only when he has returned to his Father that we will really 'touch' him, through faith and the sacraments.

[364]

The other episode, the symbolic catch of fish (21:1-13), shows us how Christ comes to the assistance of his followers in their apostolic ministry. This is not just another miracle of Christ; it is an act of the Church, accomplished with the all-powerful aid of its Founder.

Both episodes follow the passion, in which the apparent victory of the forces of darkness has in reality marked their defeat. No other evangelist shows as well as John, that Calvary is a kind of epiphany of Christ the King, that it means the beginning of his kingship—a kingship not of this world but nonetheless completely victorious over earthly powers. Thus it is that the Easter appearances of Christ found in John are much more than perceptible testimonials to the fact of his resurrection. The appearances both proclaim and symbolize the permanent presence and action of the Son of God, a presence and action which are to characterize the Church from the ascension to the parousia. And the joy and peace of those present at the appearances of the risen Christ are a foretaste of the joy and peace promised in the Last Discourse and offered through the Church to all Christians of all times.

Father with Men

The action and the being of the Son are inseparable from the action and being of the Father. If Christ must maintain the tie with his own after he leaves, the Father too will look after them. When faith encounters the Son, it will simultaneously find the Father (14:9-11). Keeping the word of Jesus will assure the disciples of the love of the Father and of his presence in them together with the Son (14:23). The Father will protect them because of the love they show for his glorified Son (16:26-28). The prayers of those commissioned to continue Christ's work will unfailingly be heard (cf. 14: 13-14) and will result in their doing deeds greater than those Christ worked during his earthly life (14:12), on a par with the powers given to him in his resurrection. They will be invested with the power given the Son so that they can work effectively for the establishment of the Kingdom.

When the risen Christ says to Mary Magdalen, "Go to my brothers and say to them, 'I ascend to my Father and your Father, to my God and your God'" (20:17), he is really saying that the cross and resurrection have established a new covenant, extending to all believers the privilege of divine sonship. Christ has become our brother and his Father ours. The 'my brothers' is very likely an allusion to Ps 22:23: "I will proclaim your name to my brothers;" and it has an excellent parallel in Hebrews (2:9-12): "Made a little lower than the angels . . . crowned with glory and honor . . . [Christ] is not ashamed to call them brothers, saying, 'I will declare your name to my brothers; in the midst of the Church will I praise you.'" Catherinet has indicated, moreover, the similarity between Jo 20:17 and the words of Ruth when she proposed that Noemi return to Moab: "Wherever you go I will go, wherever you lodge I will lodge, your people shall be my people and your God my God" (1:16). The "I ascend to my Father" shows that, under the covenant of grace, both Father and Son will be much closer to the disciples than they were before.

Spirit with Men

The Fourth Gospel insists often that the departure and glorification of Jesus coincide with the giving of the Spirit. The role to be played in the future Church by this intercessor or advocate—this Paraclete—is explained in chapters fourteen to sixteen. Not only will the Spirit put carnal man in touch with supernatural reality; he will give him a deeper understanding of the Son of God made flesh, of his heavenly Father and of Christ his brother, forming with man a family. The Spirit will give witness of Christ to Christians living in an unbelieving world; and he will show them that Christ's apparent defeat is really glorious victory, the pattern and foreshadowing of their own triumph-in-defeat through persecution.

The apostles are the first to benefit by the promises made at the farewell discourse (14:16-17, 26; 15:26; 16:7-15); yet these promises hold true for all Christians of all times. It is like the passion narrative, where Jesus is described as "giving up his spirit"; the words are very probably ambivalent. He does not merely *yield up* his spirit. He gives his Spirit to all the world—founds the Church with its sacraments in the blood and water that flow from his side. It is here we see his death as a victory, a victory to which (as John tells us in a closely parallel passage) "There are three that bear witness in heaven: the Spirit, and the water, and the blood—and these three are one" (I Jo 5:7).

Man with Men

Just as Christians are joined to the Trinity through a faith and love manifested in the keeping of the commandments, they are joined to one another by observance of the new commandment of fraternal love. There is a convergence of the many different works of Jesus upon his one supreme work—the redemption and founding of the Church. We can find the same sort of convergence of the many different commandments given Christians upon the single overriding commandment of love; it corresponds in turn to the Father's command to the Son that he give his life for the world. Thus Calvary specifies the content of the command to love: what we must give for our brothers is our own lives.

The synoptics put the stress on the universal love we ought to display for our fellowmen, enemies included.

John instead emphasizes the reciprocal love which ought to unite the disciples of Christ—a communion only to be found among God's people, possibly in function of a Eucharistic communion. Not that John envisions a ghetto; rather, he points to a basis in reality for the new love which is to be characteristic of this new people during the age of their separation from Christ. "Little children, yet a little while I am with you. . . . Where I go you cannot come. A new commandment I give you, that as I have loved you, you also love one another" (13:33-34). The underlying concrete reality is a sharing in the bond of love which unites the Father and the Son. "That the love with which you have loved me may be in them, and I in them" (17:26). Far from making Christianity a closed society, this love is to be the principal means of its expansion. This love will be the mark by which the world will recognize in the Church the presence of Christ as envoy and Son of the Father. Unity and fraternal charity are built into the structure of the Church, and they also assure her development.

To understand the religious message of the author of the Apocalypse, it is extremely important to recall the burning issues to which he sought to offer a solution. These problems were two: one concerning the Christian-Jewish relationships, the other concerning the Christian-pagan conflict. Only the second will concern us here.

Christian vs. Pagan

In those days the pagan world for all practical purposes meant the Roman empire, since it was in this vast empire that Christians of the epoch had to live their lives. At first the Roman authorities were not unfavorable to Christianity; historically Rome had always been tolerant of religion. There was some little change with the burning of Rome in 64 A.D.; Christians were held responsible and so persecuted by Nero. But the definitive clash came only with Domitian's edict that divine honors be paid him during his lifetime.

This new cult met little resistance among the general population. What was one god more or one god less in those polytheistic times? The Jews had relatively little trouble adjusting; they easily got a dispensation from cultic observances contrary to their beliefs. For Christians, however, the situation was entirely different. They saw Domitian's edict as an act directly hostile to the religion of Christ—in fact, an *aping* of it. Here was a simple mortal man acting as though he were, like Christ, an incarnation of the divinity, a Savior to be worshiped by all men regardless of race or class. Christians reacted vigorously against this satanic notion. A constantly growing supernational religious body like the Christians could expect no such exemption as favored the Jews. So there immediately ensued a bloody persecution which with interruptions was to last a very long time.

It was toward the end of the reign of Domitian, when this persecution was at its height, that the Apocalypse was written. It laid down the line of conduct to be followed in the crisis: inviolable fidelity to Christ, true king of the world, resistance to the point of martyrdom against the totalitarian state which claimed to set itself up in place of God. The Apocalypse description of the fall of Babylon (pagan Rome) may not have been verified in every detail; but it certainly has held true in its general outline: A handful of Christians prevailed over the mighty empire of Rome. Today, when totalitarian states, armed with instruments of terrible destruction, threaten anew a frail and unarmed Church of Christ, there is no New Testament book so timely as the Apocalypse. It is in this context of imminent and tragic crisis that we must understand the author's conception of the Age of the Church.

Christ—Lord of History

The Age of the Church signifies principally and primarily *the presence in history* of the risen Christ. Unlike the wholly future-oriented Jewish apocalypses, John's book sees the parousia of Christ only in relation to his first coming. It insists that the summit of the world's religious history has already been reached, that salvation and victory over the powers of evil have already in principle been achieved. Christ, who has overcome by his blood all hostile powers, is in actual fact the risen and glorious king of the universe—the real and sovereign Lord of history. To sustain the Christians through persecution, the author emphasizes that it is not totalitarian despots who will decide the destiny of mankind. Only the victorious Christ holds the divine book of the elect; only he can open it.

Christ the King

We have already seen in John's narrative of the passion a kind of epiphany of Christ the King. Jesus reminded Pilate that political power is limited by and subject to a higher transcendent sovereignty and power. If political power remains neutral, like Pilate, it invites its own destruction. The same points are made by the author of the Apocalypse; but his tone is, in the context of crisis and persecution, much more aggressive.

Scholars have remarked how similar in style are the letters at the beginning of the Apocalypse and the edicts of Domitian. A heavenly emperor is spoken of. He sends messages through ambassadors accredited to the Churches fighting for him on earth. There are the solemn imperial titles pointedly bestowed on Christ: sovereign among the kings of the earth (1:5), King of kings, Lord of lords (17:14; 19:16). We have the solemn description of the Lamb's enthronement and the extraordinary prominence given the royalty of Christ. Schutz has noted the almost exact correspondence between the titles applied to Christ in the Apocalypse and those applied to Domitian in Martial.

Essentially a manual of combat, the Apocalypse presents the Age of the Church as a *time of terrible war between Christ and Antichrist*. Though the bitterest assault against the Church will not be unleashed until just before the parousia (20:7-10), the battle is already raging. True, the Serpent was mortally wounded when Christ vanquished him (cf. ch. 12), but he is still able to wield his unholy flail. This flail is described under the two symbols of the beast which rises from the sea and the beast which rises from the land.

Symbols of Paganism

The beast which rises from the sea (the West), of which the divinized emperor of the times was only a partial incarnation, is presented as a mockery of the Lamb. Its wounding and healing are a caricature of the passion and resurrection of Christ (13:3; cf. 5:6). Its enthronement by the dragon is a ridiculous parody of the enthronement of the Lamb. Its adorers are marked with a sign just as are the adorers of Christ and God (cf. 13:4, 16-17; 5:8-9; 7:2; 14:1). The beast which rises from the land (Asia) has a prophetical office; it puts its religious power at the service of the first beast. This symbol was doubtless conceived by John as an incarnation of contemporary philosophic-religious paganism, which accepted and advanced the cult of divinized despots. This second beast gives the tyrannical state its ideology and spirit; and there are good reasons to see in it, as Rissi does, a caricature of the Holy Spirit, who makes known the teaching and person of Christ the King. A third symbol (17-18) is the Babylon of the prophets, described as a courtesan of unheard-of power

and riches, who leads nations astray by her wiles and se-
duces men with an illusion of eternal happiness: "I sit a
queen, I am no widow, and I shall not see mourning"
(18:7).

It should be noted that John, obviously describing the
pagan Rome of his time, is in no sense driven by blind
fanaticism. He appreciates and even in a certain fashion
glorifies the grandeur of Rome. But he sees what no one
else of his time saw—that Rome in all her splendor was
headed for ruin. Christians needed his convincing presentation of Rome's imminent downfall to strengthen them
in their terrible trials. He in fact anticipated all the other
similar crises which would plague the Church throughout
her future existence, supplying a corrective to naive and
infantile faith in a kind of automatic and continual progress. He foretold that the satanic beast would slaughter
Christians, but at the same time he taught that it was by
their immolation, not by military arms, that the martyrs
of Christ would, as Christ did, vanquish the devil and his
forces.

The philosopher of history studies the present *in reference to the past*. The author of the Apocalypse like the
prophets of Israel explains his own times *in reference to
the future*. He is well aware that present happenings can
be properly understood only in the light of their eventual
outcome. The prophet of Patmos showed how the contemporary trials of the Church—colliding with an omnip-
otent totalitarian state—fitted into a larger and divine
plan. The terrible assaults of the ancient dragon were only
the death throes of a creature already defeated and mortally wounded.

Liturgy Celebrates Sonship

This second part of our study should include one final
remark. Commentators have underlined the profound

inter-relationships between the teaching of the Fourth Gospel and the sacramental life of the Church. But the Apocalypse presents a liturgical character even more sharply defined. We have pointed out in an article in *Revue Biblique* (65 [1958], pp. 5-32) how the twenty-four ancients or presbyters surrounding the divine throne are a kind of celestial prototype of the hierarchy of the Church. It is clear that the doxologies, acclamations, and hymns sprinkled throughout the Apocalypse are an echo of the liturgical Christian chants. It is *primarily in the liturgy* that the Christian expresses and celebrates his divine sonship and the permanent presence and action in him of the risen Christ and the Holy Spirit. It is in the liturgy that he becomes certain of his victory over the forces of evil. The first chapters of the Book contain many of these wonderful promises: "Him who overcomes I will permit to eat of the tree of life. . . . To him who overcomes I will give the hidden manna" (2:7, 17; cf. Jo 6). "Behold, I stand at the door and knock. If any man listens to my voice and opens the door to me, I will come in to him and will sup with him, and he with me" (3:20).

The Woman: Church or Mary?

Before concluding this sketchy study, we would like to say something of the symbol of the woman used in the Fourth Gospel and the Apocalypse to represent the Church and to characterize the conditions of its present-day existence. In recent times much has been written about the woman in Apoc 12. Some authors like to think that this symbol represents primarily or even exclusively the Virgin Mary. The references to the Old Testament (the Isaian texts on the glorified Sion giving birth: 66:7-8; 26:17-18; cf. Songs 6:10) show clearly, however, that the woman of this wonderfully enchanting vision is the ideal Sion of the prophets who, once she has given Christ to the world, becomes the Christian Church. Like the people of the old covenant, she lives in the desert, protected and fed by God while awaiting the parousia (6:14).

If the Virgin Mary is seen here secondarily (and we think she ought to be, at least in the first verses of the chapter) this can be only as an incarnation of the people of God: in fact it is through her that the Church has given the Messias to the world. As Mother of the Messias, Mary is simultaneously the image of the Christian Church through which her Son is daily given to souls through preaching and the sacraments. Considering the woman as both militant and victorious, we cannot help thinking that it is chiefly through Mary that the Church is already triumphant in heaven. But while such a secondary Marian interpretation of the text is legitimate, we must be careful not to substitute our modern, anachronistic, individual conceptions of Marian piety for the essentially salvation-history point of view of the sacred author.

The Fourth Gospel's narrations of the passion and the Easter Christophanies have as their main point that the Church is both the fruit of Christ's messianic work and the privileged setting of his subsequent saving action. The scene (19:25-27) where Christ bids farewell to his mother is no exception. Even a Protestant like Hoskyns, however, does not hesitate to admit that here Mary stands for the Church, in perfect keeping with the spirit of Apoc 12. Deprived of the sensible presence of Jesus, Christians will be loved by God as by the most gentle of mothers—and this because of the Church which Mary represents and which prolongs on earth the saving work of Christ.

The two Gospel texts—20:17 (Magdalen) and 19:25-27 (Mary)—are fundamentally in harmony. They reinforce and complete one another in giving us a full picture of this decisive stage in the history of salvation which is called the Age of the Church. We learn on the one hand that after the departure of Jesus the disciples will have as their Father the heavenly Father himself; on the other hand that they will have a mother while they remain on earth. This is the privileged life of Christians here below from the time of the ascension to the parousia.

Index of Persons

Index of Subjects

[379]

A NOTE ON THE TEXT

IN WHICH THIS BOOK IS SET

This book is set in Baskerville, a Linotype face, created from the original types used by John Baskerville, the eighteenth-century typefounder and printer. This type has long been considered one of the finest book types ever developed. The letters are wide and open and have a businesslike approach. The finer hairlines give exquisite delicacy. The heavier strokes give color and strength. The relation of the two in combination gives a brilliant effect and makes for easy reading. The book was composed and printed by the Wickersham Printing Company of Lancaster, Penna., and bound by Moore and Company of Baltimore. The typography and design are by Howard N. King.